X-MEN
WORLDS APART

WRITER: **CHRISTOPHER YOST**
PENCILER: **DIOGENES NEVES**
INKER: **ED TADEO**
COLORIST: **RAÚL TREVIÑO**
LETTERER: **VC'S CORY PETIT**
EDITOR: **DANIEL KETCHUM**
EXECUTIVE EDITOR: **AXEL ALONSO**

COVER ARTISTS:
**J. SCOTT CAMPBELL & EDGAR DELGADO;
DAVID YARDIN & JASON KEITH; MIKE DEODATO
& MORRY HOLLOWELL; AND STEPHANE ROUX**

"STURM UND DRANG: A STORY OF LOVE AND
WAR, BOOK ONE: ECHOES"
FROM *BLACK PANTHER #26* (JANUARY 2001)
WRITER: **PRIEST**
PENCILER: **SAL VELLUTO**
INKER: **BOB ALMOND**
COLORIST: **STEVE OLIFF**
LETTERER: **SHARPEFONT & PT**
ASSISTANT EDITOR: **MARC SUMERAK**
EDITOR: **TOM BREVOORT**

"CRY -- VENGEANCE!"
FROM *MARVEL TEAM-UP #100* (DECEMBER 1980)
WRITER: **CHRIS CLAREMONT**
CO-PLOTTER & PENCILER: **JOHN BYRNE**
INKER: **BOB McLEOD**
COLORIST: **ROBBIE CAROSELLA**
LETTERER: **ANNETTE KAWECKI**
EDITOR: **DENNY O'NEIL**

Collection Editor:
MARK D. BEAZLEY
Editorial Assistant:
ALEX STARBUCK
Assistant Editors:
CORY LEVINE & JOHN DENNING
Editor, Special Projects:
JENNIFER GRÜNWALD
Senior Editor, Special Projects:
JEFF YOUNGQUIST
Senior Vice President of Sales:
DAVID GABRIEL
Book Designers:
**RODOLFO MURAGUCHI
& SPRING HOTELING**
Production:
JERRY KALINOWSKI

Editor in Chief:
JOE QUESADA
Publisher:
DAN BUCKLEY
Executive Producer:
ALAN FINE

D0884838

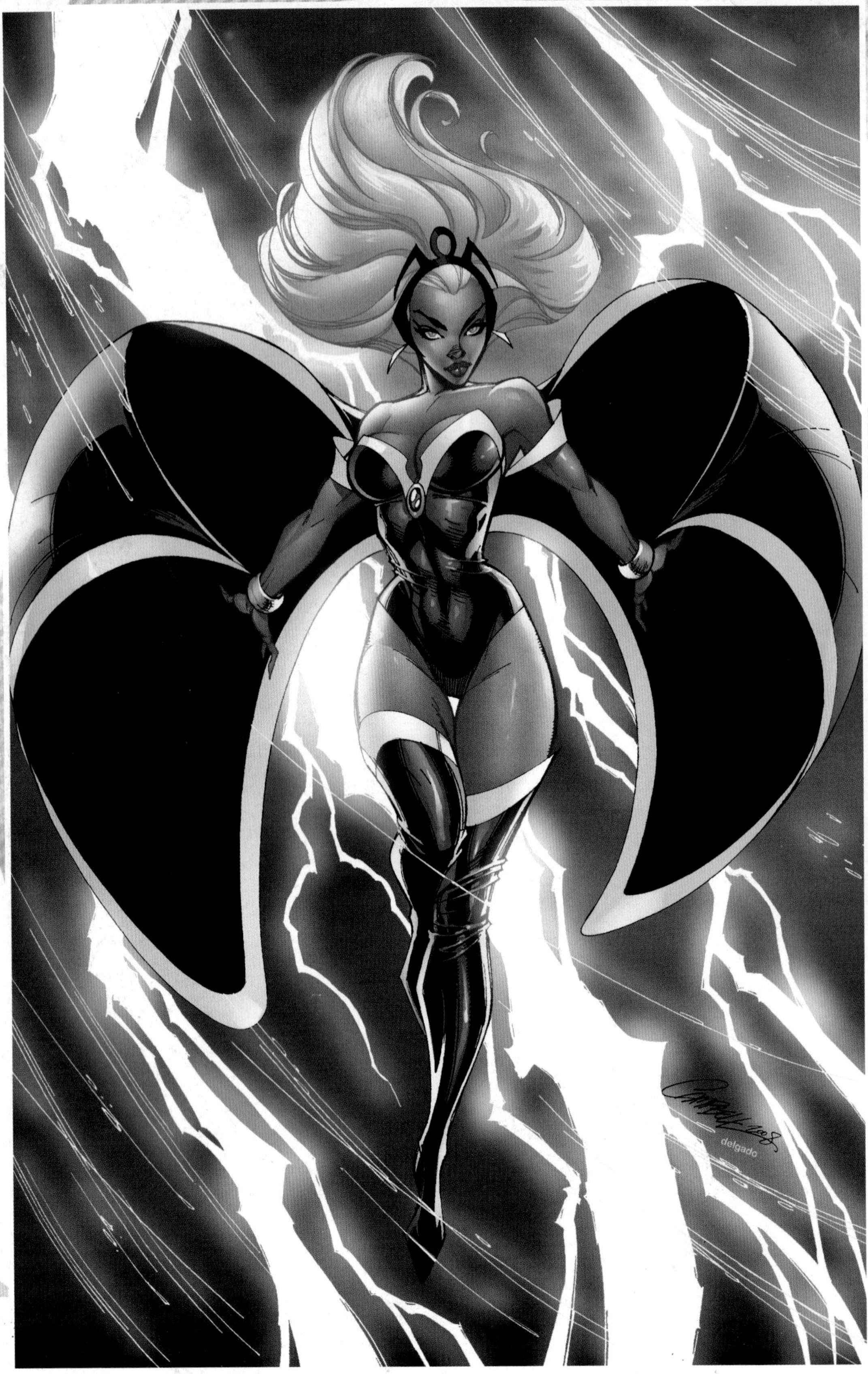
delgado

X-MEN: WORLDS APART #1

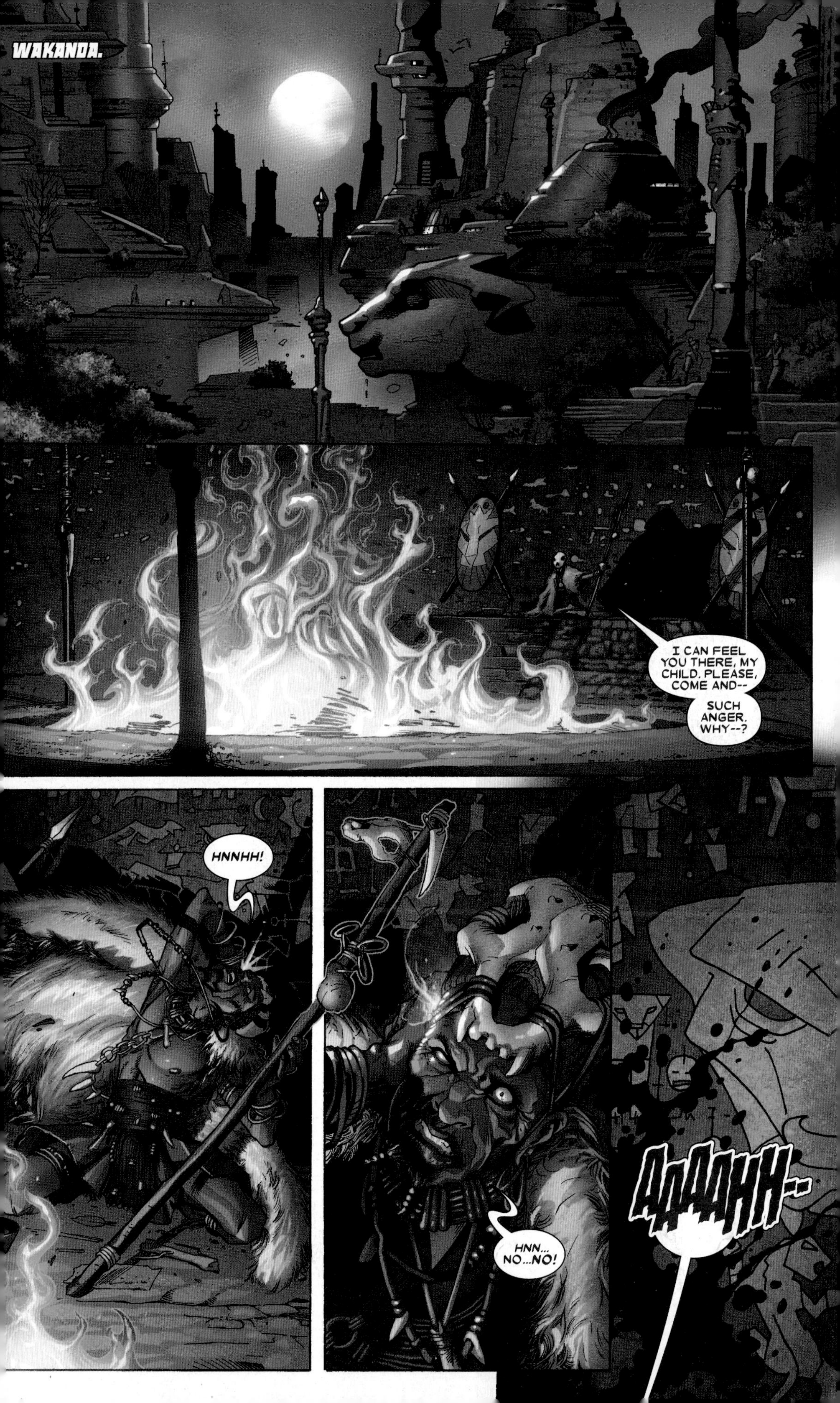
WAKANDA.
I CAN FEEL YOU THERE, MY CHILD. PLEASE, COME AND--
SUCH ANGER. WHY--?
HNNHH!
HNN... NO...NO!
AAAAHH--

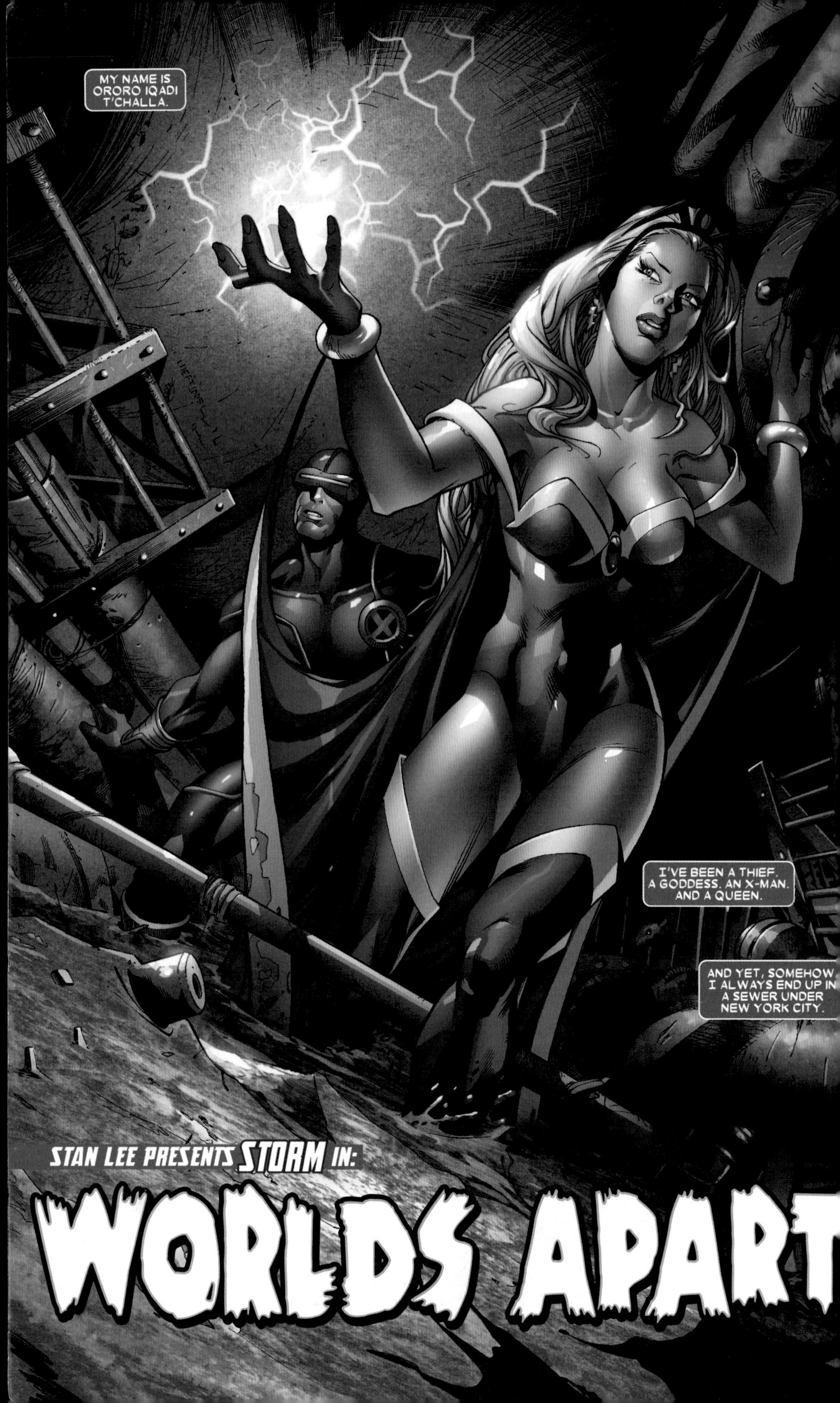

MY NAME IS ORORO IQADI T'CHALLA.
I'VE BEEN A THIEF. A GODDESS. AN X-MAN. AND A QUEEN.
AND YET, SOMEHOW, I ALWAYS END UP IN A SEWER UNDER NEW YORK CITY.
STAN LEE PRESENTS STORM IN:
WORLDS APART

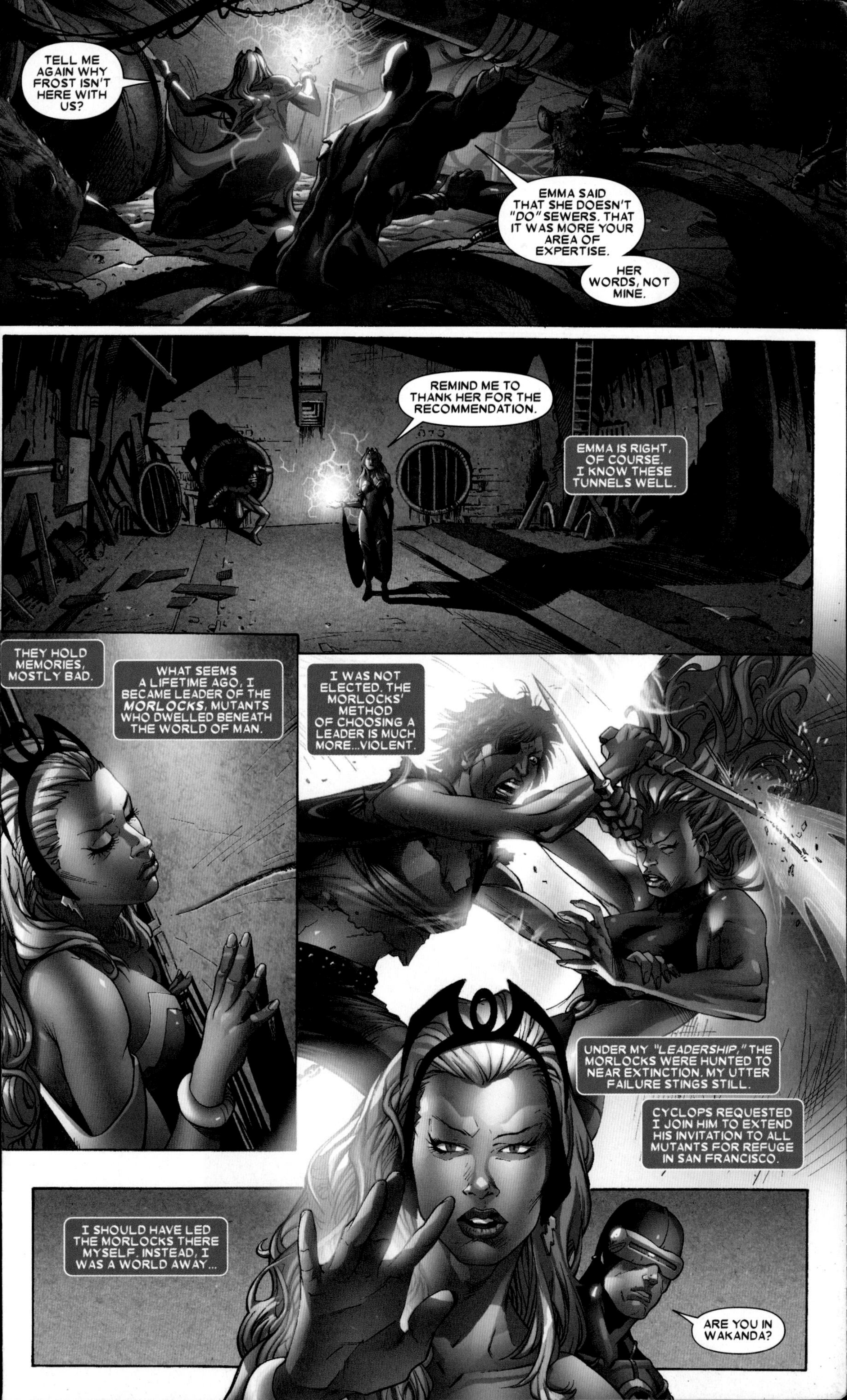
TELL ME AGAIN WHY FROST ISN'T HERE WITH US?
EMMA SAID THAT SHE DOESN'T "DO" SEWERS. THAT IT WAS MORE YOUR AREA OF EXPERTISE.
HER WORDS, NOT MINE.
REMIND ME TO THANK HER FOR THE RECOMMENDATION.
EMMA IS RIGHT, OF COURSE. I KNOW THESE TUNNELS WELL.
THEY HOLD MEMORIES, MOSTLY BAD.
WHAT SEEMS A LIFETIME AGO, I BECAME LEADER OF THE MORLOCKS, MUTANTS WHO DWELLED BENEATH THE WORLD OF MAN.
I WAS NOT ELECTED. THE MORLOCKS' METHOD OF CHOOSING A LEADER IS MUCH MORE...VIOLENT.
UNDER MY "LEADERSHIP," THE MORLOCKS WERE HUNTED TO NEAR EXTINCTION. MY UTTER FAILURE STINGS STILL.
CYCLOPS REQUESTED I JOIN HIM TO EXTEND HIS INVITATION TO ALL MUTANTS FOR REFUGE IN SAN FRANCISCO.
I SHOULD HAVE LED THE MORLOCKS THERE MYSELF. INSTEAD, I WAS A WORLD AWAY...
ARE YOU IN WAKANDA?

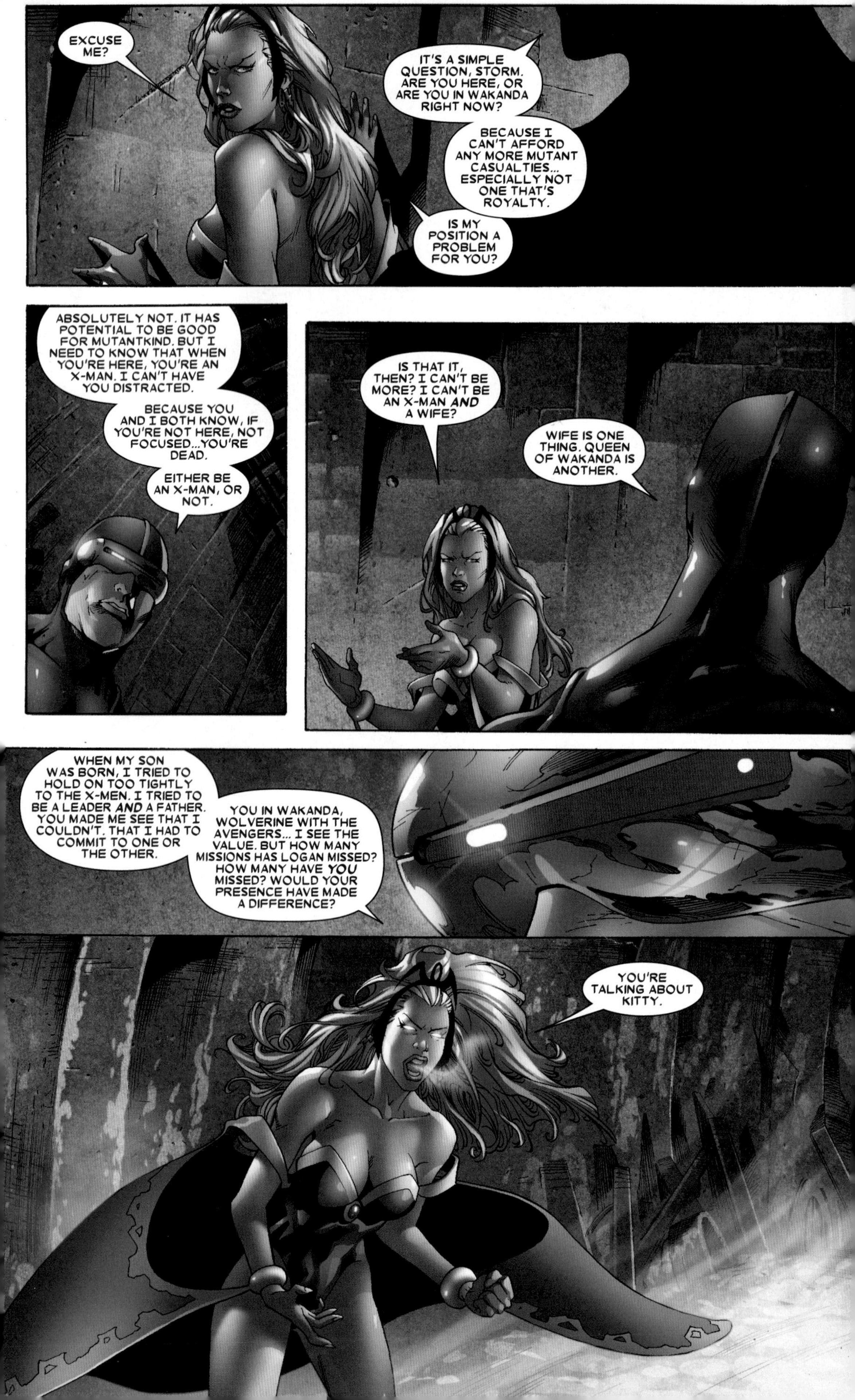
EXCUSE ME?
IT'S A SIMPLE QUESTION, STORM. ARE YOU HERE, OR ARE YOU IN WAKANDA RIGHT NOW?
BECAUSE I CAN'T AFFORD ANY MORE MUTANT CASUALTIES... ESPECIALLY NOT ONE THAT'S ROYALTY.
IS MY POSITION A PROBLEM FOR YOU?
ABSOLUTELY NOT. IT HAS POTENTIAL TO BE GOOD FOR MUTANTKIND. BUT I NEED TO KNOW THAT WHEN YOU'RE HERE, YOU'RE AN X-MAN. I CAN'T HAVE YOU DISTRACTED.
BECAUSE YOU AND I BOTH KNOW, IF YOU'RE NOT HERE, NOT FOCUSED...YOU'RE DEAD.
EITHER BE AN X-MAN, OR NOT.
IS THAT IT, THEN? I CAN'T BE MORE? I CAN'T BE AN X-MAN *AND* A WIFE?
WIFE IS ONE THING. QUEEN OF WAKANDA IS ANOTHER.
WHEN MY SON WAS BORN, I TRIED TO HOLD ON TOO TIGHTLY TO THE X-MEN. I TRIED TO BE A LEADER *AND* A FATHER. YOU MADE ME SEE THAT I COULDN'T. THAT I HAD TO COMMIT TO ONE OR THE OTHER.
YOU IN WAKANDA, WOLVERINE WITH THE AVENGERS... I SEE THE VALUE. BUT HOW MANY MISSIONS HAS LOGAN MISSED? HOW MANY HAVE *YOU* MISSED? WOULD YOUR PRESENCE HAVE MADE A DIFFERENCE?
YOU'RE TALKING ABOUT KITTY.

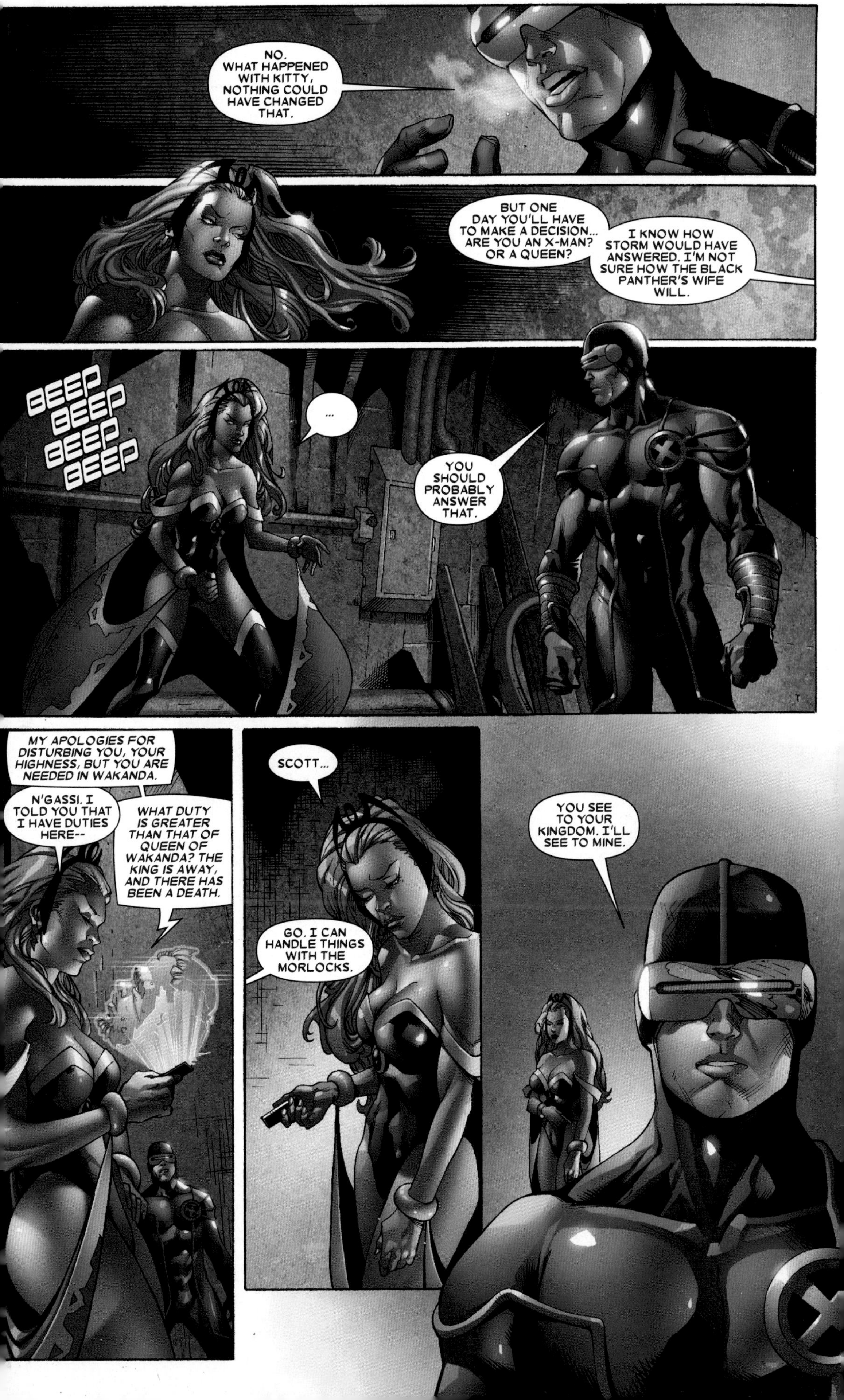
NO. WHAT HAPPENED WITH KITTY, NOTHING COULD HAVE CHANGED THAT.
BUT ONE DAY YOU'LL HAVE TO MAKE A DECISION... ARE YOU AN X-MAN? OR A QUEEN?
I KNOW HOW STORM WOULD HAVE ANSWERED. I'M NOT SURE HOW THE BLACK PANTHER'S WIFE WILL.
BEEP BEEP BEEP BEEP
...
YOU SHOULD PROBABLY ANSWER THAT.
MY APOLOGIES FOR DISTURBING YOU, YOUR HIGHNESS, BUT YOU ARE NEEDED IN WAKANDA.
N'GASSI. I TOLD YOU THAT I HAVE DUTIES HERE--
WHAT DUTY IS GREATER THAN THAT OF QUEEN OF WAKANDA? THE KING IS AWAY, AND THERE HAS BEEN A DEATH.
SCOTT...
GO. I CAN HANDLE THINGS WITH THE MORLOCKS.
YOU SEE TO YOUR KINGDOM. I'LL SEE TO MINE.

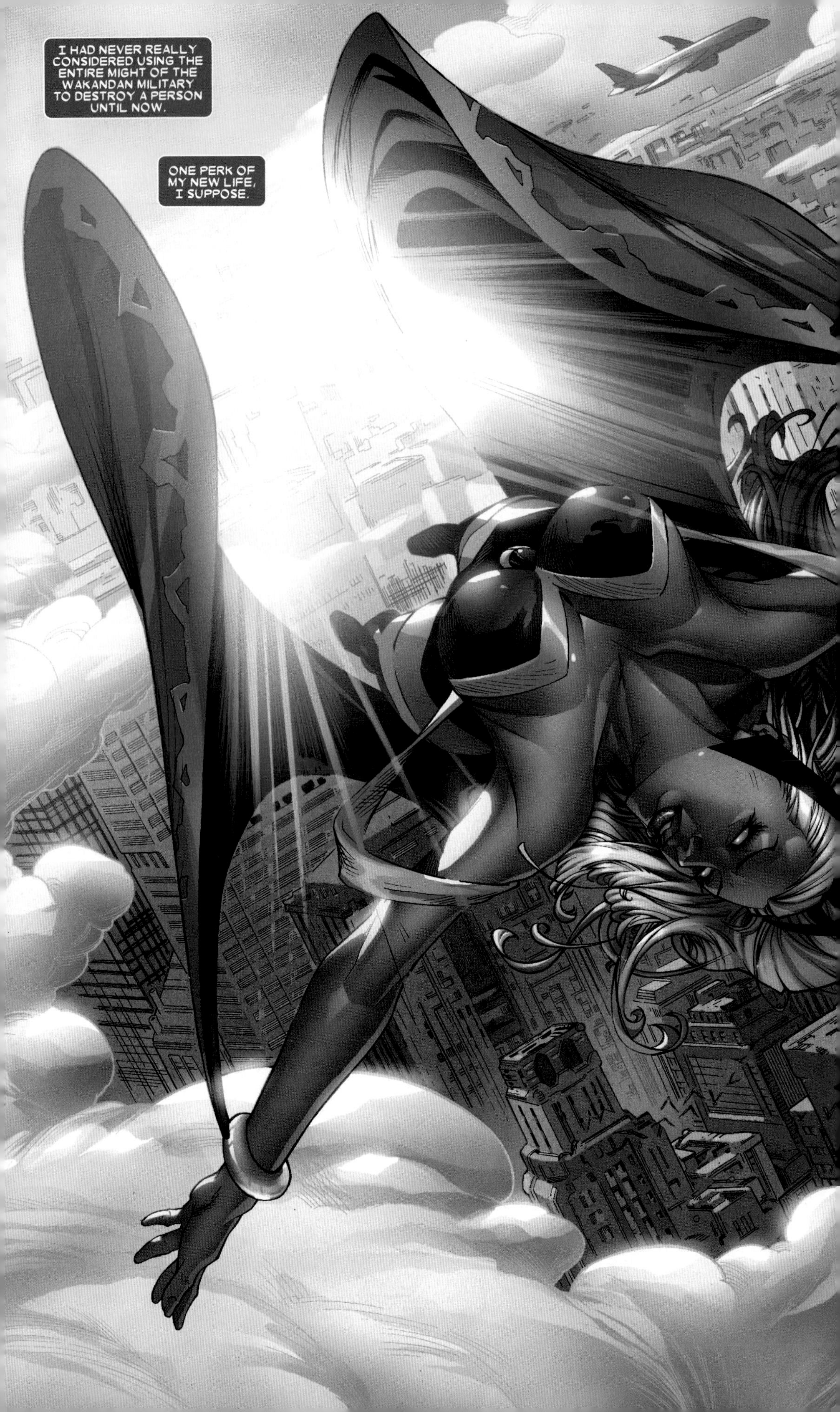
I HAD NEVER REALLY CONSIDERED USING THE ENTIRE MIGHT OF THE WAKANDAN MILITARY TO DESTROY A PERSON UNTIL NOW.
ONE PERK OF MY NEW LIFE, I SUPPOSE.

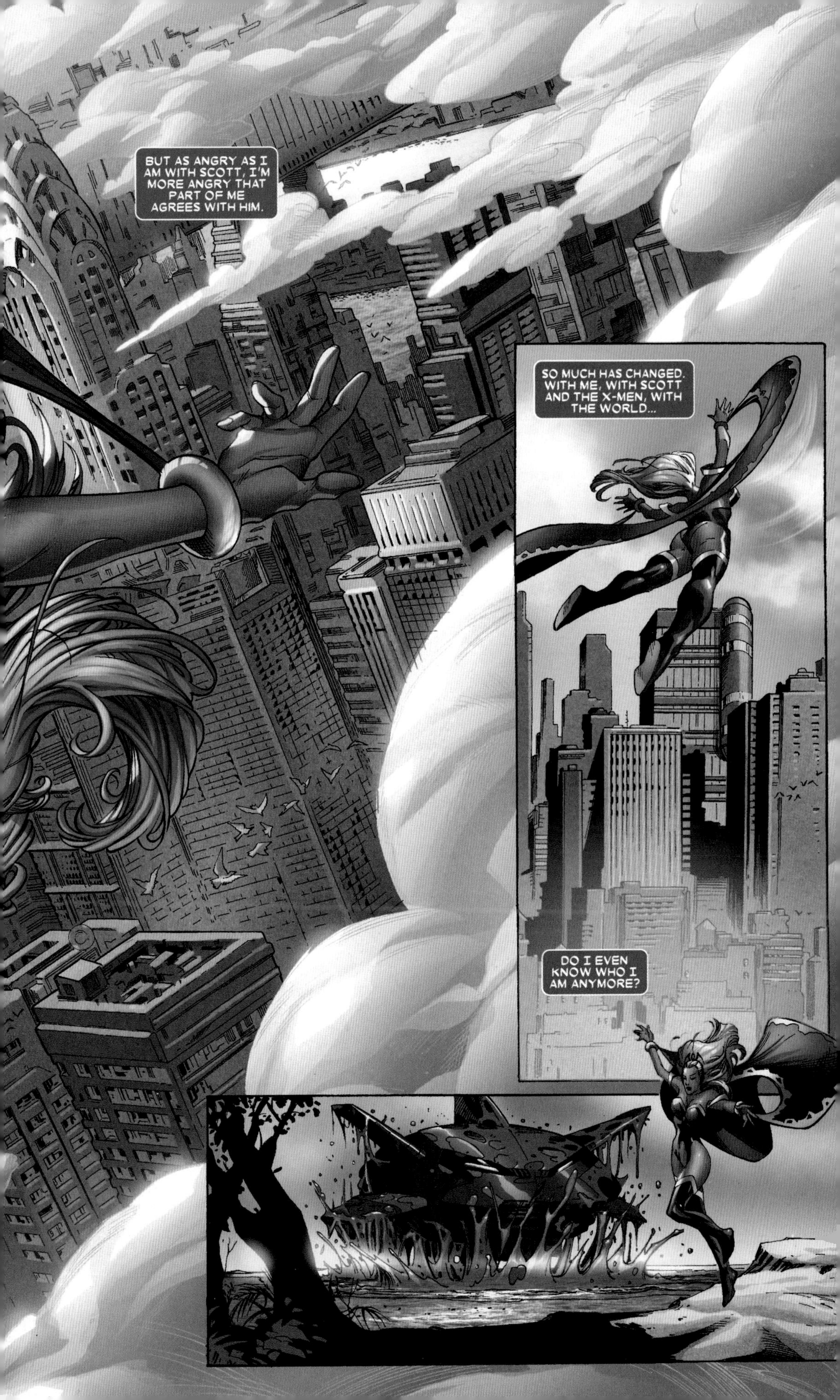

BUT AS ANGRY AS I AM WITH SCOTT, I'M MORE ANGRY THAT PART OF ME AGREES WITH HIM.
SO MUCH HAS CHANGED. WITH ME, WITH SCOTT AND THE X-MEN, WITH THE WORLD...
DO I EVEN KNOW WHO I AM ANYMORE?

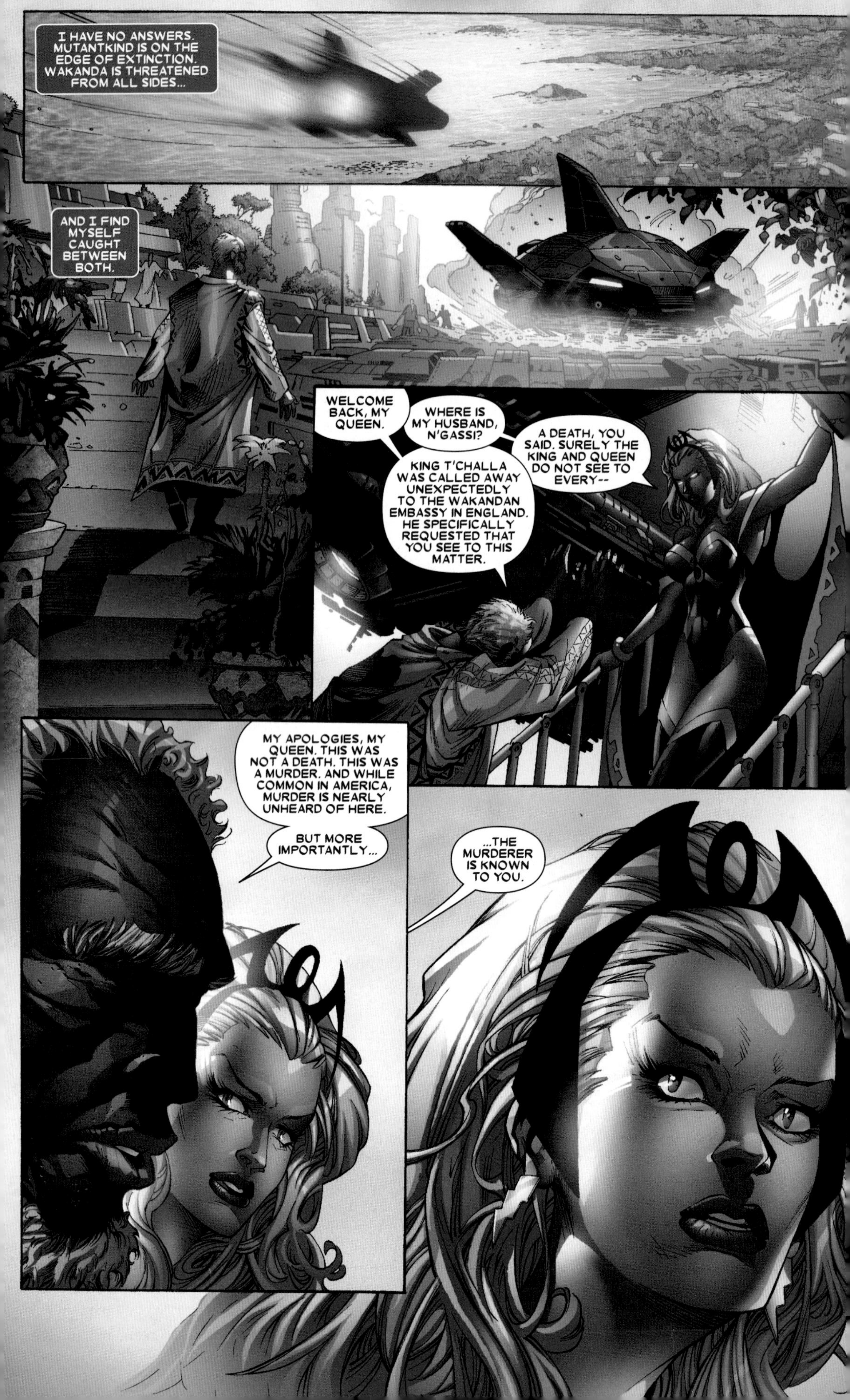

I HAVE NO ANSWERS. MUTANTKIND IS ON THE EDGE OF EXTINCTION. WAKANDA IS THREATENED FROM ALL SIDES...
AND I FIND MYSELF CAUGHT BETWEEN BOTH.
WELCOME BACK, MY QUEEN.
WHERE IS MY HUSBAND, N'GASSI?
KING T'CHALLA WAS CALLED AWAY UNEXPECTEDLY TO THE WAKANDAN EMBASSY IN ENGLAND. HE SPECIFICALLY REQUESTED THAT YOU SEE TO THIS MATTER.
A DEATH, YOU SAID. SURELY THE KING AND QUEEN DO NOT SEE TO EVERY--
MY APOLOGIES, MY QUEEN. THIS WAS NOT A DEATH. THIS WAS A MURDER. AND WHILE COMMON IN AMERICA, MURDER IS NEARLY UNHEARD OF HERE.
BUT MORE IMPORTANTLY...
...THE MURDERER IS KNOWN TO YOU.

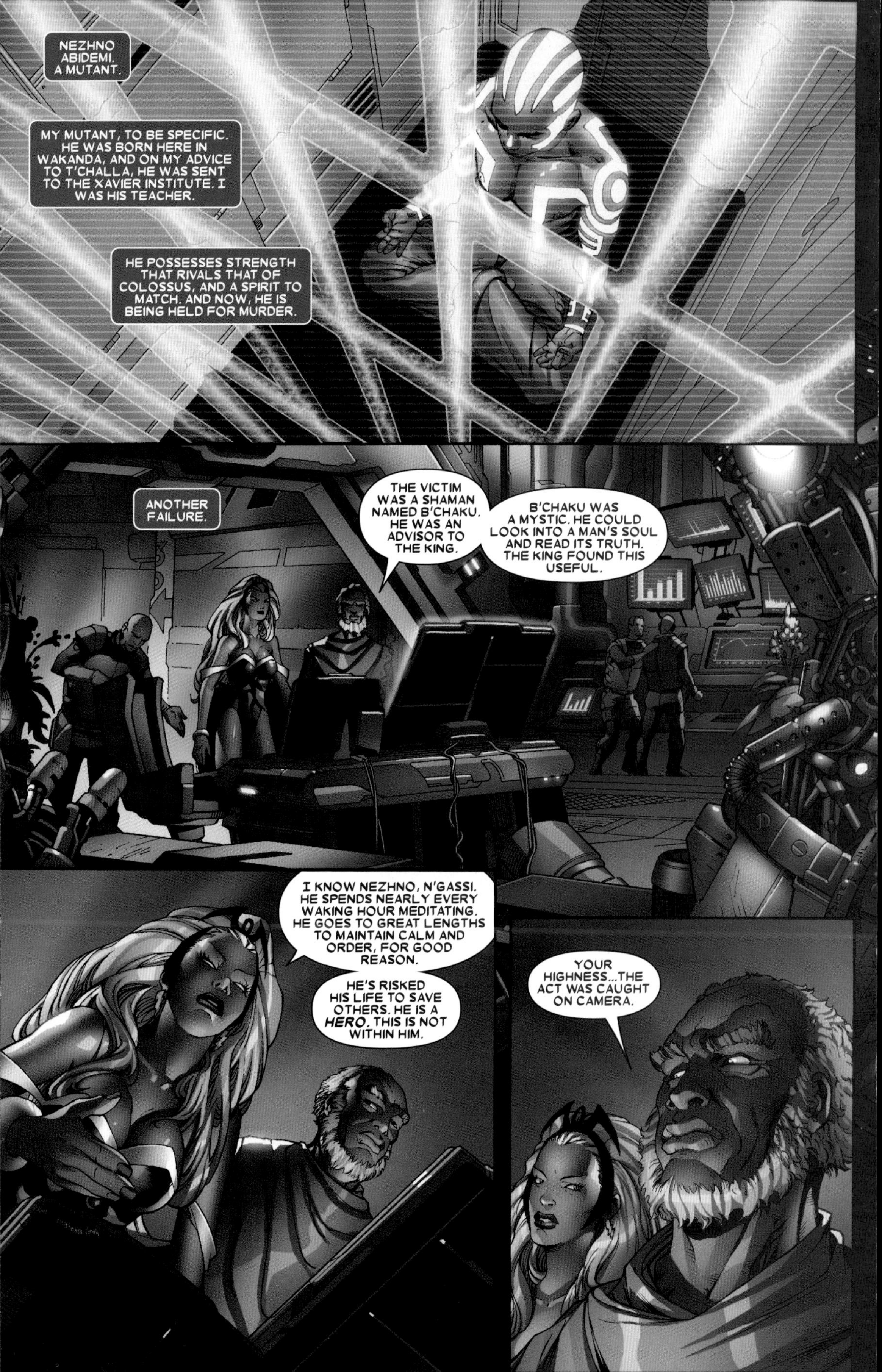
NEZHNO ABIDEMI. A MUTANT.
MY MUTANT, TO BE SPECIFIC. HE WAS BORN HERE IN WAKANDA, AND ON MY ADVICE TO T'CHALLA, HE WAS SENT TO THE XAVIER INSTITUTE. I WAS HIS TEACHER.
HE POSSESSES STRENGTH THAT RIVALS THAT OF COLOSSUS, AND A SPIRIT TO MATCH. AND NOW, HE IS BEING HELD FOR MURDER.
ANOTHER FAILURE.
THE VICTIM WAS A SHAMAN NAMED B'CHAKU. HE WAS AN ADVISOR TO THE KING.
B'CHAKU WAS A MYSTIC. HE COULD LOOK INTO A MAN'S SOUL AND READ ITS TRUTH. THE KING FOUND THIS USEFUL.
I KNOW NEZHNO, N'GASSI. HE SPENDS NEARLY EVERY WAKING HOUR MEDITATING. HE GOES TO GREAT LENGTHS TO MAINTAIN CALM AND ORDER, FOR GOOD REASON.
HE'S RISKED HIS LIFE TO SAVE OTHERS. HE IS A HERO. THIS IS NOT WITHIN HIM.
YOUR HIGHNESS...THE ACT WAS CAUGHT ON CAMERA.

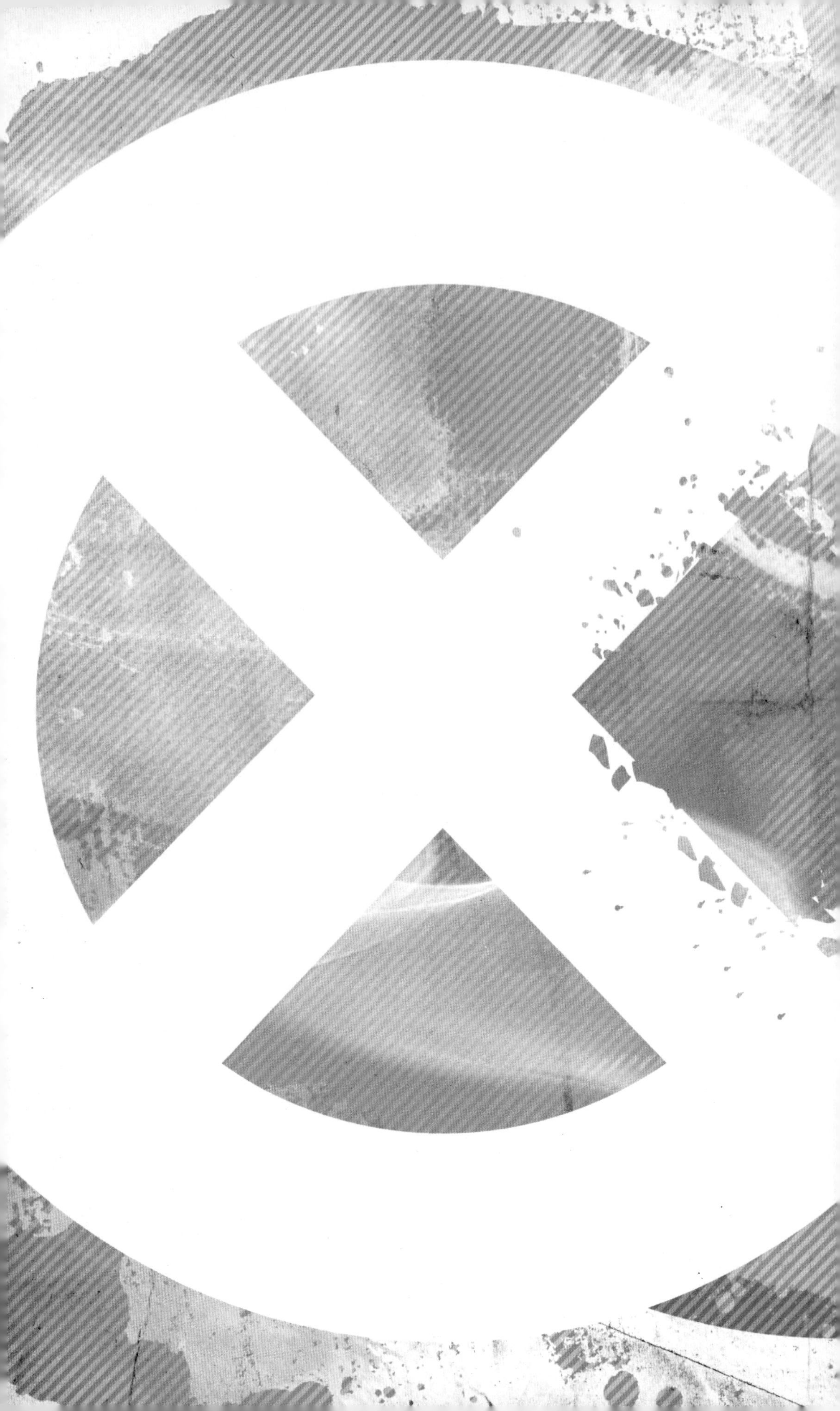

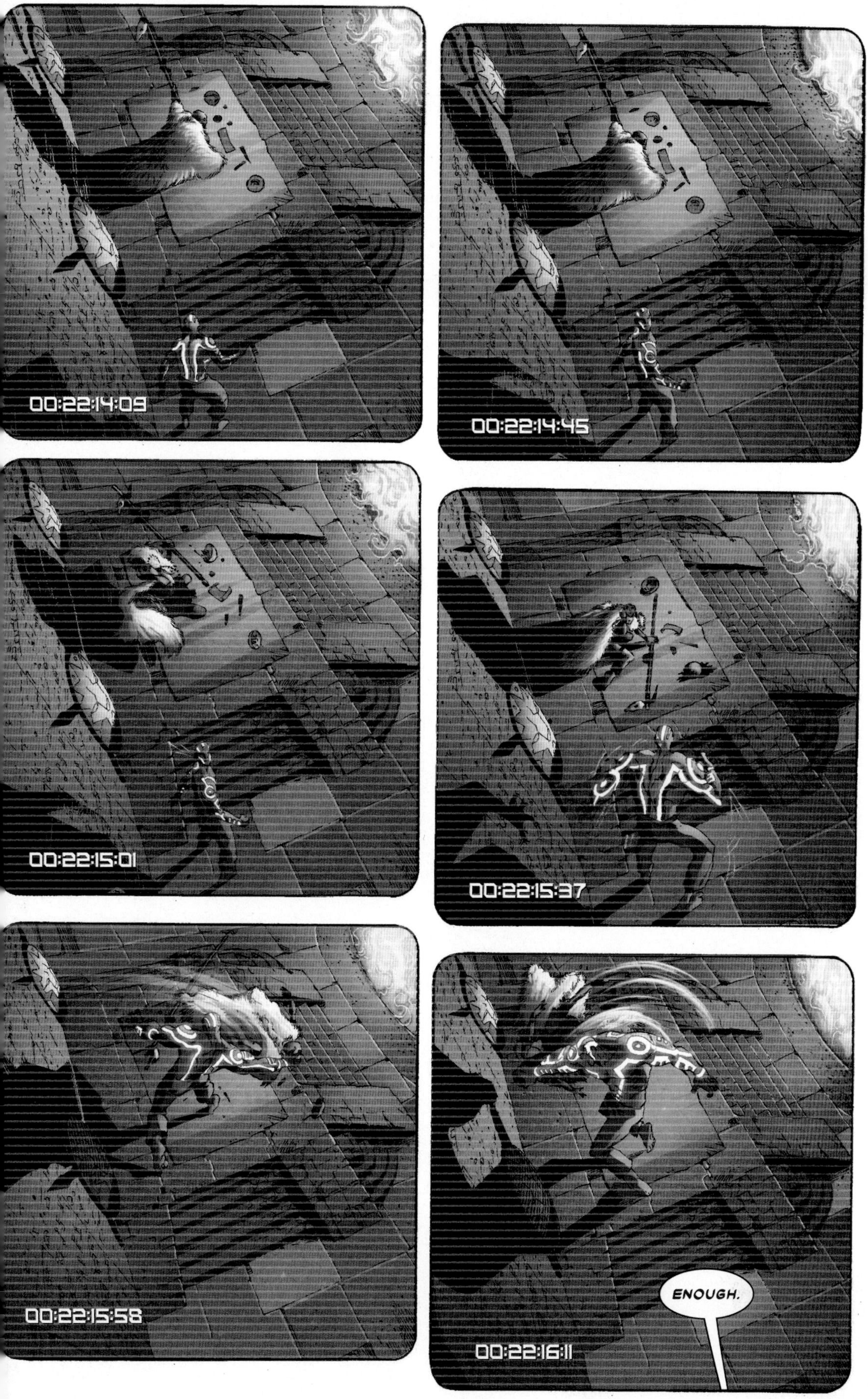
00:22:14:09
00:22:14:45
00:22:15:01
00:22:15:37
00:22:15:58
ENOUGH.
00:22:16:11

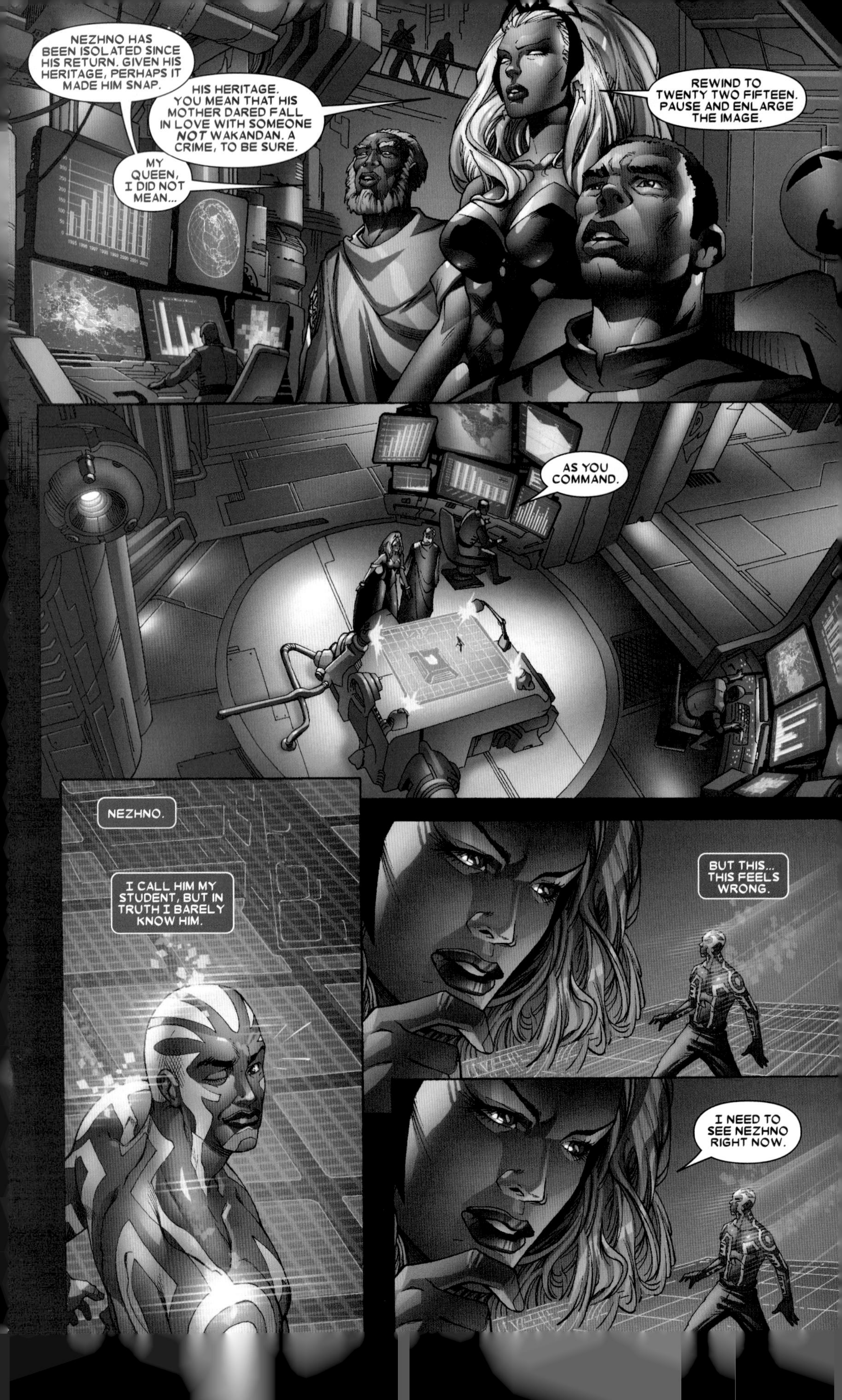
NEZHNO HAS BEEN ISOLATED SINCE HIS RETURN. GIVEN HIS HERITAGE, PERHAPS IT MADE HIM SNAP.
HIS HERITAGE. YOU MEAN THAT HIS MOTHER DARED FALL IN LOVE WITH SOMEONE NOT WAKANDAN. A CRIME, TO BE SURE.
MY QUEEN, I DID NOT MEAN...
REWIND TO TWENTY TWO FIFTEEN. PAUSE AND ENLARGE THE IMAGE.
AS YOU COMMAND.
NEZHNO.
I CALL HIM MY STUDENT, BUT IN TRUTH I BARELY KNOW HIM.
BUT THIS... THIS FEELS WRONG.
I NEED TO SEE NEZHNO RIGHT NOW.

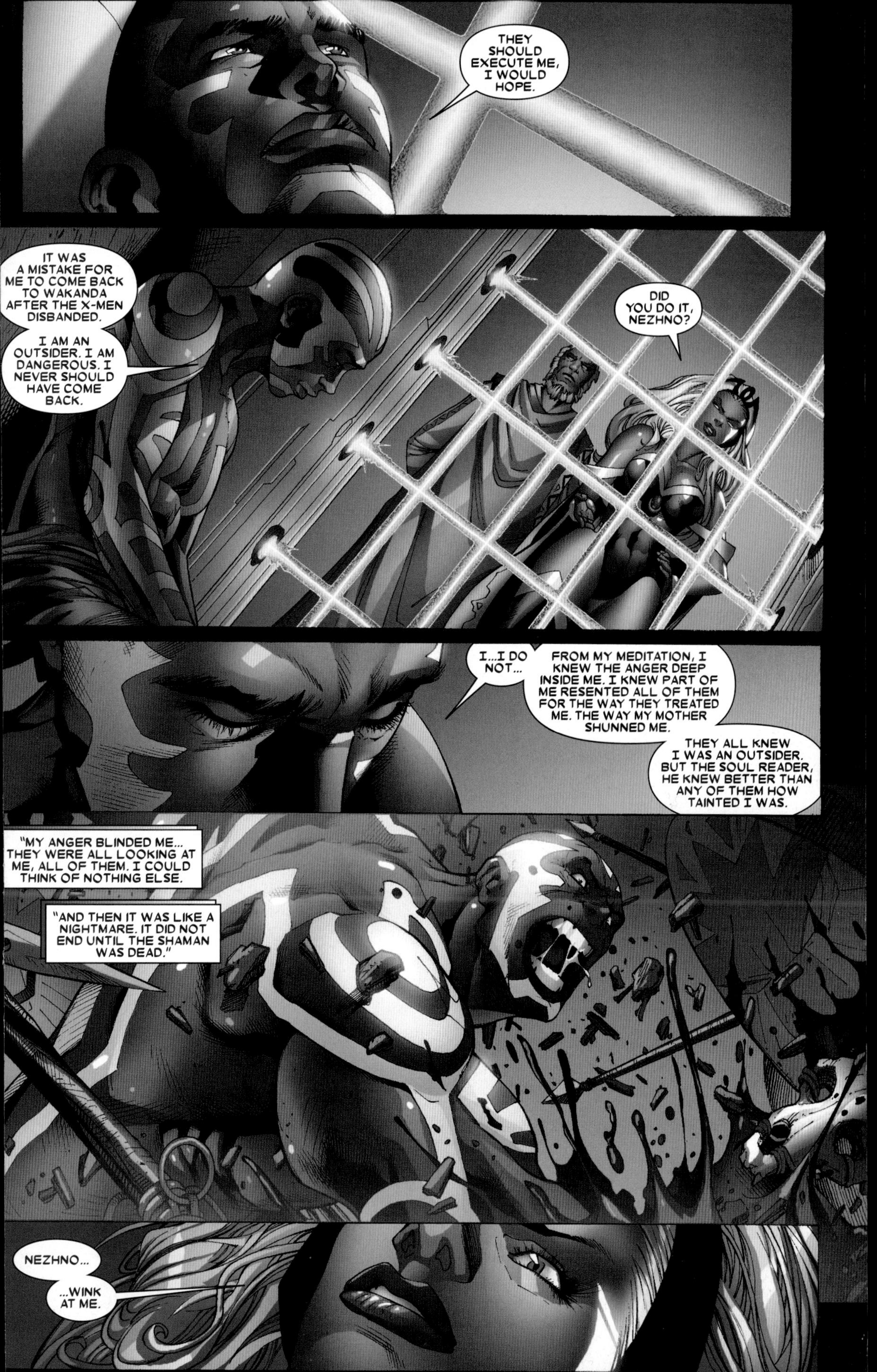
THEY SHOULD EXECUTE ME, I WOULD HOPE.
IT WAS A MISTAKE FOR ME TO COME BACK TO WAKANDA AFTER THE X-MEN DISBANDED.
I AM AN OUTSIDER. I AM DANGEROUS. I NEVER SHOULD HAVE COME BACK.
DID YOU DO IT, NEZHNO?
I...I DO NOT...
FROM MY MEDITATION, I KNEW THE ANGER DEEP INSIDE ME. I KNEW PART OF ME RESENTED ALL OF THEM FOR THE WAY THEY TREATED ME. THE WAY MY MOTHER SHUNNED ME.
THEY ALL KNEW I WAS AN OUTSIDER. BUT THE SOUL READER, HE KNEW BETTER THAN ANY OF THEM HOW TAINTED I WAS.
"MY ANGER BLINDED ME... THEY WERE ALL LOOKING AT ME, ALL OF THEM. I COULD THINK OF NOTHING ELSE.
"AND THEN IT WAS LIKE A NIGHTMARE. IT DID NOT END UNTIL THE SHAMAN WAS DEAD."
NEZHNO...
...WINK AT ME.

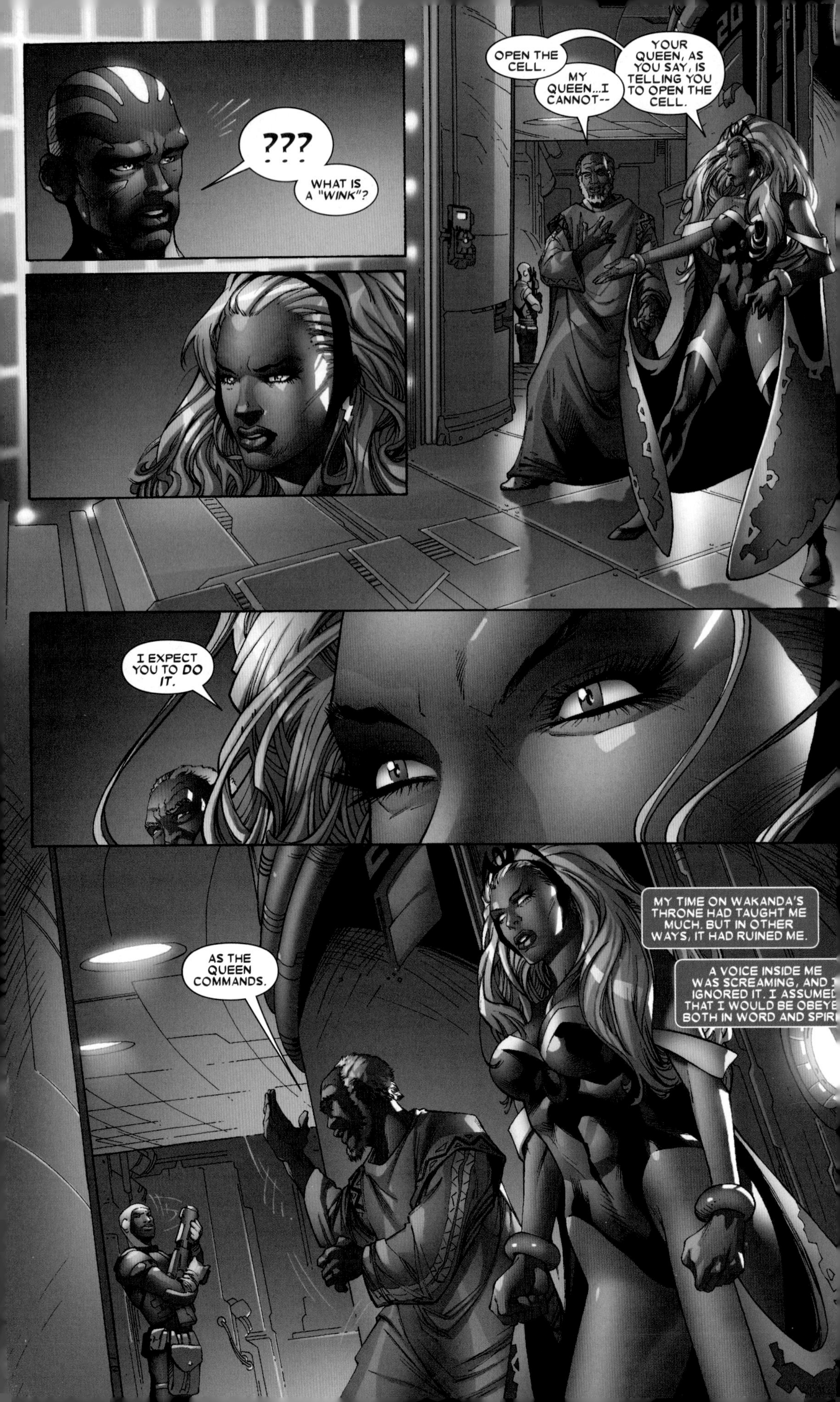
???
WHAT IS A "WINK"?
OPEN THE CELL.
MY QUEEN...I CANNOT--
YOUR QUEEN, AS YOU SAY, IS TELLING YOU TO OPEN THE CELL.
I EXPECT YOU TO DO IT.
AS THE QUEEN COMMANDS.
MY TIME ON WAKANDA'S THRONE HAD TAUGHT ME MUCH. BUT IN OTHER WAYS, IT HAD RUINED ME.
A VOICE INSIDE ME WAS SCREAMING, AND I IGNORED IT. I ASSUMED THAT I WOULD BE OBEYE BOTH IN WORD AND SPIR

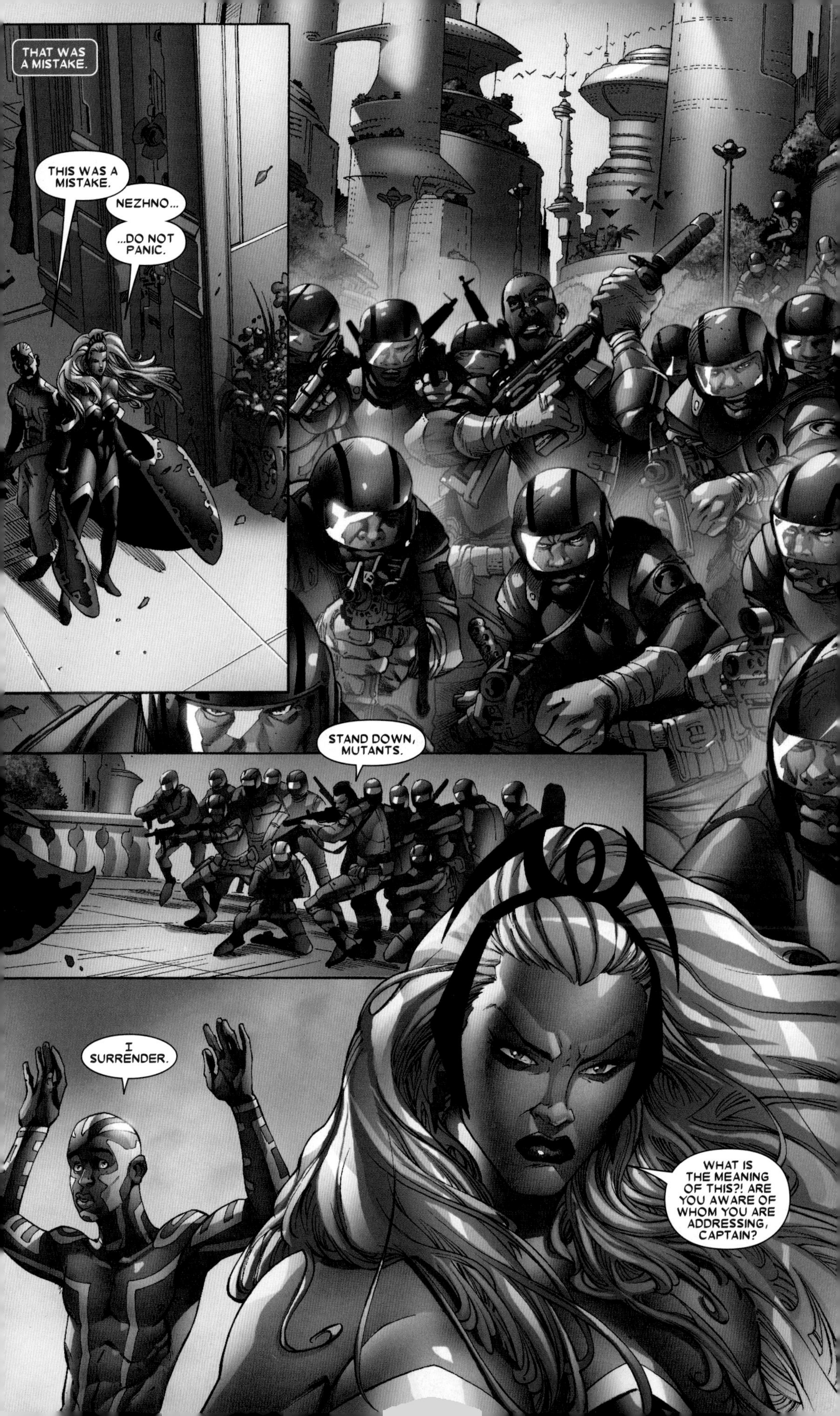
THAT WAS A MISTAKE.
THIS WAS A MISTAKE.
NEZHNO...
...DO NOT PANIC.
STAND DOWN, MUTANTS.
I SURRENDER.
WHAT IS THE MEANING OF THIS?! ARE YOU AWARE OF WHOM YOU ARE ADDRESSING, CAPTAIN?

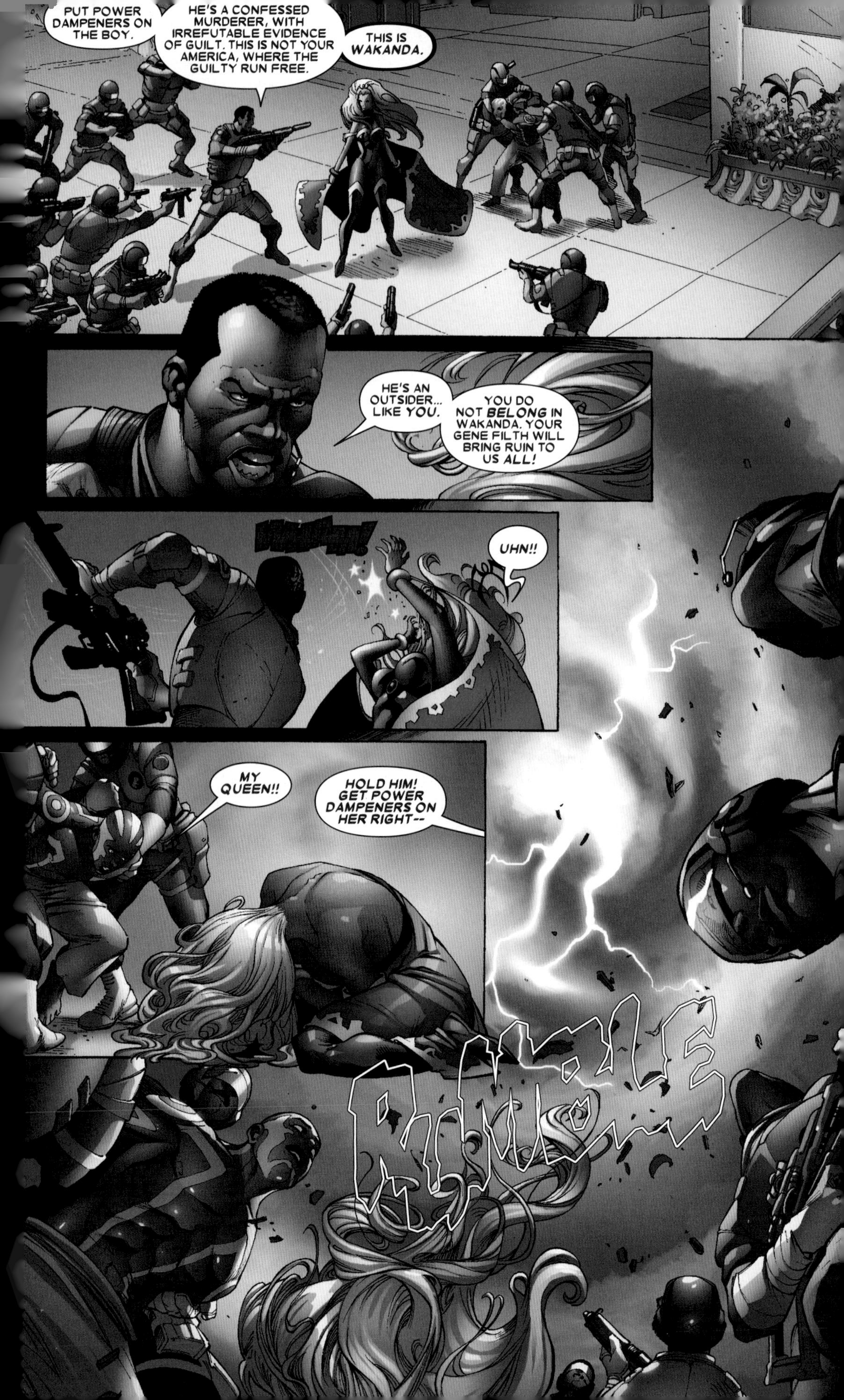
PUT POWER DAMPENERS ON THE BOY.
HE'S A CONFESSED MURDERER, WITH IRREFUTABLE EVIDENCE OF GUILT. THIS IS NOT YOUR AMERICA, WHERE THE GUILTY RUN FREE.
THIS IS WAKANDA.
HE'S AN OUTSIDER... LIKE YOU.
YOU DO NOT BELONG IN WAKANDA. YOUR GENE FILTH WILL BRING RUIN TO US ALL!
UHN!!
MY QUEEN!!
HOLD HIM! GET POWER DAMPENERS ON HER RIGHT--
RRUMBLE

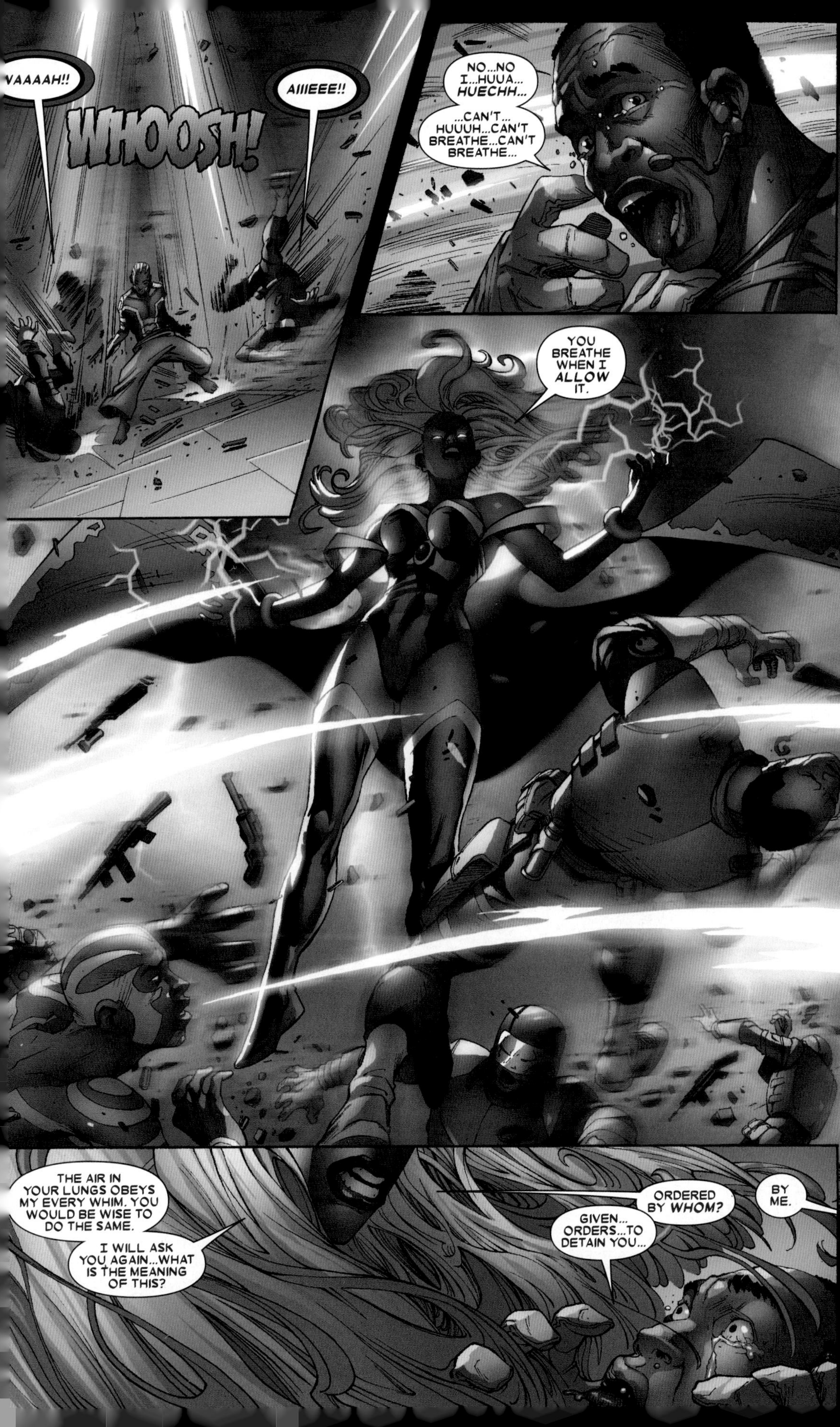
WAAAAH!!
WHOOSH!
AIIIEEE!!
NO...NO I...HUUA... HUECHH...
...CAN'T... HUUUH...CAN'T BREATHE...CAN'T BREATHE...
YOU BREATHE WHEN I ALLOW IT.
THE AIR IN YOUR LUNGS OBEYS MY EVERY WHIM. YOU WOULD BE WISE TO DO THE SAME.
I WILL ASK YOU AGAIN...WHAT IS THE MEANING OF THIS?
GIVEN... ORDERS...TO DETAIN YOU...
ORDERED BY WHOM?
BY ME.

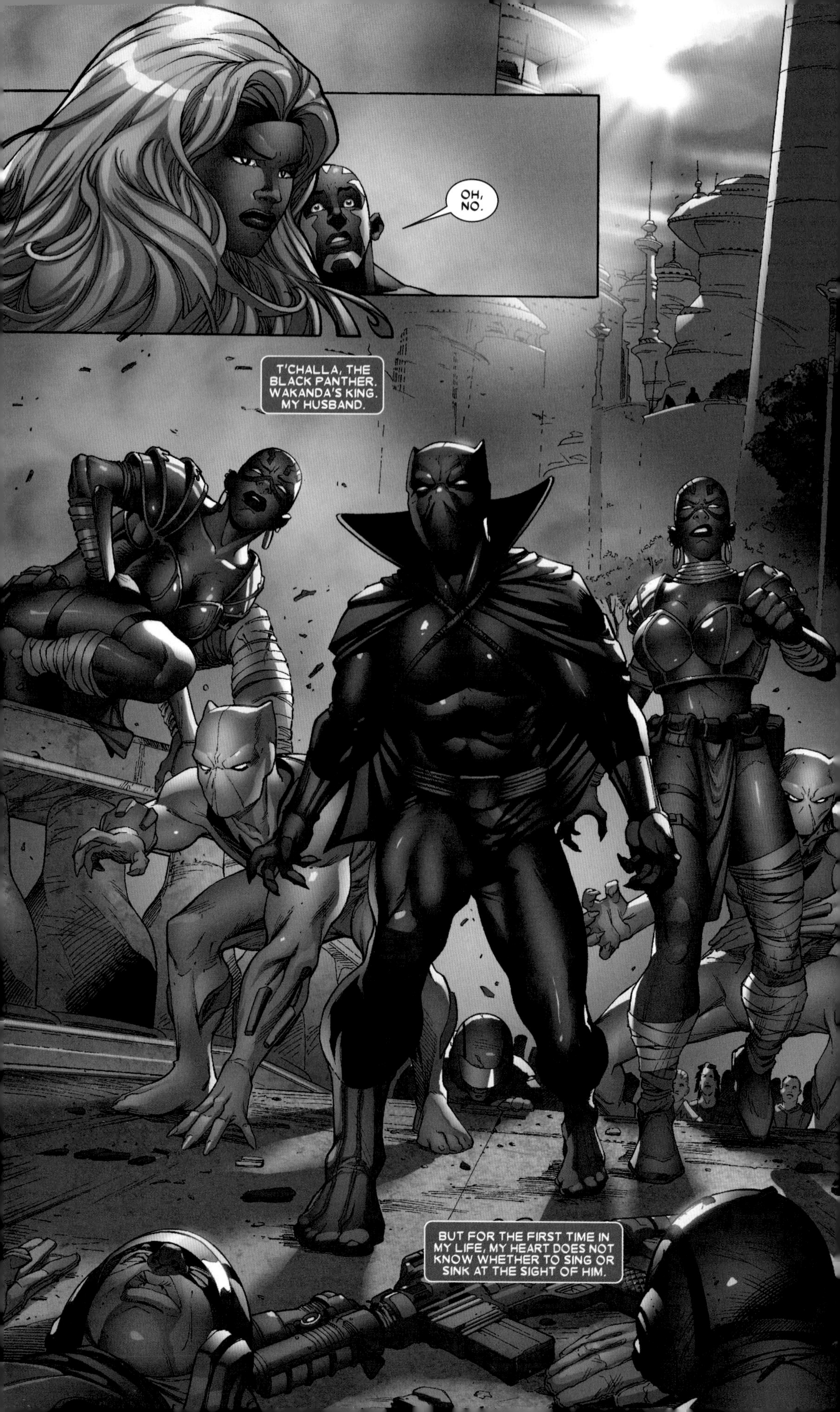

OH, NO.
T'CHALLA, THE BLACK PANTHER. WAKANDA'S KING. MY HUSBAND.
BUT FOR THE FIRST TIME IN MY LIFE, MY HEART DOES NOT KNOW WHETHER TO SING OR SINK AT THE SIGHT OF HIM.

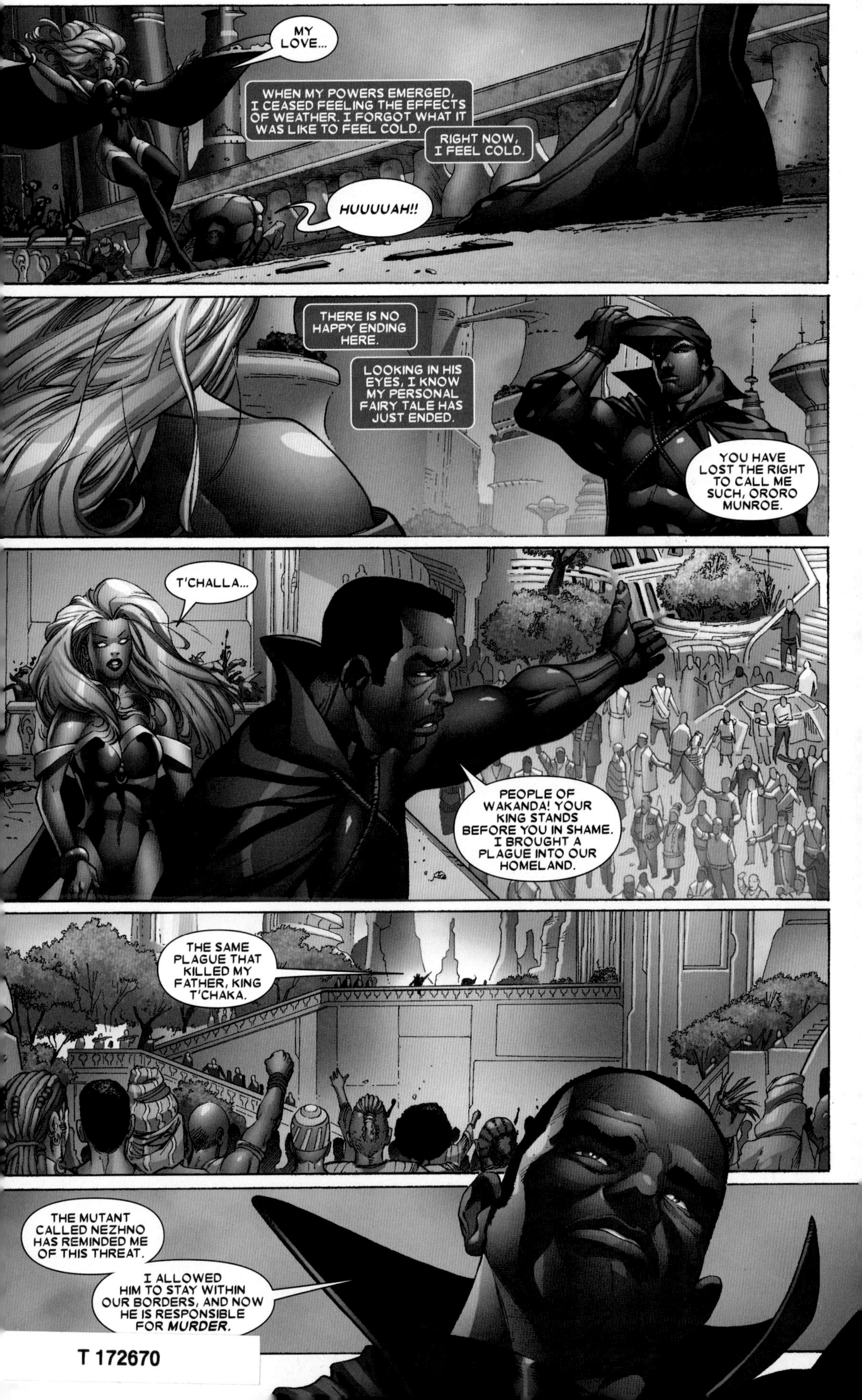
MY LOVE...
WHEN MY POWERS EMERGED, I CEASED FEELING THE EFFECTS OF WEATHER. I FORGOT WHAT IT WAS LIKE TO FEEL COLD.
RIGHT NOW, I FEEL COLD.
HUUUUAH!!
THERE IS NO HAPPY ENDING HERE.
LOOKING IN HIS EYES, I KNOW MY PERSONAL FAIRY TALE HAS JUST ENDED.
YOU HAVE LOST THE RIGHT TO CALL ME SUCH, ORORO MUNROE.
T'CHALLA...
PEOPLE OF WAKANDA! YOUR KING STANDS BEFORE YOU IN SHAME. I BROUGHT A PLAGUE INTO OUR HOMELAND.
THE SAME PLAGUE THAT KILLED MY FATHER, KING T'CHAKA.
THE MUTANT CALLED NEZHNO HAS REMINDED ME OF THIS THREAT.
I ALLOWED HIM TO STAY WITHIN OUR BORDERS, AND NOW HE IS RESPONSIBLE FOR *MURDER.*

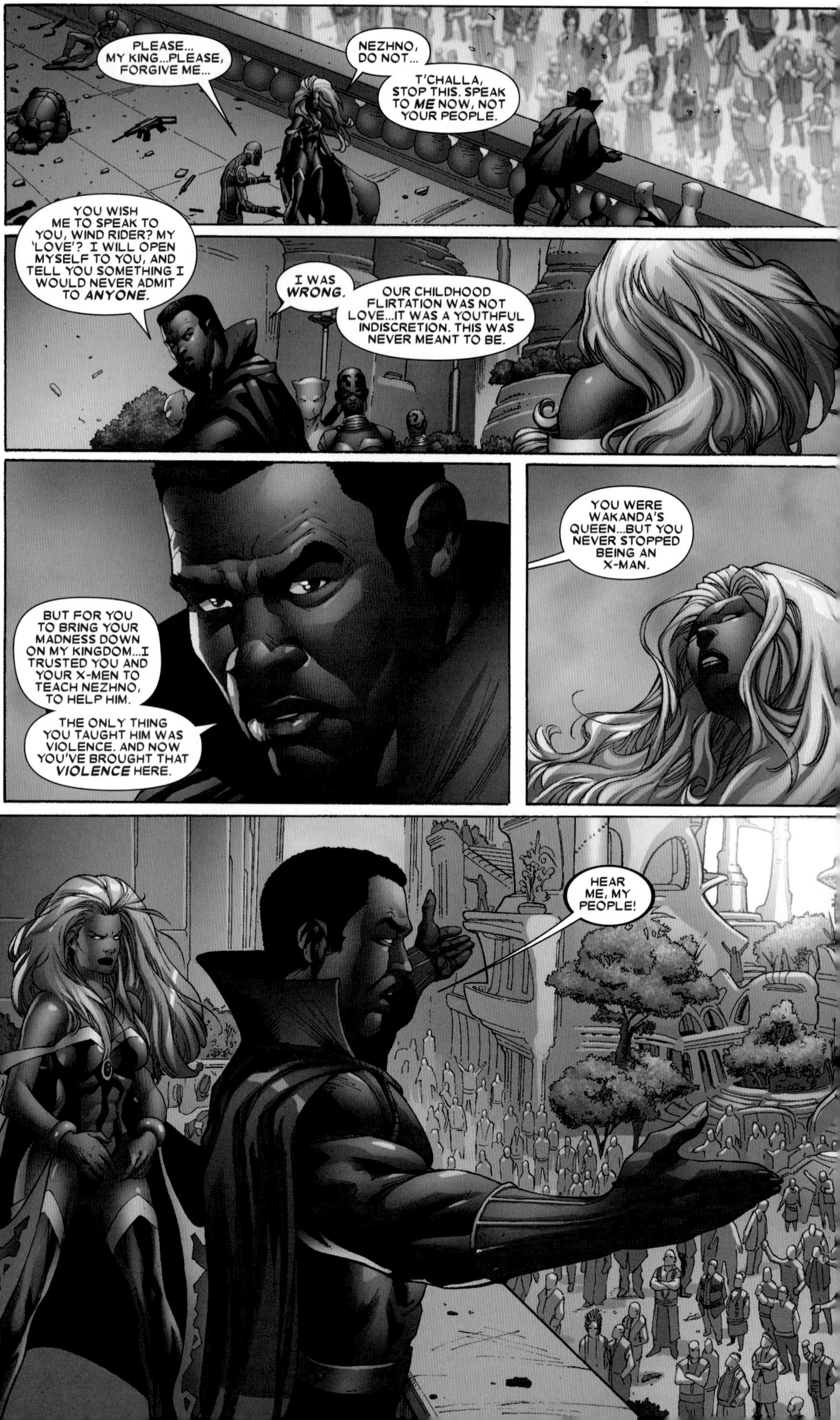
PLEASE... MY KING...PLEASE, FORGIVE ME...
NEZHNO, DO NOT...
T'CHALLA, STOP THIS. SPEAK TO *ME* NOW, NOT YOUR PEOPLE.
YOU WISH ME TO SPEAK TO YOU, WIND RIDER? MY 'LOVE'? I WILL OPEN MYSELF TO YOU, AND TELL YOU SOMETHING I WOULD NEVER ADMIT TO *ANYONE.*
I WAS *WRONG*.
OUR CHILDHOOD FLIRTATION WAS NOT LOVE...IT WAS A YOUTHFUL INDISCRETION. THIS WAS NEVER MEANT TO BE.
BUT FOR YOU TO BRING YOUR MADNESS DOWN ON MY KINGDOM...I TRUSTED YOU AND YOUR X-MEN TO TEACH NEZHNO, TO HELP HIM.
THE ONLY THING YOU TAUGHT HIM WAS VIOLENCE. AND NOW YOU'VE BROUGHT THAT *VIOLENCE* HERE.
YOU WERE WAKANDA'S QUEEN...BUT YOU NEVER STOPPED BEING AN X-MAN.
HEAR ME, MY PEOPLE!

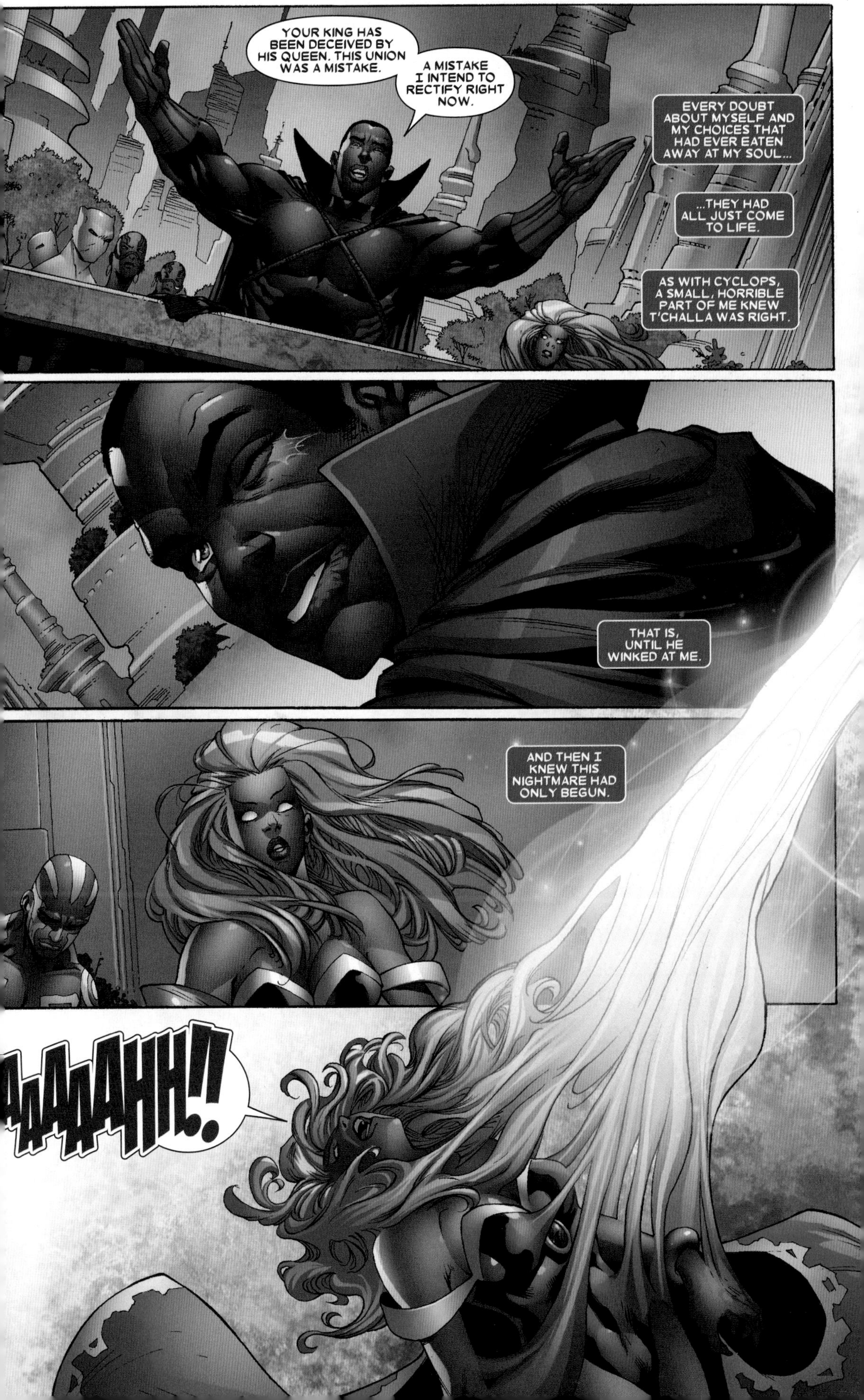
YOUR KING HAS BEEN DECEIVED BY HIS QUEEN. THIS UNION WAS A MISTAKE.
A MISTAKE I INTEND TO RECTIFY RIGHT NOW.
EVERY DOUBT ABOUT MYSELF AND MY CHOICES THAT HAD EVER EATEN AWAY AT MY SOUL...
...THEY HAD ALL JUST COME TO LIFE.
AS WITH CYCLOPS, A SMALL, HORRIBLE PART OF ME KNEW T'CHALLA WAS RIGHT.
THAT IS, UNTIL HE WINKED AT ME.
AND THEN I KNEW THIS NIGHTMARE HAD ONLY BEGUN.
AAAAAHH!?!

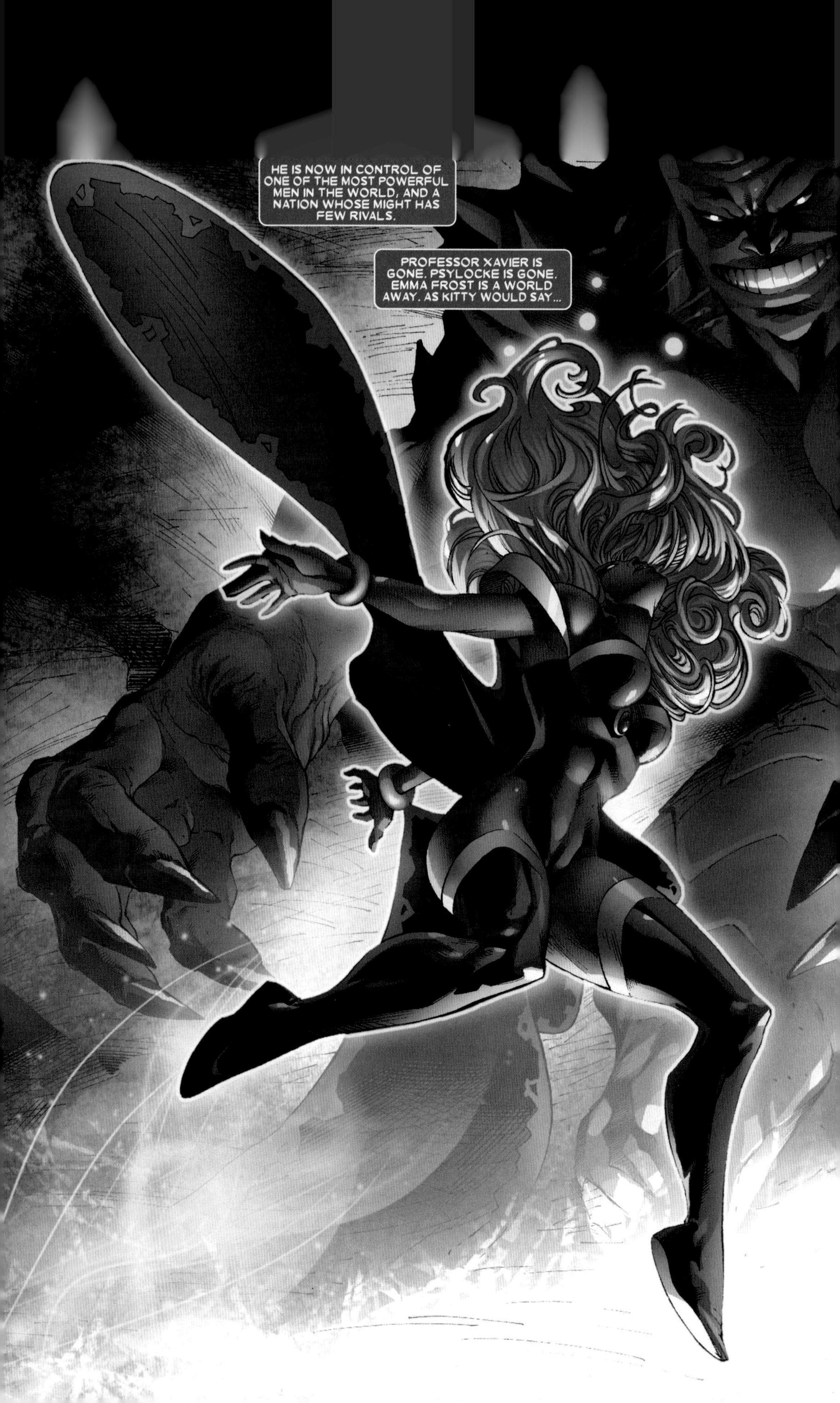
HE IS NOW IN CONTROL OF ONE OF THE MOST POWERFUL MEN IN THE WORLD, AND A NATION WHOSE MIGHT HAS FEW RIVALS.
PROFESSOR XAVIER IS GONE. PSYLOCKE IS GONE. EMMA FROST IS A WORLD AWAY. AS KITTY WOULD SAY...

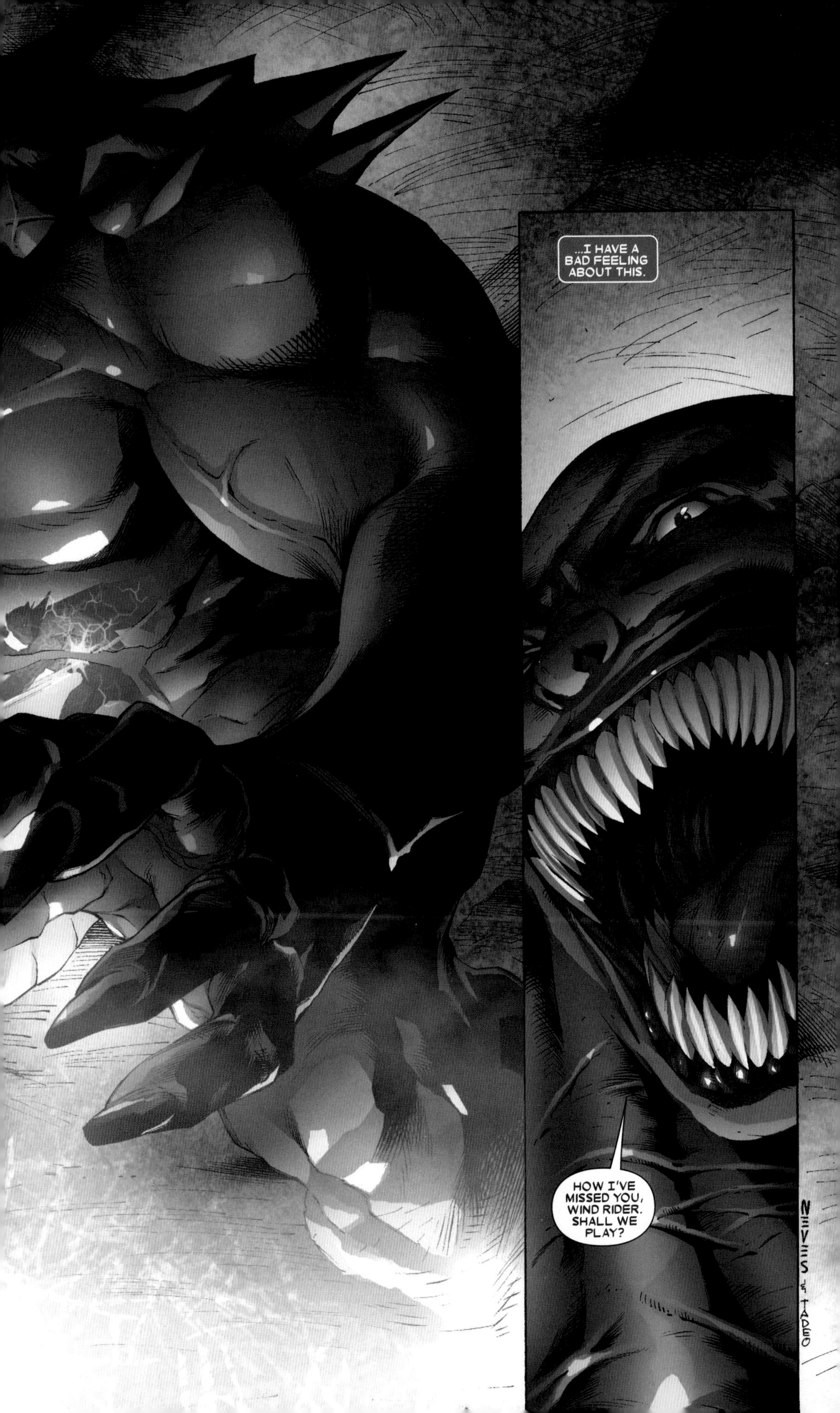
...I HAVE A BAD FEELING ABOUT THIS.
HOW I'VE MISSED YOU, WIND RIDER. SHALL WE PLAY?
NEVES TADEO

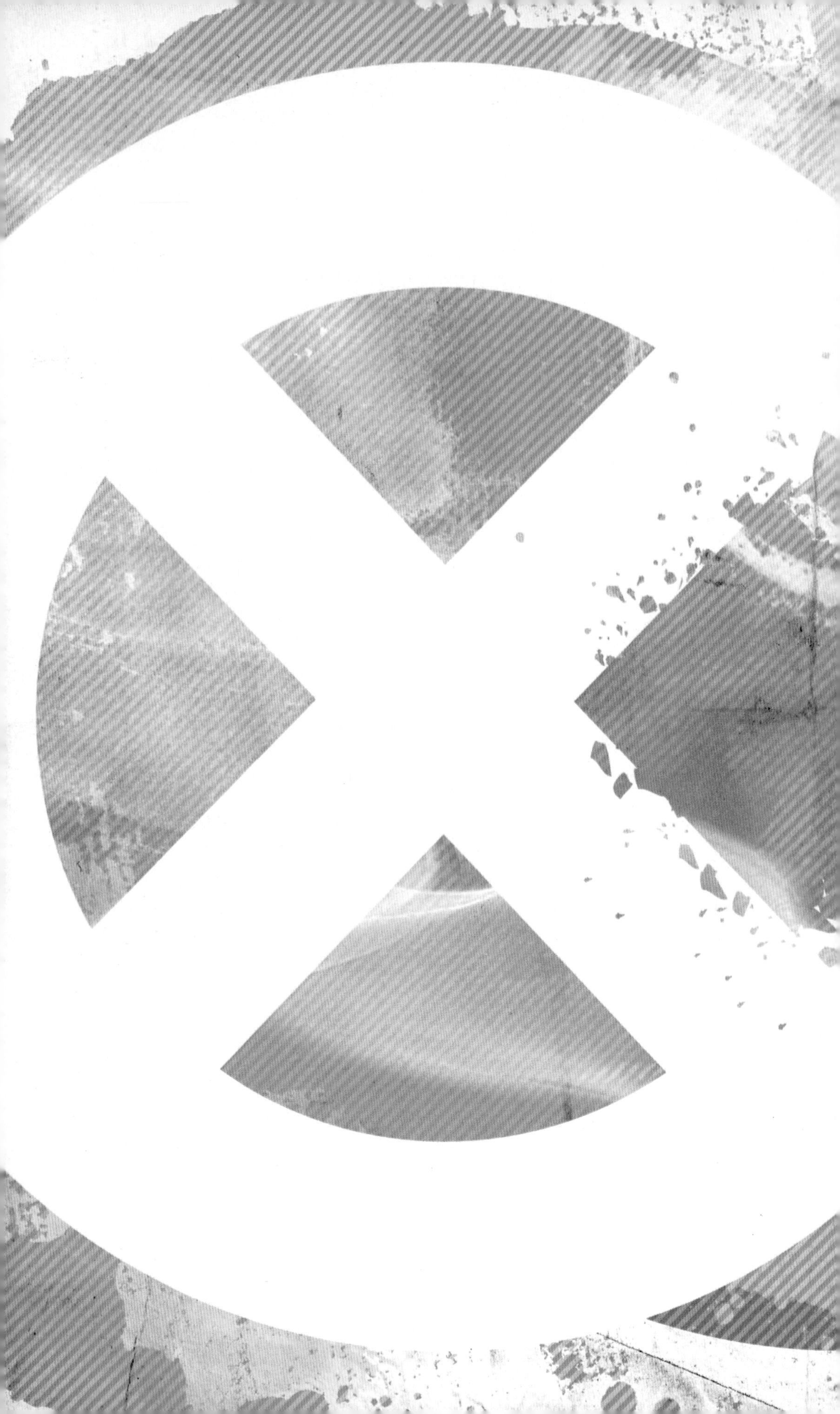

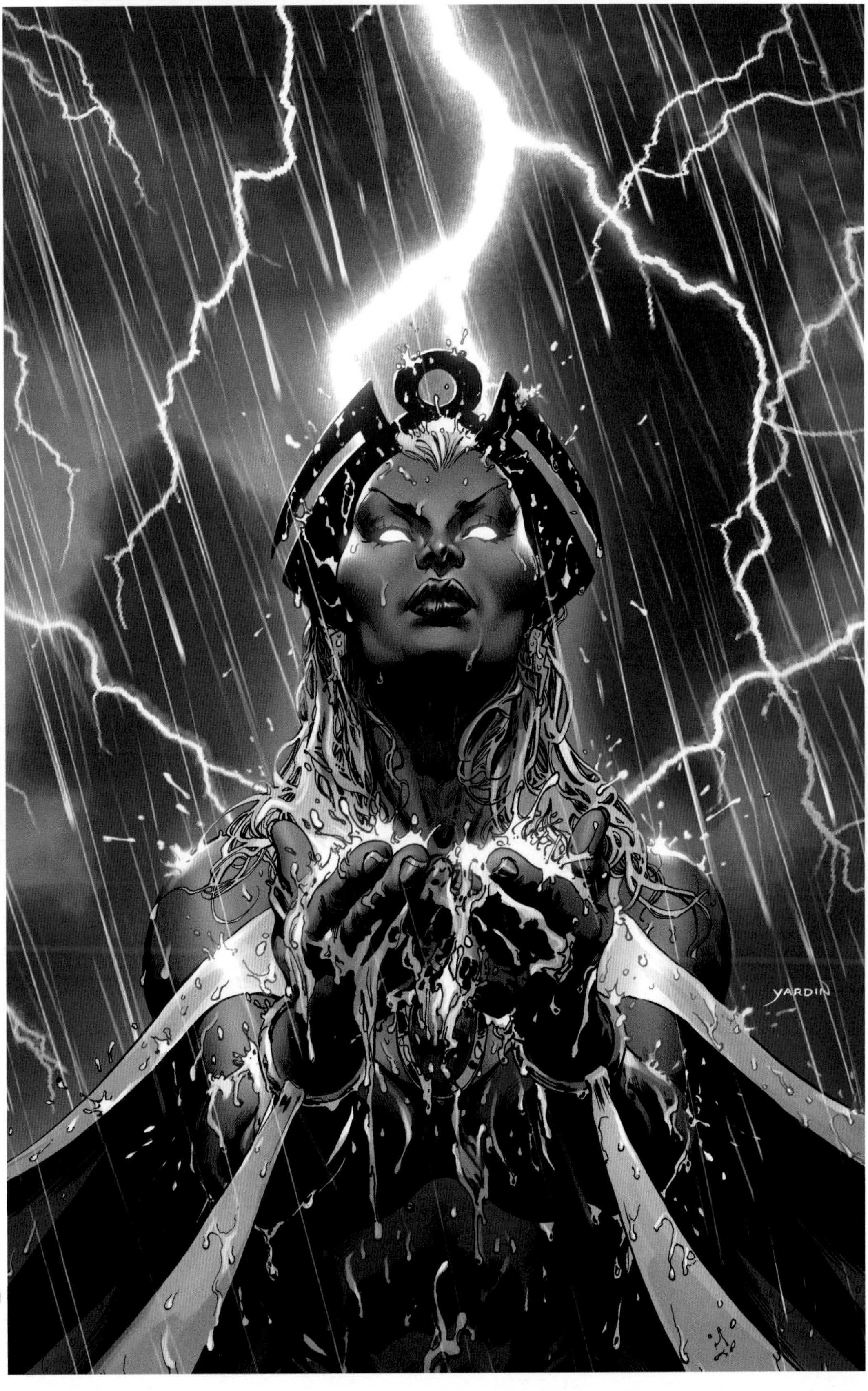
YARDIN

X-MEN: WORLDS APART #2

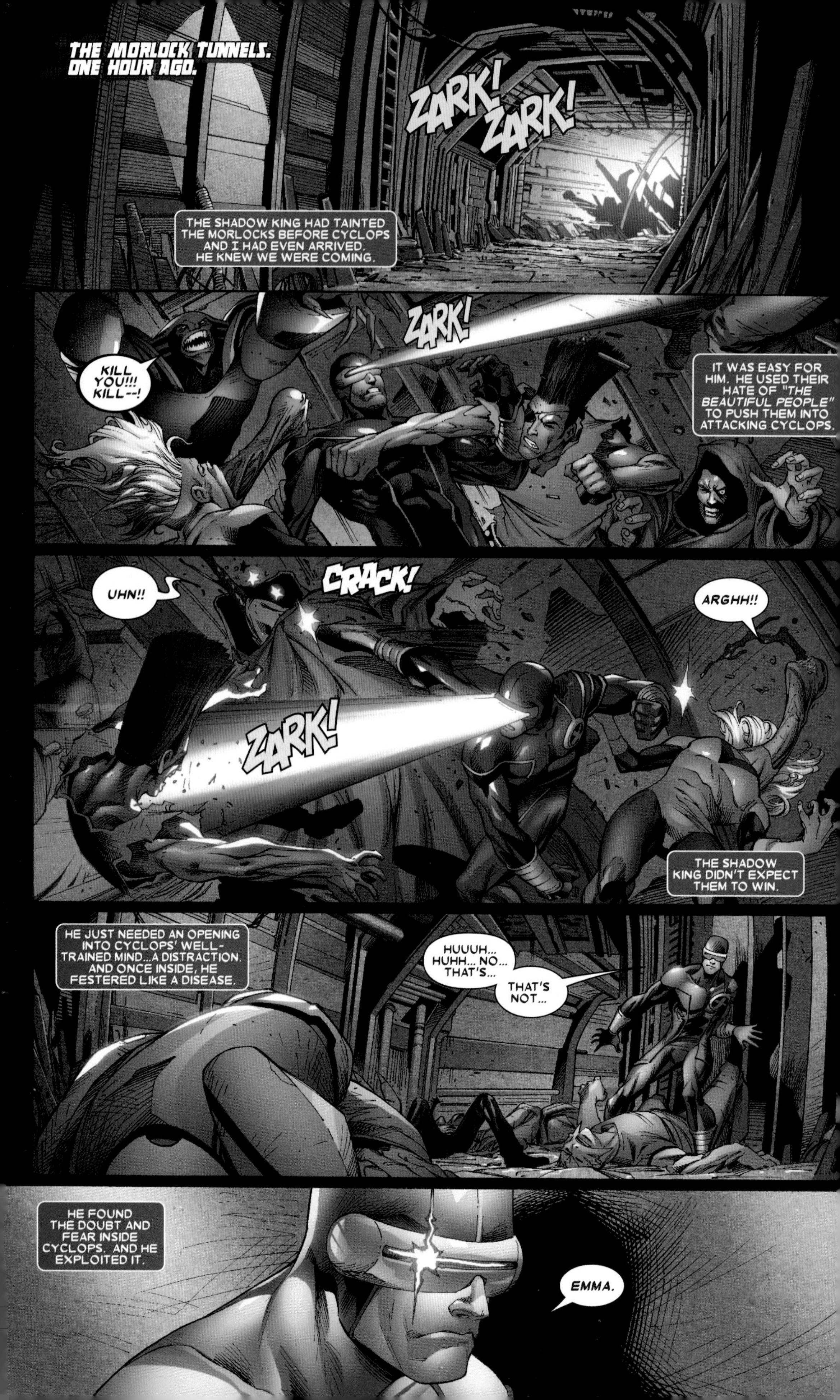

THE MORLOCK TUNNELS. ONE HOUR AGO.
ZARK! ZARK!
THE SHADOW KING HAD TAINTED THE MORLOCKS BEFORE CYCLOPS AND I HAD EVEN ARRIVED. HE KNEW WE WERE COMING.
KILL YOU!!! KILL--!
ZARK!
IT WAS EASY FOR HIM. HE USED THEIR HATE OF "THE BEAUTIFUL PEOPLE" TO PUSH THEM INTO ATTACKING CYCLOPS.
UHN!!
CRACK!
ARGHH!!
ZARK!
THE SHADOW KING DIDN'T EXPECT THEM TO WIN.
HE JUST NEEDED AN OPENING INTO CYCLOPS' WELL-TRAINED MIND...A DISTRACTION. AND ONCE INSIDE, HE FESTERED LIKE A DISEASE.
HUUUH... HUHH... NO... THAT'S...
THAT'S NOT...
HE FOUND THE DOUBT AND FEAR INSIDE CYCLOPS. AND HE EXPLOITED IT.
EMMA.

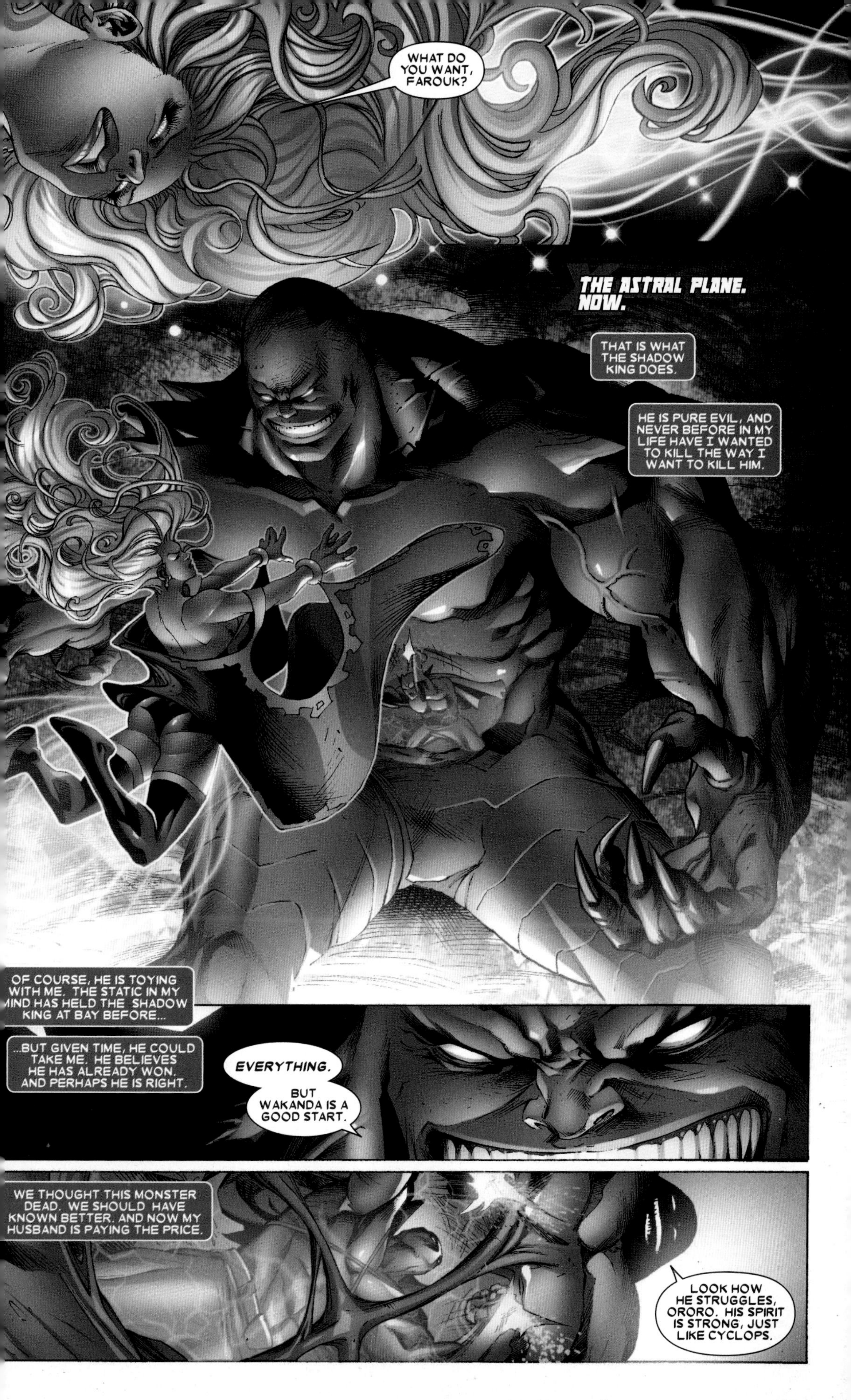
WHAT DO YOU WANT, FAROUK?
THE ASTRAL PLANE. NOW.
THAT IS WHAT THE SHADOW KING DOES.
HE IS PURE EVIL, AND NEVER BEFORE IN MY LIFE HAVE I WANTED TO KILL THE WAY I WANT TO KILL HIM.
OF COURSE, HE IS TOYING WITH ME. THE STATIC IN MY MIND HAS HELD THE SHADOW KING AT BAY BEFORE...
...BUT GIVEN TIME, HE COULD TAKE ME. HE BELIEVES HE HAS ALREADY WON. AND PERHAPS HE IS RIGHT.
EVERYTHING.
BUT WAKANDA IS A GOOD START.
WE THOUGHT THIS MONSTER DEAD. WE SHOULD HAVE KNOWN BETTER. AND NOW MY HUSBAND IS PAYING THE PRICE.
LOOK HOW HE STRUGGLES, ORORO. HIS SPIRIT IS STRONG, JUST LIKE CYCLOPS.

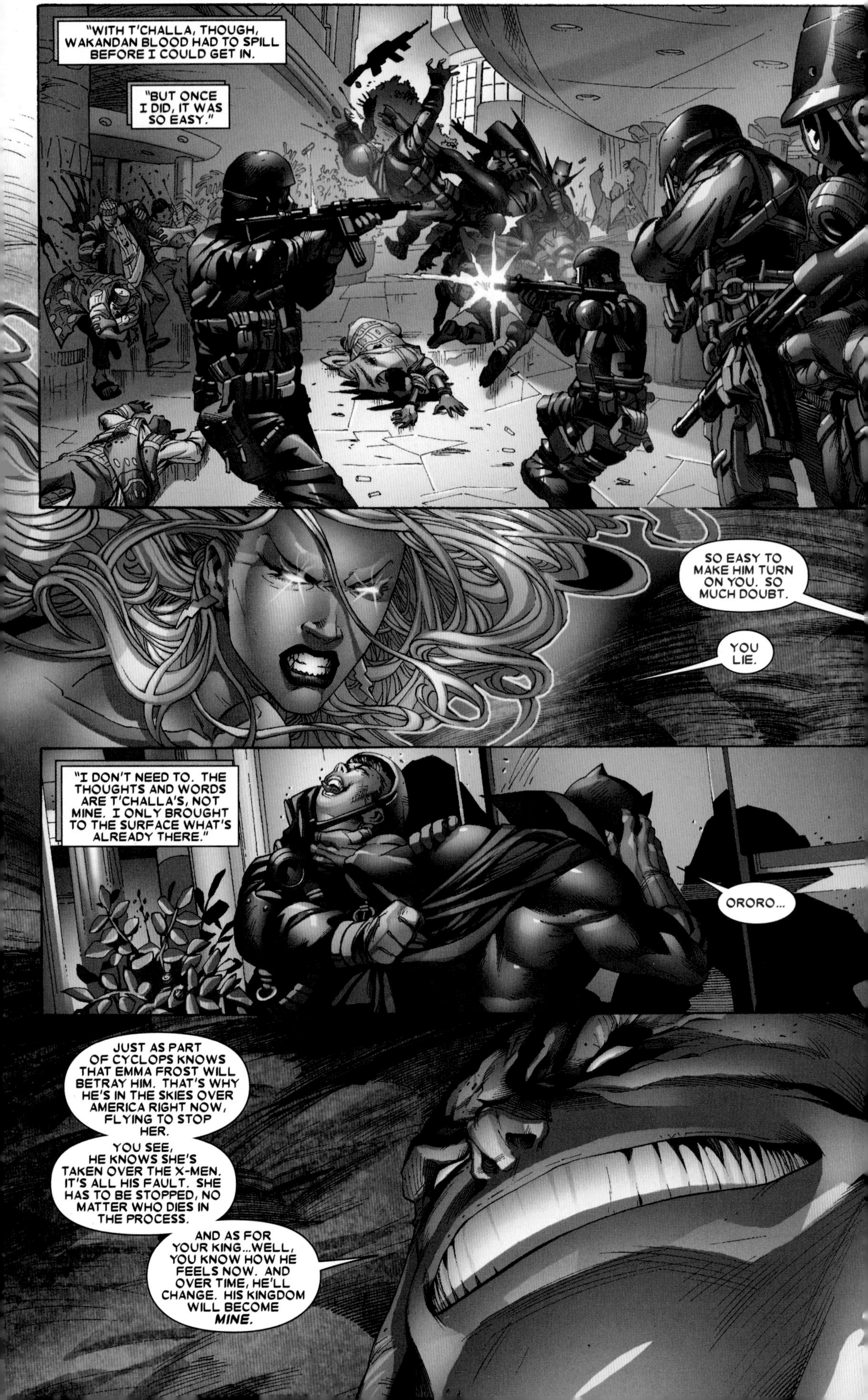

"WITH T'CHALLA, THOUGH, WAKANDAN BLOOD HAD TO SPILL BEFORE I COULD GET IN.
"BUT ONCE I DID, IT WAS SO EASY."
SO EASY TO MAKE HIM TURN ON YOU. SO MUCH DOUBT.
YOU LIE.
"I DON'T NEED TO. THE THOUGHTS AND WORDS ARE T'CHALLA'S, NOT MINE. I ONLY BROUGHT TO THE SURFACE WHAT'S ALREADY THERE."
ORORO...
JUST AS PART OF CYCLOPS KNOWS THAT EMMA FROST WILL BETRAY HIM. THAT'S WHY HE'S IN THE SKIES OVER AMERICA RIGHT NOW, FLYING TO STOP HER.
YOU SEE, HE KNOWS SHE'S TAKEN OVER THE X-MEN. IT'S ALL HIS FAULT. SHE HAS TO BE STOPPED, NO MATTER WHO DIES IN THE PROCESS.
AND AS FOR YOUR KING...WELL, YOU KNOW HOW HE FEELS NOW. AND OVER TIME, HE'LL CHANGE. HIS KINGDOM WILL BECOME MINE.

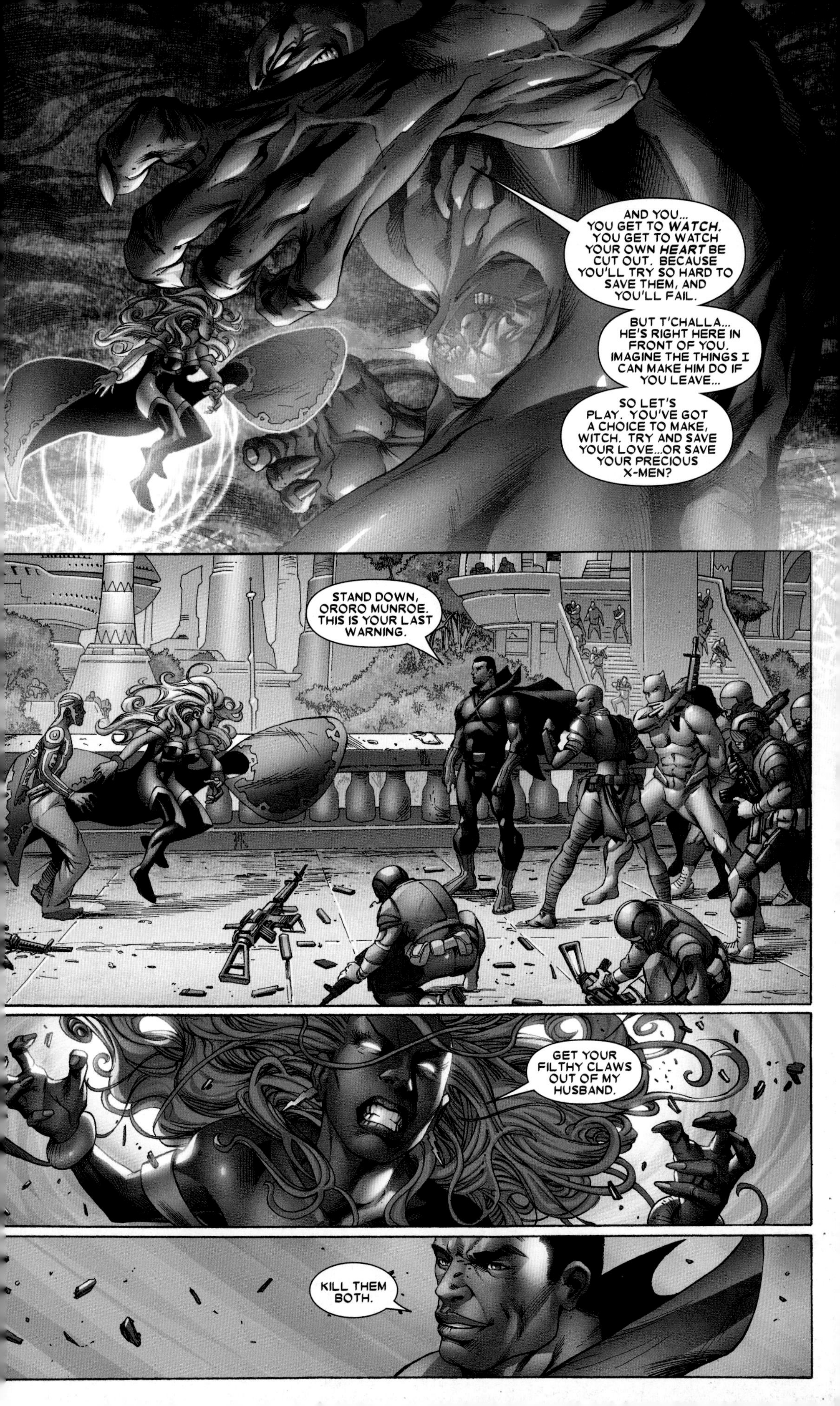
AND YOU... YOU GET TO WATCH. YOU GET TO WATCH YOUR OWN HEART BE CUT OUT. BECAUSE YOU'LL TRY SO HARD TO SAVE THEM, AND YOU'LL FAIL.
BUT T'CHALLA... HE'S RIGHT HERE IN FRONT OF YOU. IMAGINE THE THINGS I CAN MAKE HIM DO IF YOU LEAVE...
SO LET'S PLAY. YOU'VE GOT A CHOICE TO MAKE, WITCH. TRY AND SAVE YOUR LOVE...OR SAVE YOUR PRECIOUS X-MEN?
STAND DOWN, ORORO MUNROE. THIS IS YOUR LAST WARNING.
GET YOUR FILTHY CLAWS OUT OF MY HUSBAND.
KILL THEM BOTH.

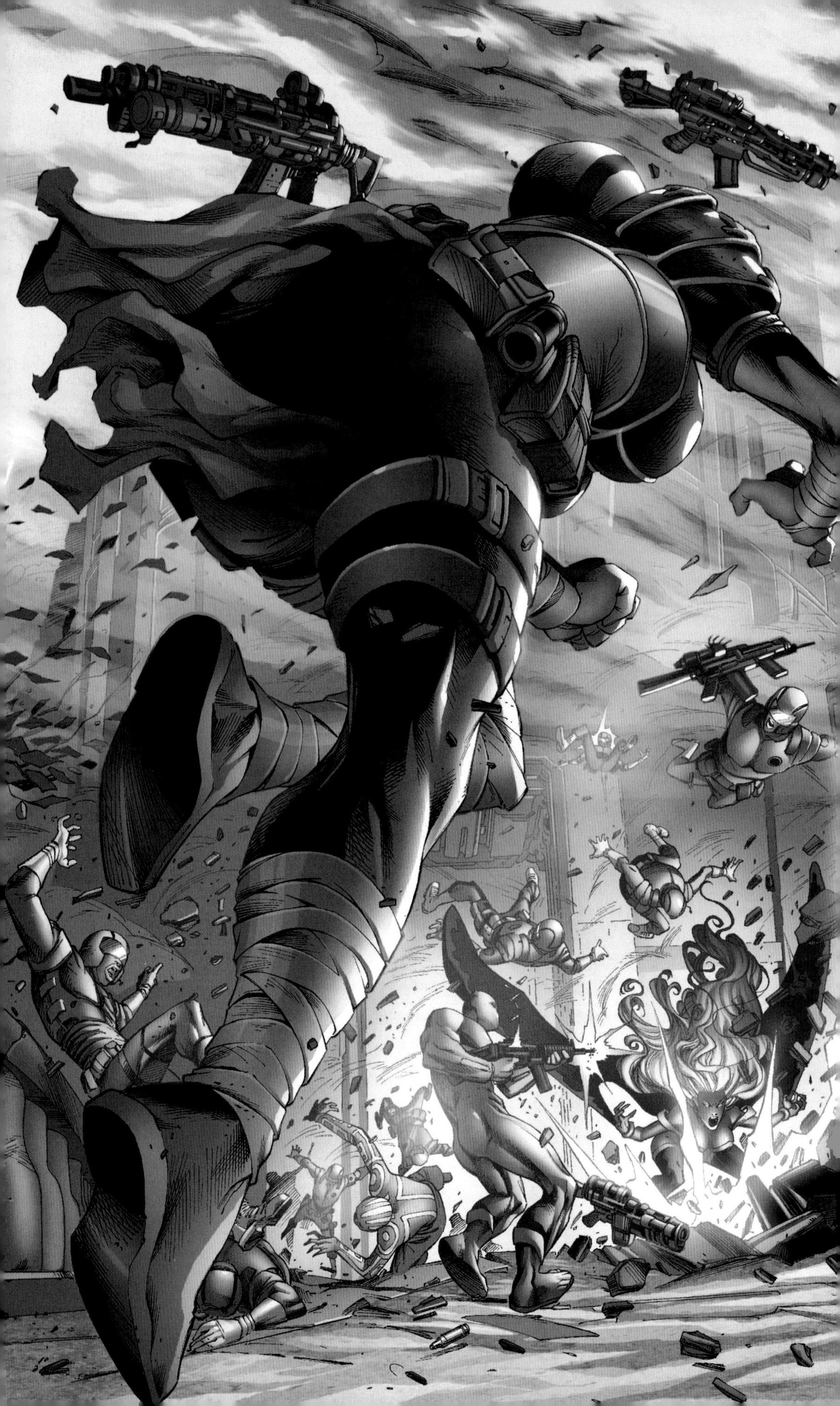

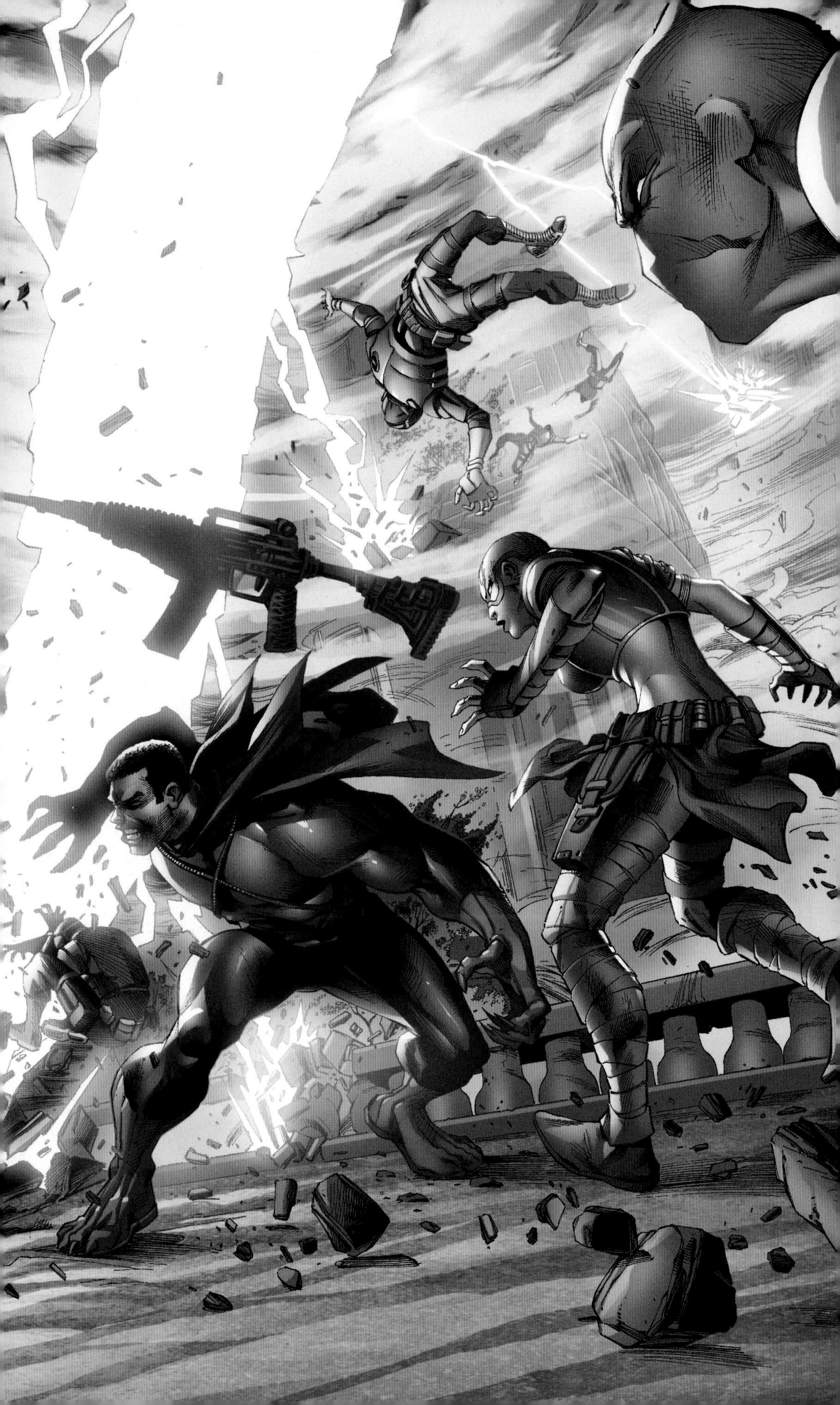

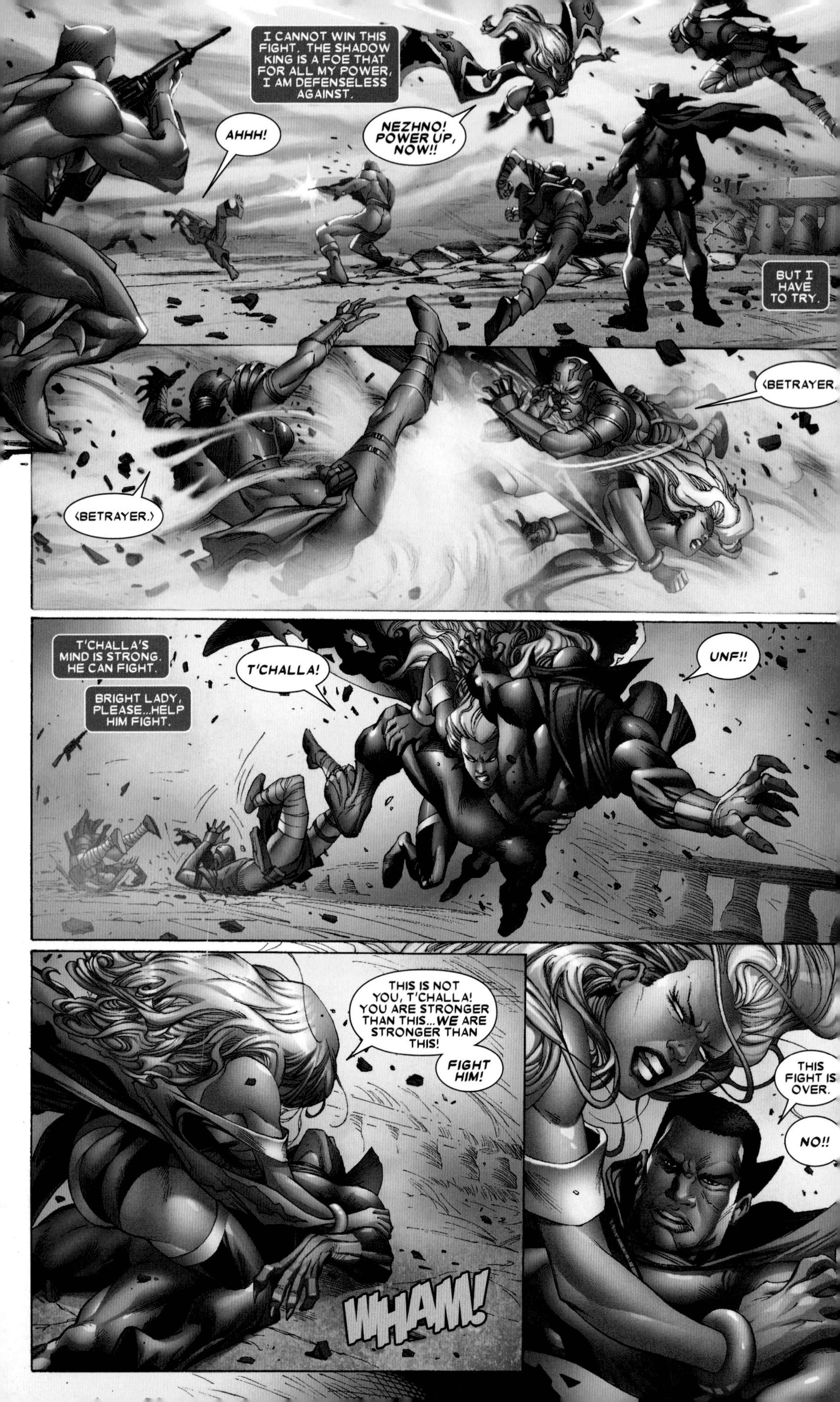

I CANNOT WIN THIS FIGHT. THE SHADOW KING IS A FOE THAT FOR ALL MY POWER, I AM DEFENSELESS AGAINST.
AHHH!
NEZHNO! POWER UP, NOW!!
BUT I HAVE TO TRY.
‹BETRAYER.›
‹BETRAYER.›
T'CHALLA'S MIND IS STRONG. HE CAN FIGHT.
BRIGHT LADY, PLEASE...HELP HIM FIGHT.
T'CHALLA!
UNF!!
THIS IS NOT YOU, T'CHALLA! YOU ARE STRONGER THAN THIS...WE ARE STRONGER THAN THIS!
FIGHT HIM!
WHAM!
THIS FIGHT IS OVER.
NO!!

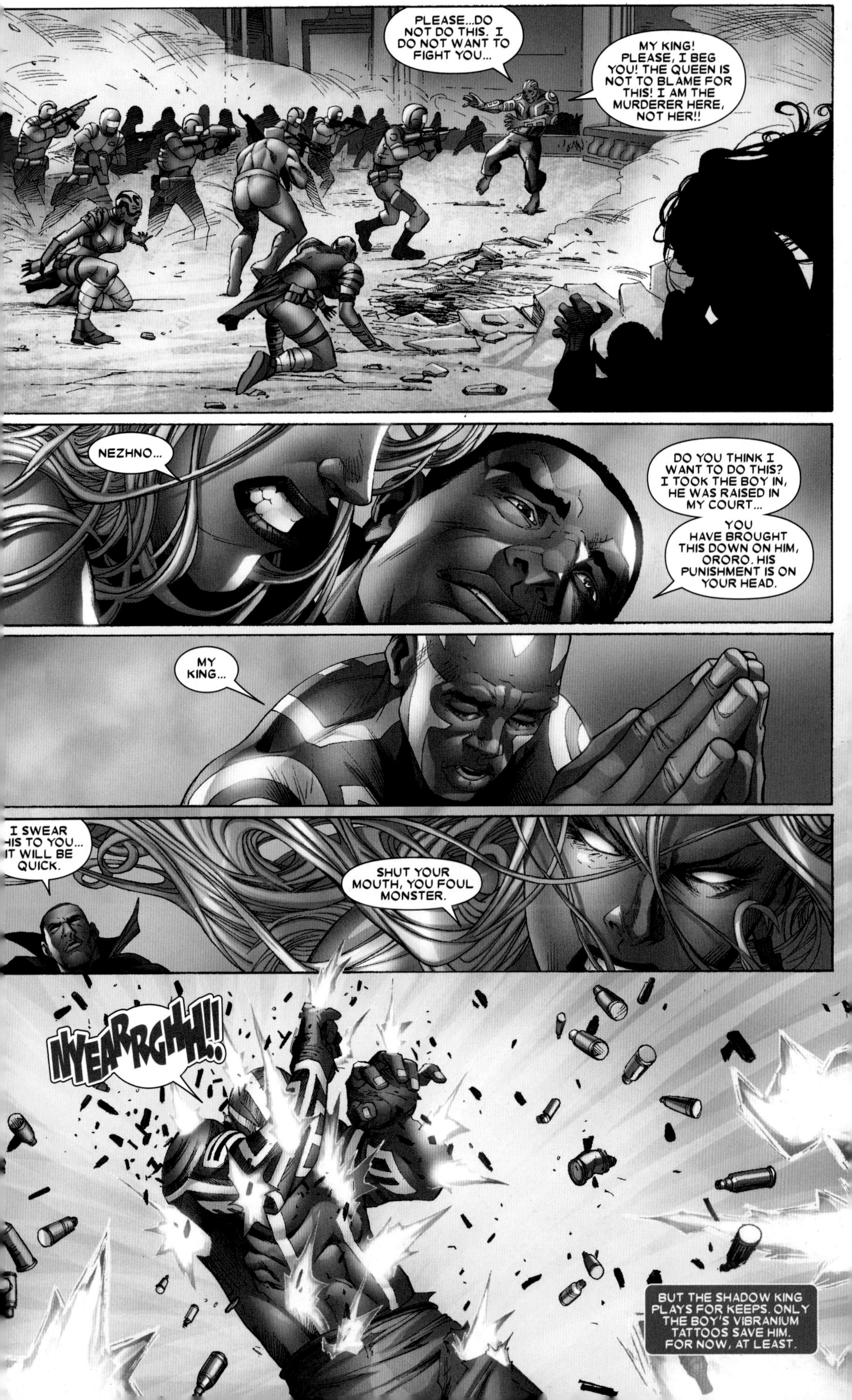

PLEASE...DO NOT DO THIS. I DO NOT WANT TO FIGHT YOU...
MY KING! PLEASE, I BEG YOU! THE QUEEN IS NOT TO BLAME FOR THIS! I AM THE MURDERER HERE, NOT HER!!
NEZHNO...
DO YOU THINK I WANT TO DO THIS? I TOOK THE BOY IN, HE WAS RAISED IN MY COURT...
YOU HAVE BROUGHT THIS DOWN ON HIM, ORORO. HIS PUNISHMENT IS ON YOUR HEAD.
MY KING...
I SWEAR THIS TO YOU... IT WILL BE QUICK.
SHUT YOUR MOUTH, YOU FOUL MONSTER.
NYEARRGHH!!
BUT THE SHADOW KING PLAYS FOR KEEPS. ONLY THE BOY'S VIBRANIUM TATTOOS SAVE HIM. FOR NOW, AT LEAST.

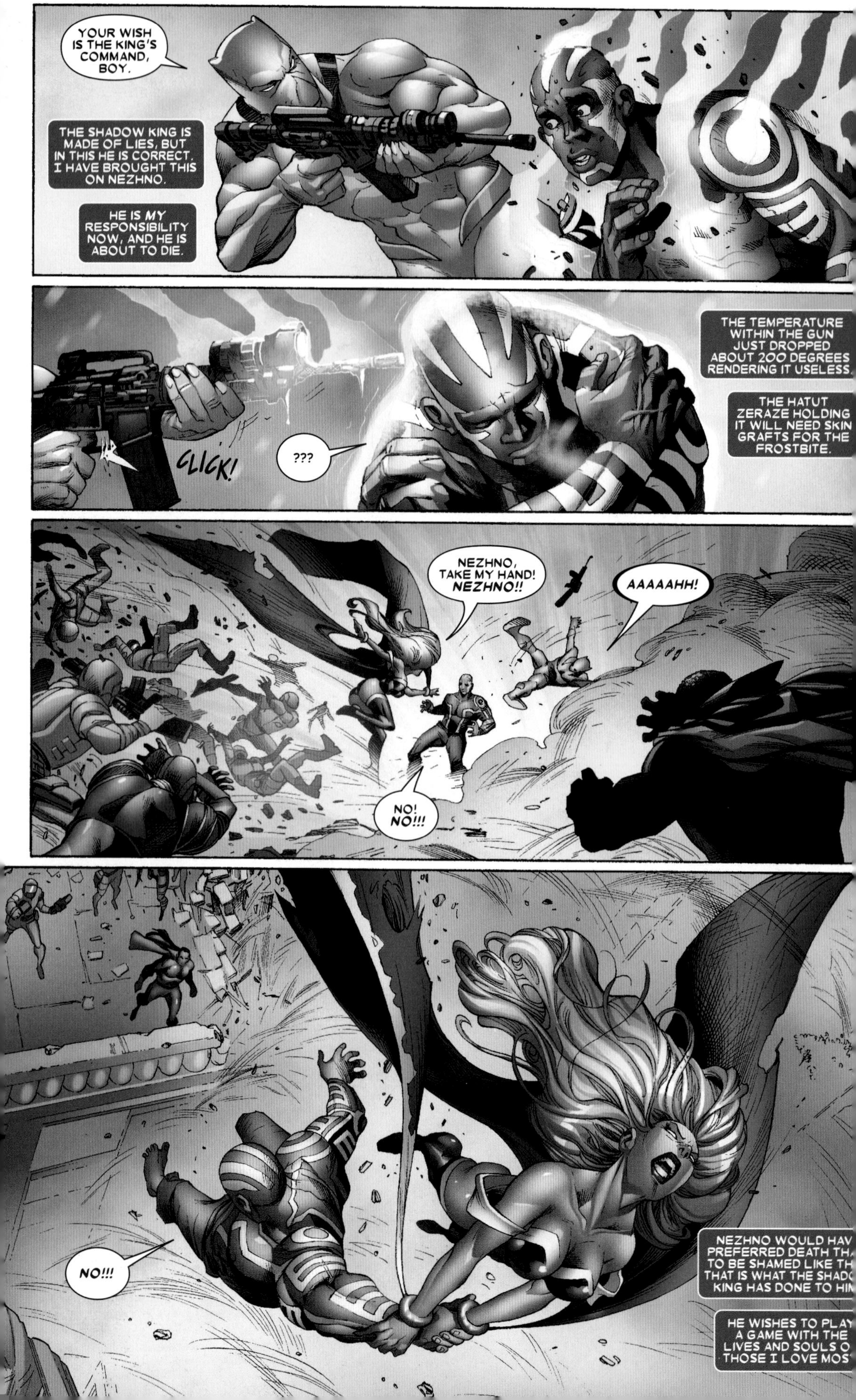
YOUR WISH IS THE KING'S COMMAND, BOY.
THE SHADOW KING IS MADE OF LIES, BUT IN THIS HE IS CORRECT. I HAVE BROUGHT THIS ON NEZHNO.
HE IS MY RESPONSIBILITY NOW, AND HE IS ABOUT TO DIE.
THE TEMPERATURE WITHIN THE GUN JUST DROPPED ABOUT 200 DEGREES RENDERING IT USELESS.
THE HATUT ZERAZE HOLDING IT WILL NEED SKIN GRAFTS FOR THE FROSTBITE.
CLICK!
???
NEZHNO, TAKE MY HAND! NEZHNO!!
AAAAAHH!
NO! NO!!!
NO!!!
NEZHNO WOULD HAV PREFERRED DEATH TH TO BE SHAMED LIKE TH THAT IS WHAT THE SHAD KING HAS DONE TO HI
HE WISHES TO PLAY A GAME WITH THE LIVES AND SOULS O THOSE I LOVE MOS

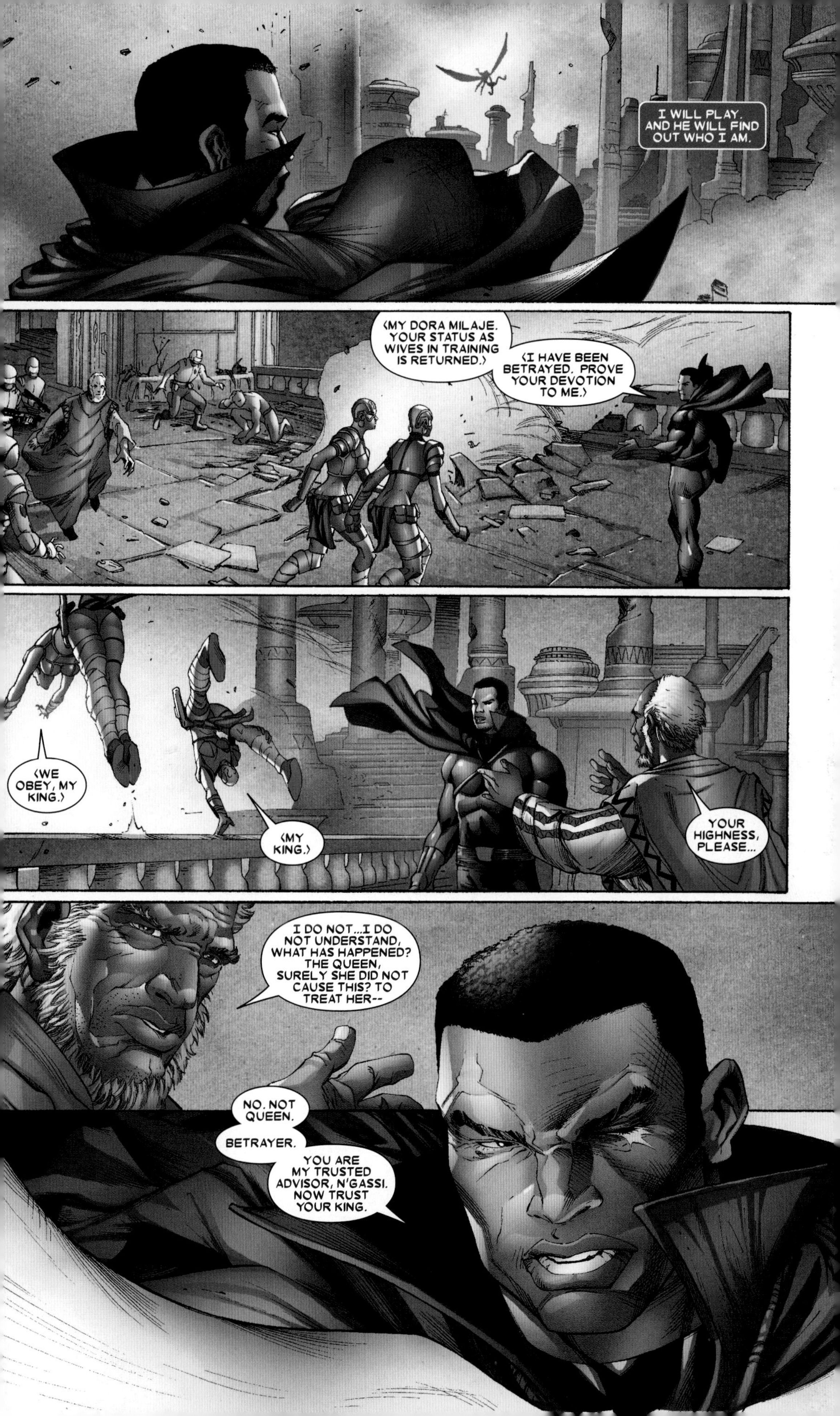
I WILL PLAY. AND HE WILL FIND OUT WHO I AM.
‹MY DORA MILAJE. YOUR STATUS AS WIVES IN TRAINING IS RETURNED.›
‹I HAVE BEEN BETRAYED. PROVE YOUR DEVOTION TO ME.›
‹WE OBEY, MY KING.›
‹MY KING.›
YOUR HIGHNESS, PLEASE...
I DO NOT...I DO NOT UNDERSTAND, WHAT HAS HAPPENED? THE QUEEN, SURELY SHE DID NOT CAUSE THIS? TO TREAT HER--
NO. NOT QUEEN.
BETRAYER.
YOU ARE MY TRUSTED ADVISOR, N'GASSI. NOW TRUST YOUR KING.

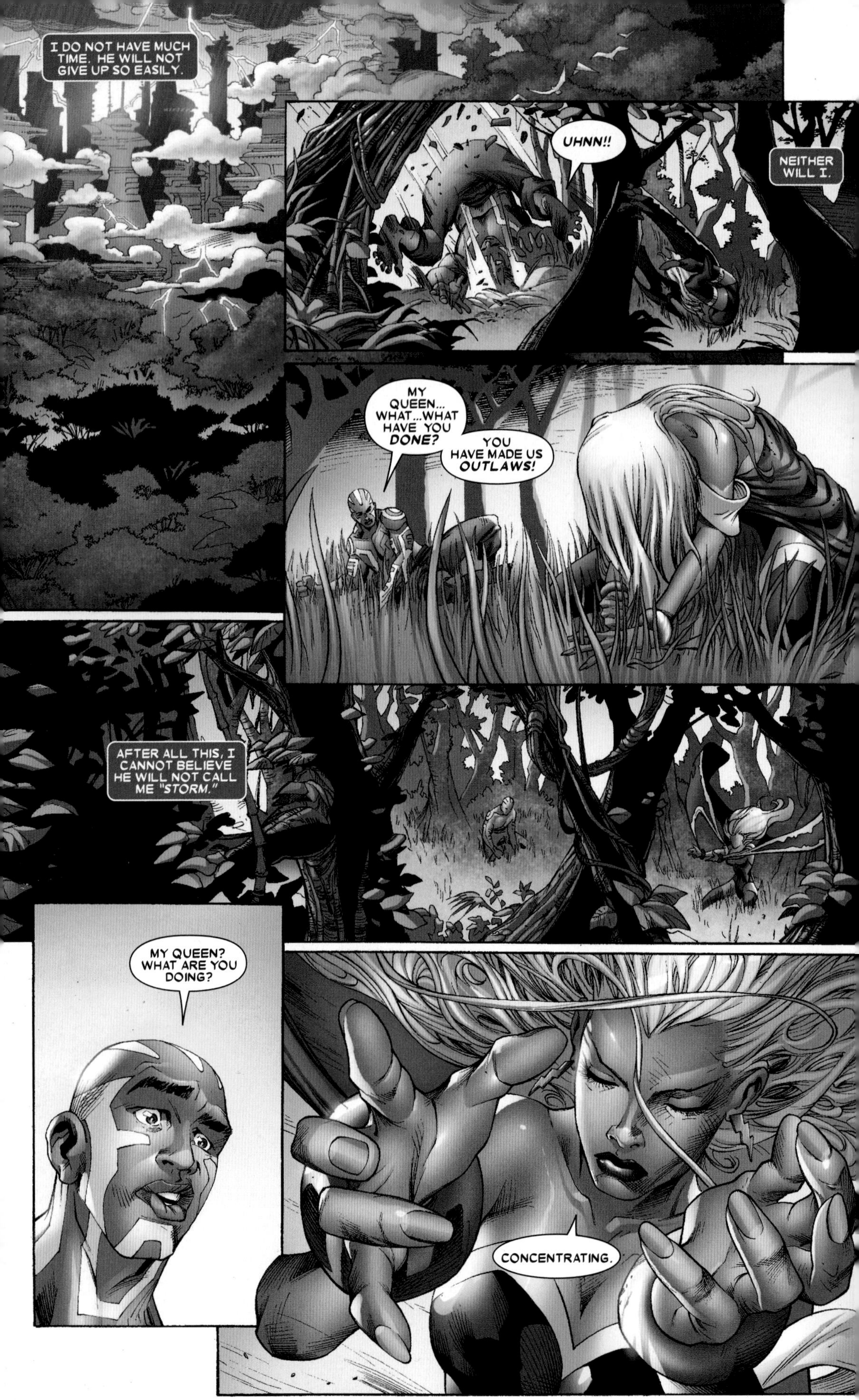
I DO NOT HAVE MUCH TIME. HE WILL NOT GIVE UP SO EASILY.
UHNN!!
NEITHER WILL I.
MY QUEEN... WHAT...WHAT HAVE YOU *DONE?*
YOU HAVE MADE US *OUTLAWS!*
AFTER ALL THIS, I CANNOT BELIEVE HE WILL NOT CALL ME *"STORM."*
MY QUEEN? WHAT ARE YOU DOING?
CONCENTRATING.

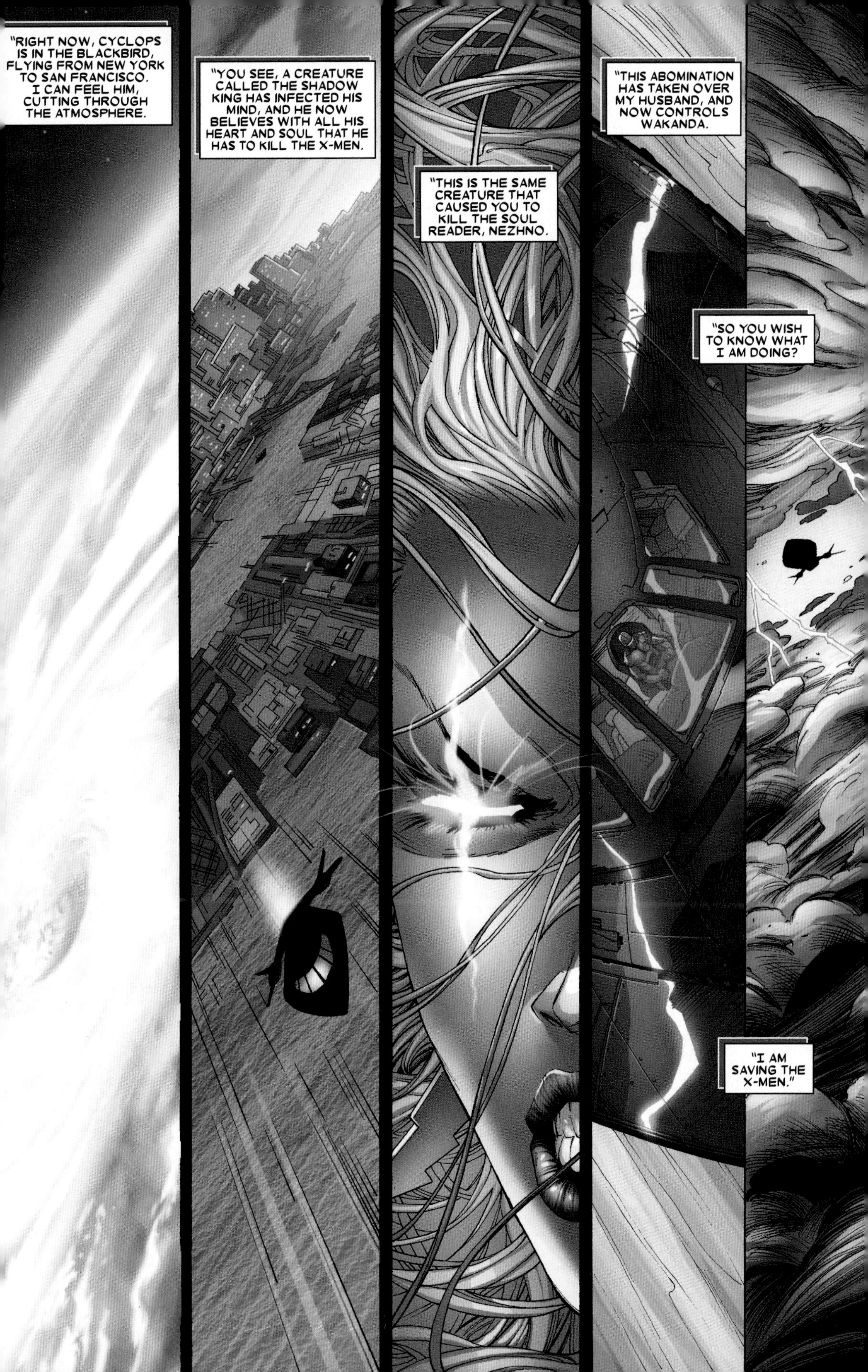
"RIGHT NOW, CYCLOPS IS IN THE BLACKBIRD, FLYING FROM NEW YORK TO SAN FRANCISCO. I CAN FEEL HIM, CUTTING THROUGH THE ATMOSPHERE.
"YOU SEE, A CREATURE CALLED THE SHADOW KING HAS INFECTED HIS MIND, AND HE NOW BELIEVES WITH ALL HIS HEART AND SOUL THAT HE HAS TO KILL THE X-MEN.
"THIS IS THE SAME CREATURE THAT CAUSED YOU TO KILL THE SOUL READER, NEZHNO.
"THIS ABOMINATION HAS TAKEN OVER MY HUSBAND, AND NOW CONTROLS WAKANDA.
"SO YOU WISH TO KNOW WHAT I AM DOING?
"I AM SAVING THE X-MEN."

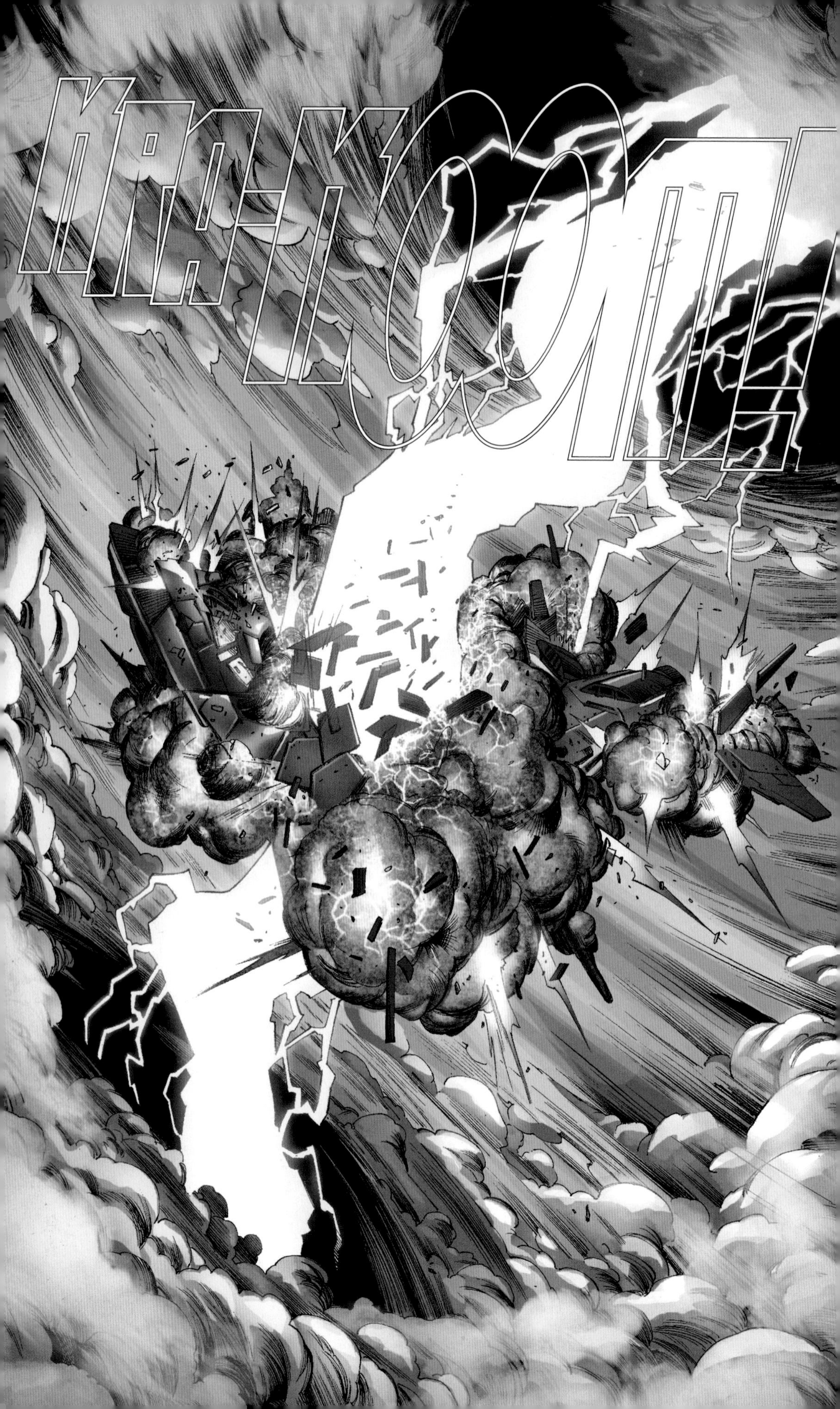
KRA-KOOM!

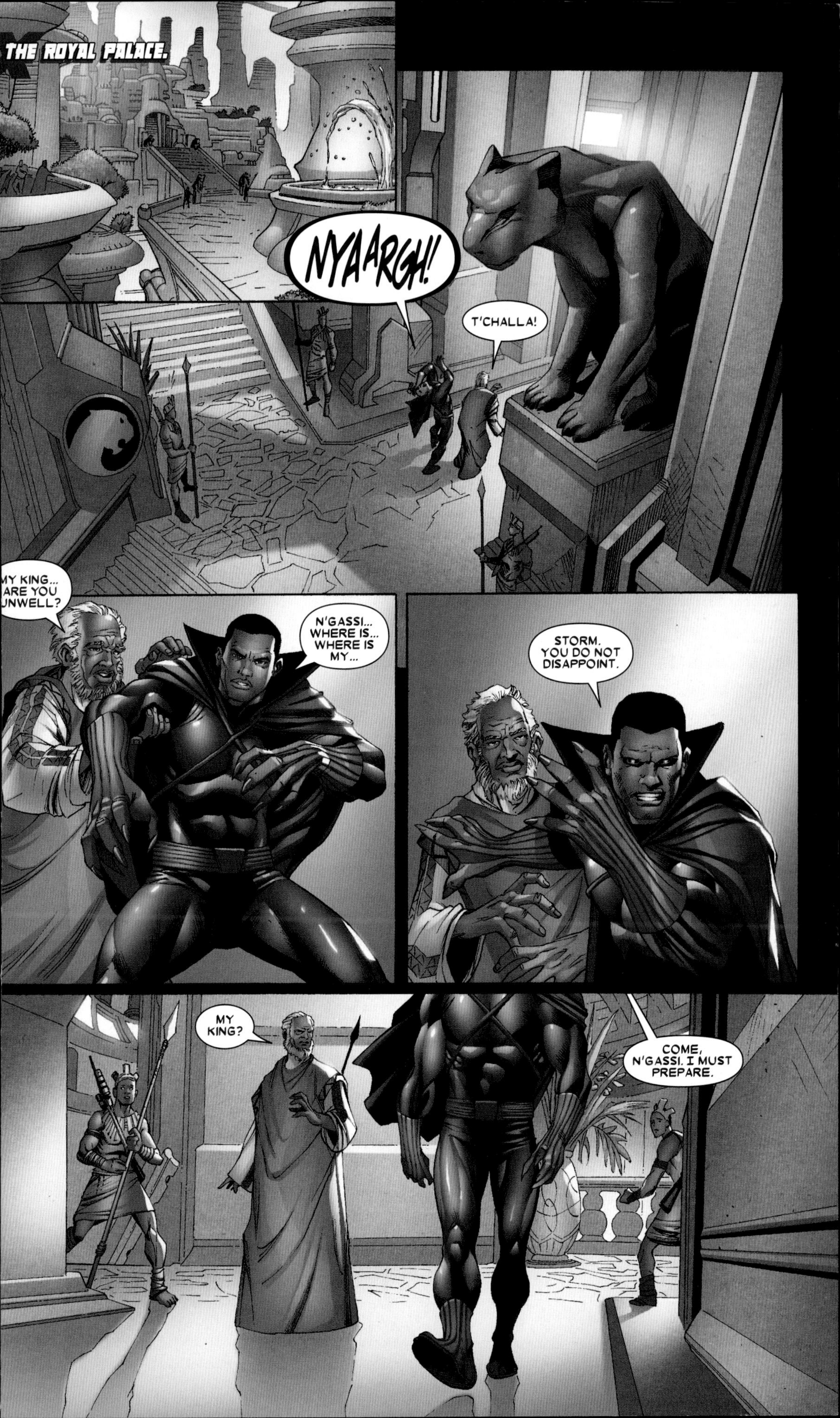
THE ROYAL PALACE.
NYAARGH!
T'CHALLA!
MY KING... ARE YOU UNWELL?
N'GASSI... WHERE IS... WHERE IS MY...
STORM. YOU DO NOT DISAPPOINT.
MY KING?
COME, N'GASSI. I MUST PREPARE.

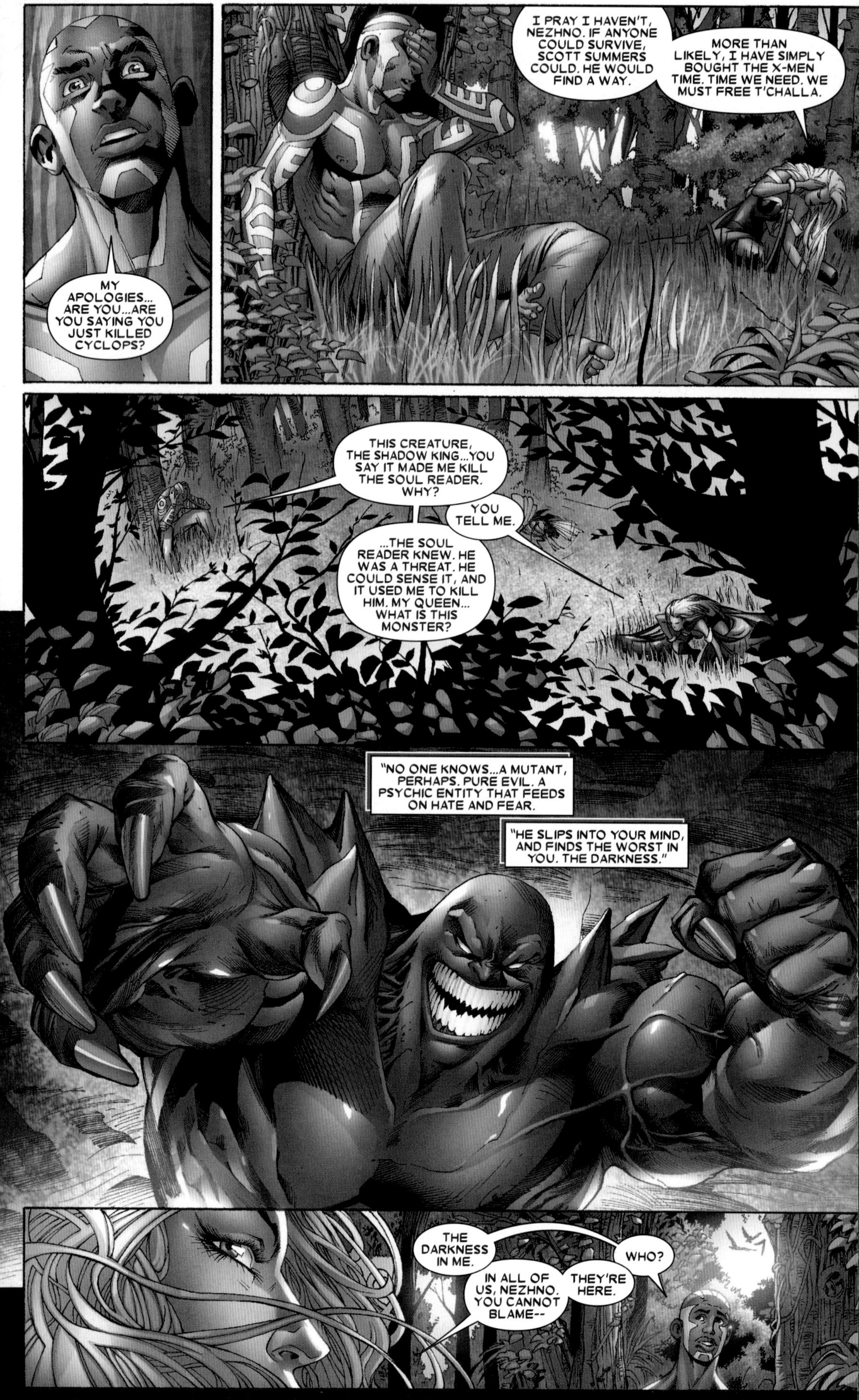
MY APOLOGIES... ARE YOU...ARE YOU SAYING YOU JUST KILLED CYCLOPS?
I PRAY I HAVEN'T, NEZHNO. IF ANYONE COULD SURVIVE, SCOTT SUMMERS COULD. HE WOULD FIND A WAY.
MORE THAN LIKELY, I HAVE SIMPLY BOUGHT THE X-MEN TIME. TIME WE NEED. WE MUST FREE T'CHALLA.
THIS CREATURE, THE SHADOW KING...YOU SAY IT MADE ME KILL THE SOUL READER. WHY?
YOU TELL ME.
...THE SOUL READER KNEW. HE WAS A THREAT. HE COULD SENSE IT, AND IT USED ME TO KILL HIM. MY QUEEN... WHAT IS THIS MONSTER?
"NO ONE KNOWS...A MUTANT, PERHAPS. PURE EVIL. A PSYCHIC ENTITY THAT FEEDS ON HATE AND FEAR.
"HE SLIPS INTO YOUR MIND, AND FINDS THE WORST IN YOU. THE DARKNESS."
THE DARKNESS IN ME.
IN ALL OF US, NEZHNO. YOU CANNOT BLAME--
WHO?
THEY'RE HERE.

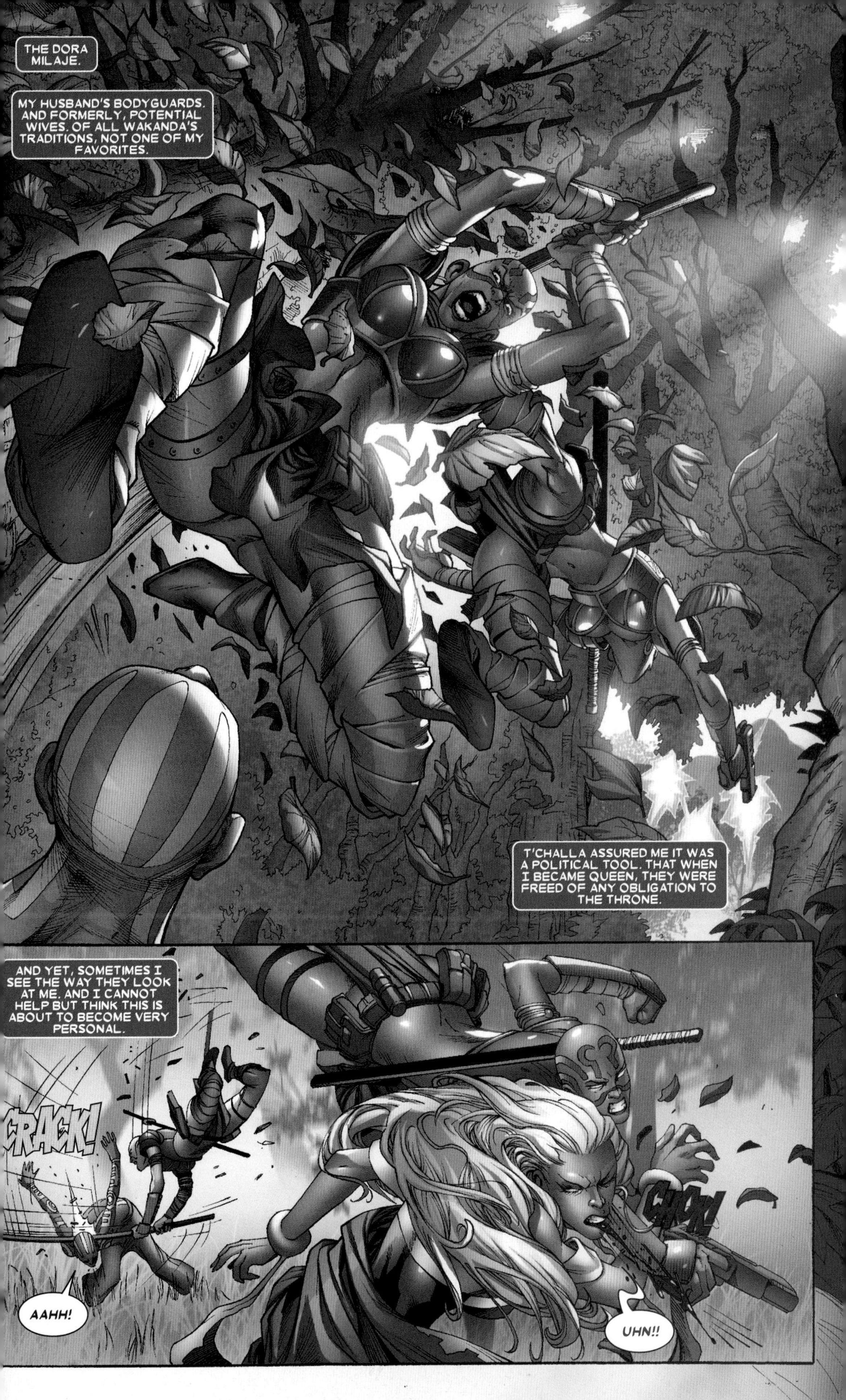
THE DORA MILAJE.
MY HUSBAND'S BODYGUARDS. AND FORMERLY, POTENTIAL WIVES. OF ALL WAKANDA'S TRADITIONS, NOT ONE OF MY FAVORITES.
T'CHALLA ASSURED ME IT WAS A POLITICAL TOOL. THAT WHEN I BECAME QUEEN, THEY WERE FREED OF ANY OBLIGATION TO THE THRONE.
AND YET, SOMETIMES I SEE THE WAY THEY LOOK AT ME. AND I CANNOT HELP BUT THINK THIS IS ABOUT TO BECOME VERY PERSONAL.
CRACK!
AAHH!
CHOK!
UHN!!

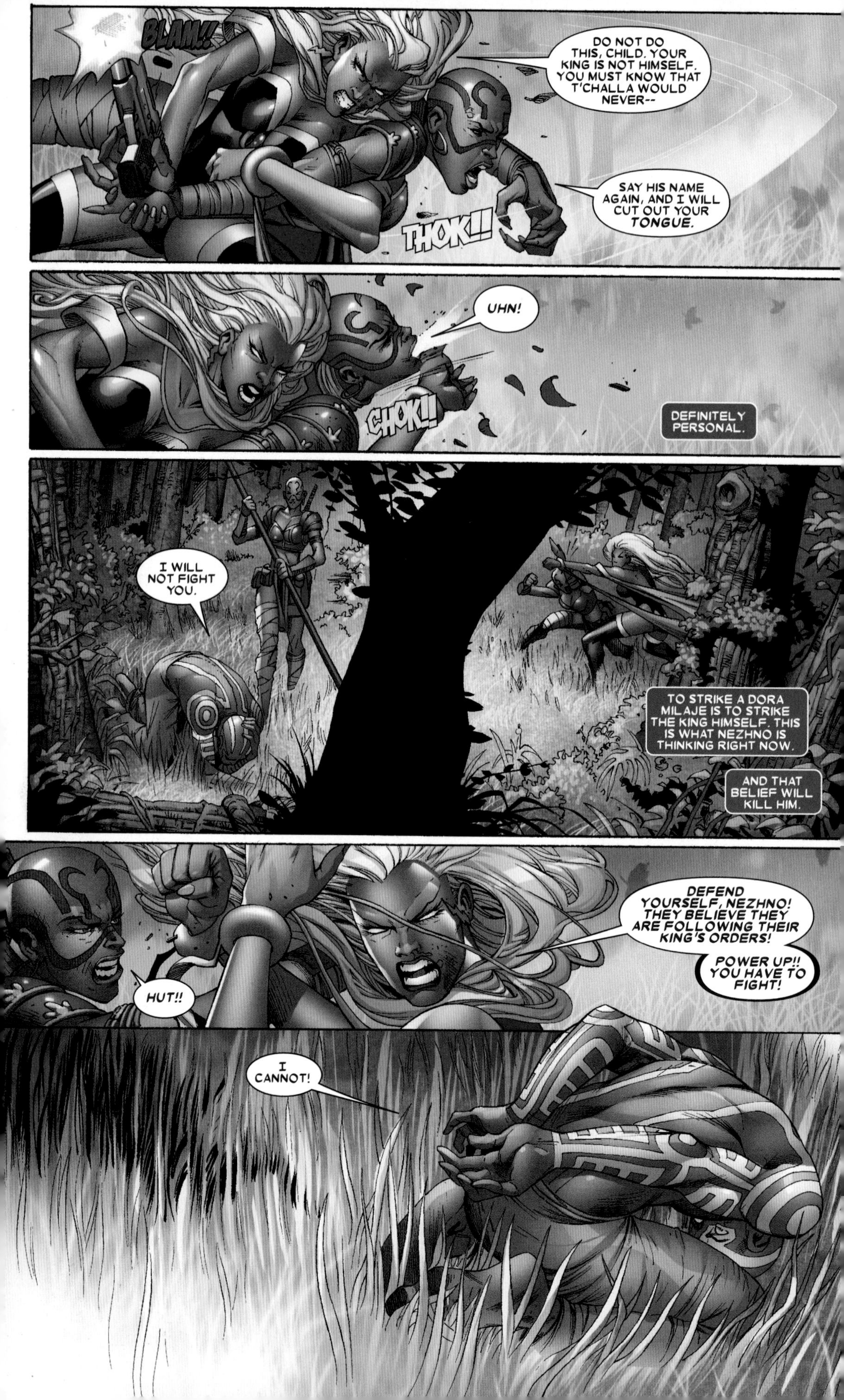
BLAM!!
DO NOT DO THIS, CHILD. YOUR KING IS NOT HIMSELF. YOU MUST KNOW THAT T'CHALLA WOULD NEVER--
SAY HIS NAME AGAIN, AND I WILL CUT OUT YOUR TONGUE.
THOK!!
UHN!
CHOK!!
DEFINITELY PERSONAL.
I WILL NOT FIGHT YOU.
TO STRIKE A DORA MILAJE IS TO STRIKE THE KING HIMSELF. THIS IS WHAT NEZHNO IS THINKING RIGHT NOW.
AND THAT BELIEF WILL KILL HIM.
DEFEND YOURSELF, NEZHNO! THEY BELIEVE THEY ARE FOLLOWING THEIR KING'S ORDERS!
POWER UP!! YOU HAVE TO FIGHT!
HUT!!
I CANNOT!

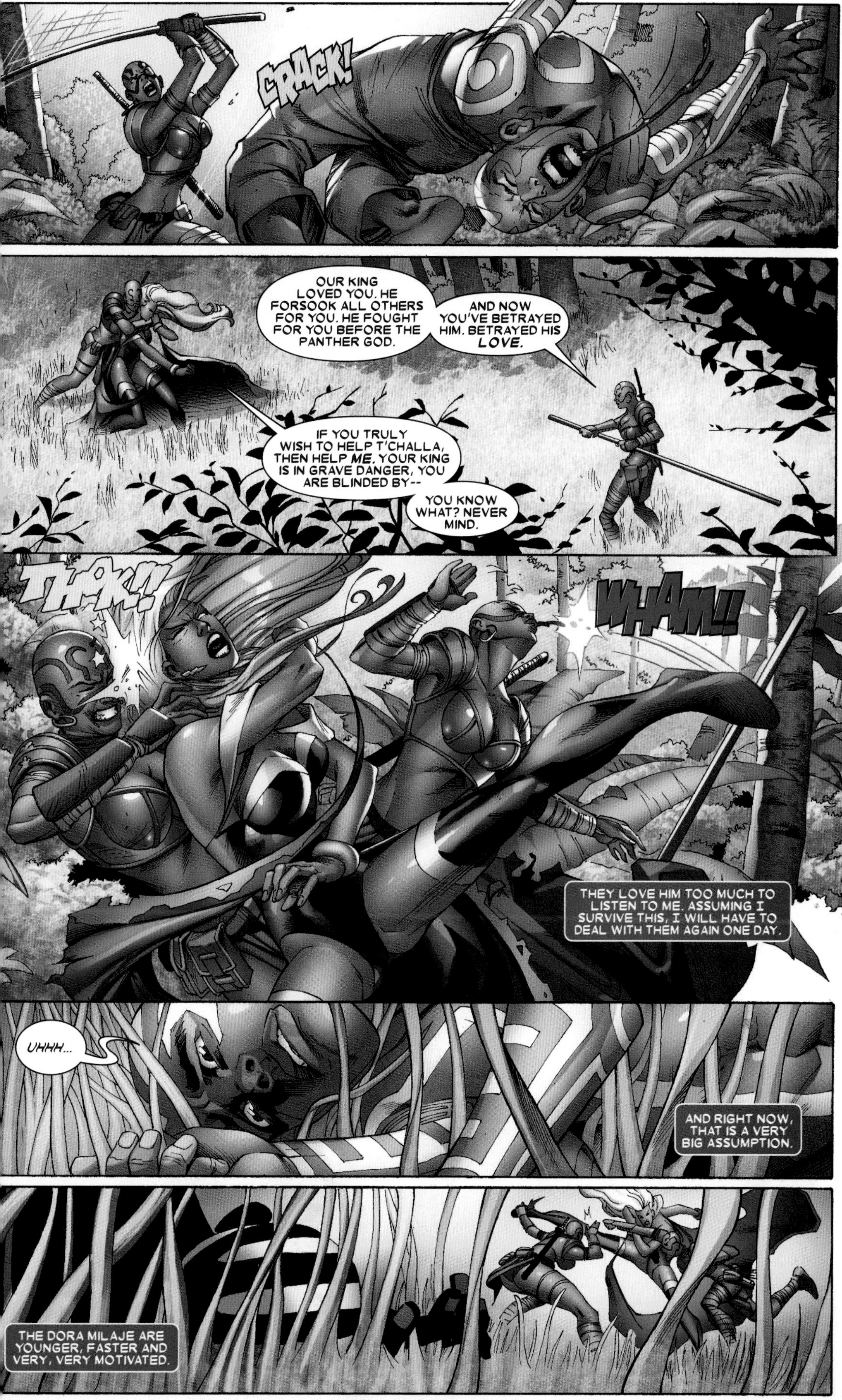

CRACK!
OUR KING LOVED YOU. HE FORSOOK ALL OTHERS FOR YOU. HE FOUGHT FOR YOU BEFORE THE PANTHER GOD.
AND NOW YOU'VE BETRAYED HIM. BETRAYED HIS LOVE.
IF YOU TRULY WISH TO HELP T'CHALLA, THEN HELP ME. YOUR KING IS IN GRAVE DANGER. YOU ARE BLINDED BY--
YOU KNOW WHAT? NEVER MIND.
THOK!!
WHAM!!
THEY LOVE HIM TOO MUCH TO LISTEN TO ME. ASSUMING I SURVIVE THIS, I WILL HAVE TO DEAL WITH THEM AGAIN ONE DAY.
UHHH...
AND RIGHT NOW, THAT IS A VERY BIG ASSUMPTION.
THE DORA MILAJE ARE YOUNGER, FASTER AND VERY, VERY MOTIVATED.

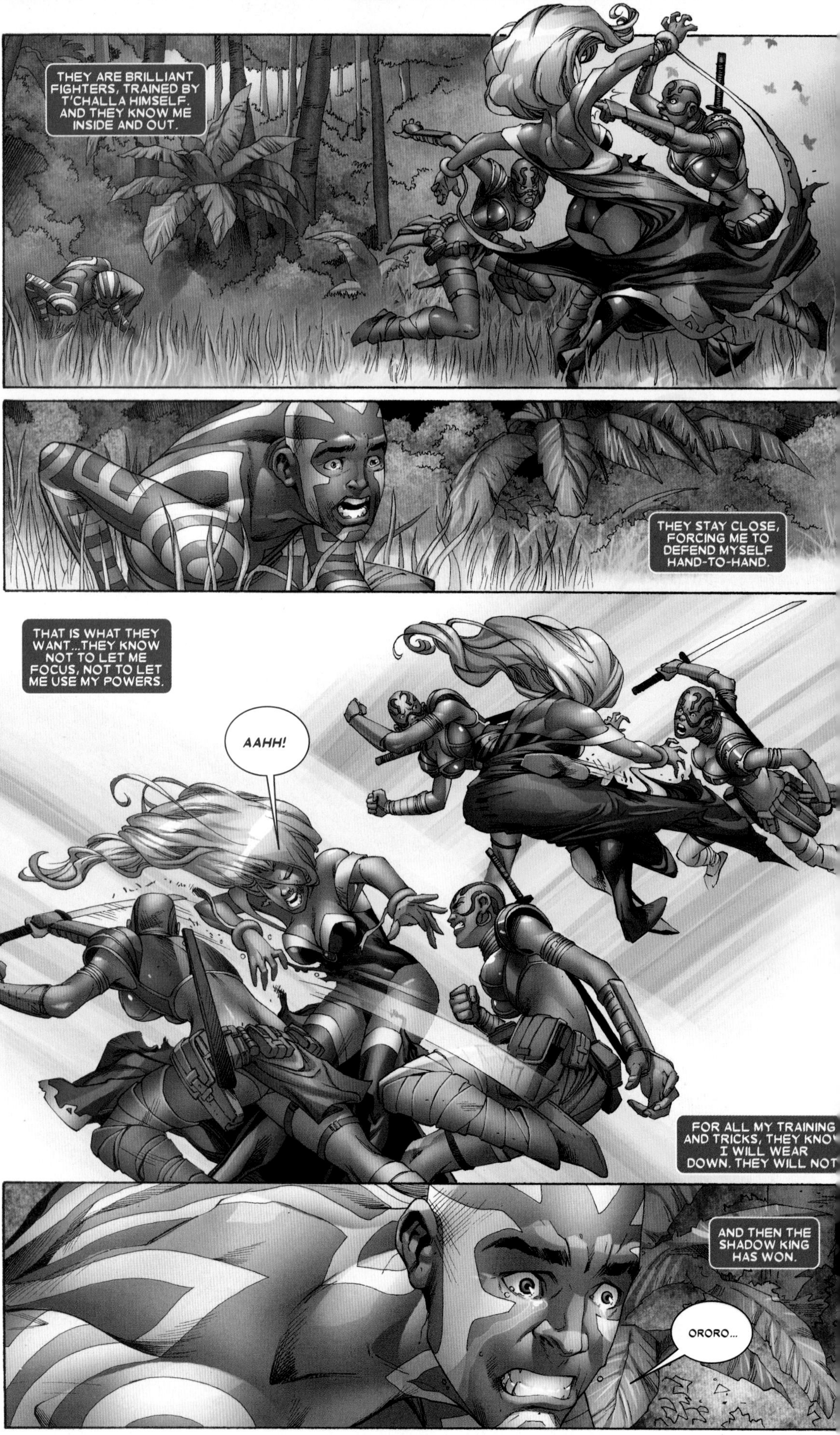
THEY ARE BRILLIANT FIGHTERS, TRAINED BY T'CHALLA HIMSELF. AND THEY KNOW ME INSIDE AND OUT.
THEY STAY CLOSE, FORCING ME TO DEFEND MYSELF HAND-TO-HAND.
THAT IS WHAT THEY WANT...THEY KNOW NOT TO LET ME FOCUS, NOT TO LET ME USE MY POWERS.
AAHH!
FOR ALL MY TRAINING AND TRICKS, THEY KNO I WILL WEAR DOWN. THEY WILL NOT
AND THEN THE SHADOW KING HAS WON.
ORORO...

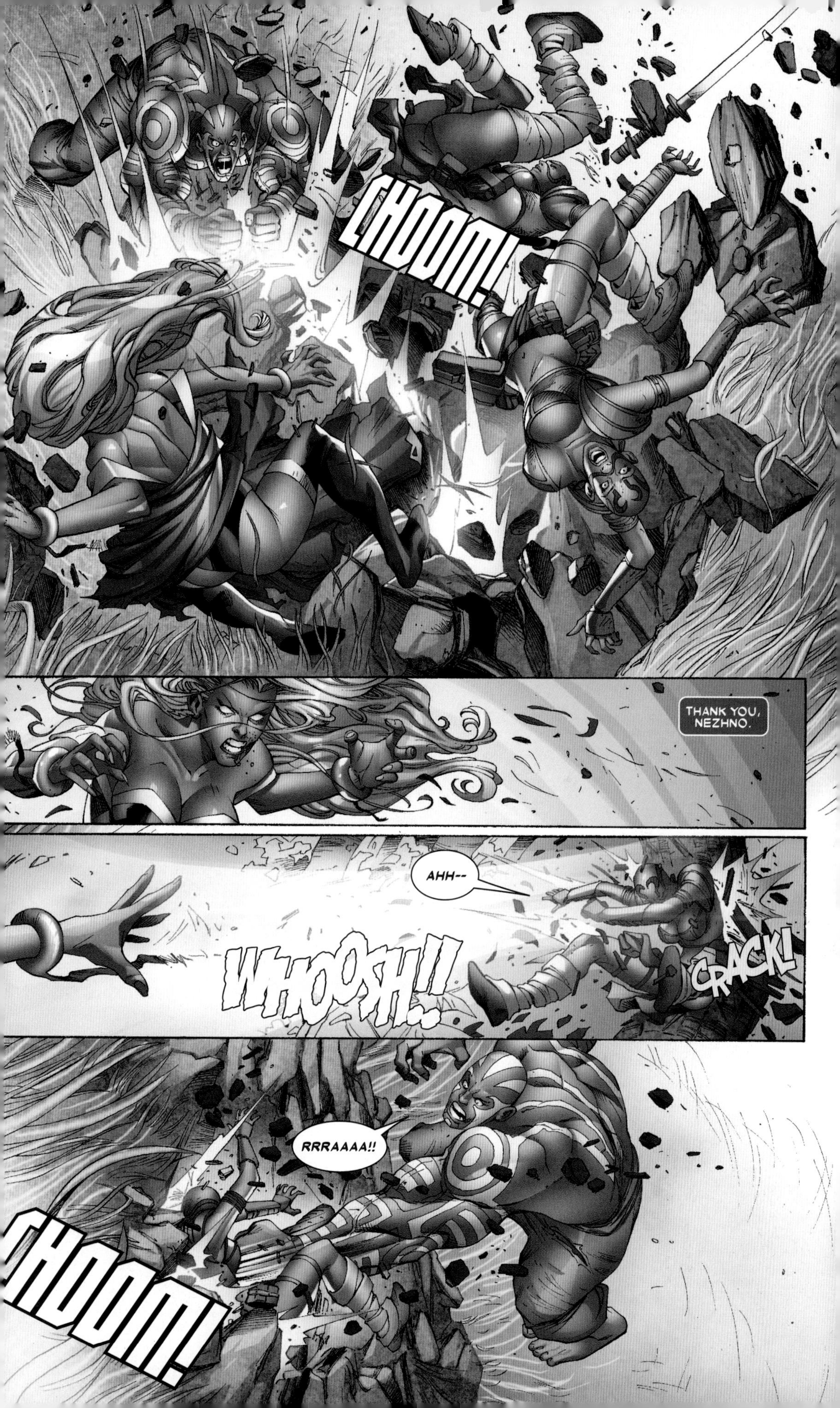
CHOOM!
THANK YOU, NEZHNO.
AHH--
WHOOSH!!
CRACK!
RRRAAAA!!
CHOOM!

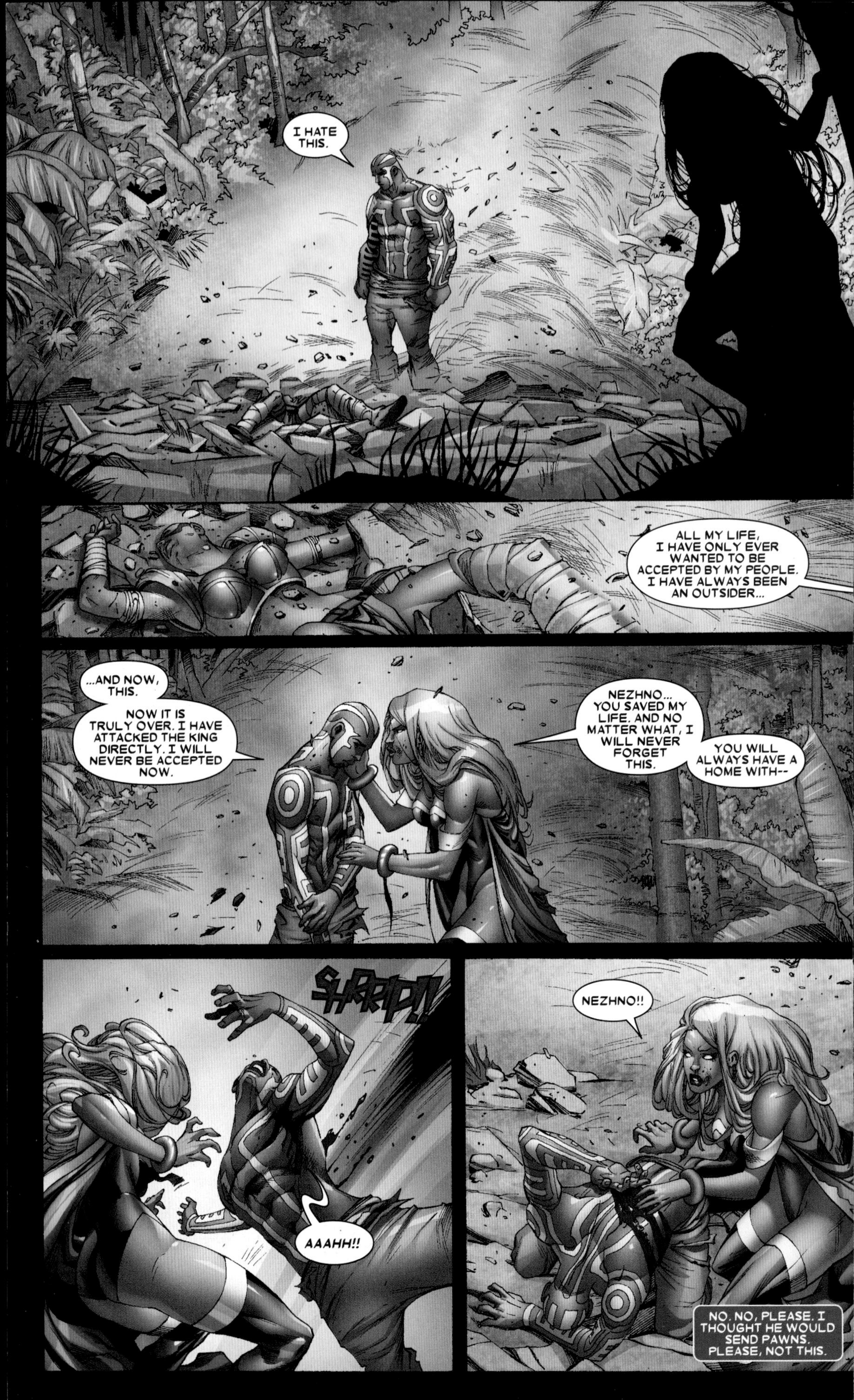
I HATE THIS.
ALL MY LIFE, I HAVE ONLY EVER WANTED TO BE ACCEPTED BY MY PEOPLE. I HAVE ALWAYS BEEN AN OUTSIDER...
...AND NOW, THIS.
NOW IT IS TRULY OVER. I HAVE ATTACKED THE KING DIRECTLY. I WILL NEVER BE ACCEPTED NOW.
NEZHNO... YOU SAVED MY LIFE. AND NO MATTER WHAT, I WILL NEVER FORGET THIS.
YOU WILL ALWAYS HAVE A HOME WITH--
SHRRRIP!!
AAAHH!!
NEZHNO!!
NO. NO, PLEASE. I THOUGHT HE WOULD SEND PAWNS. PLEASE, NOT THIS.

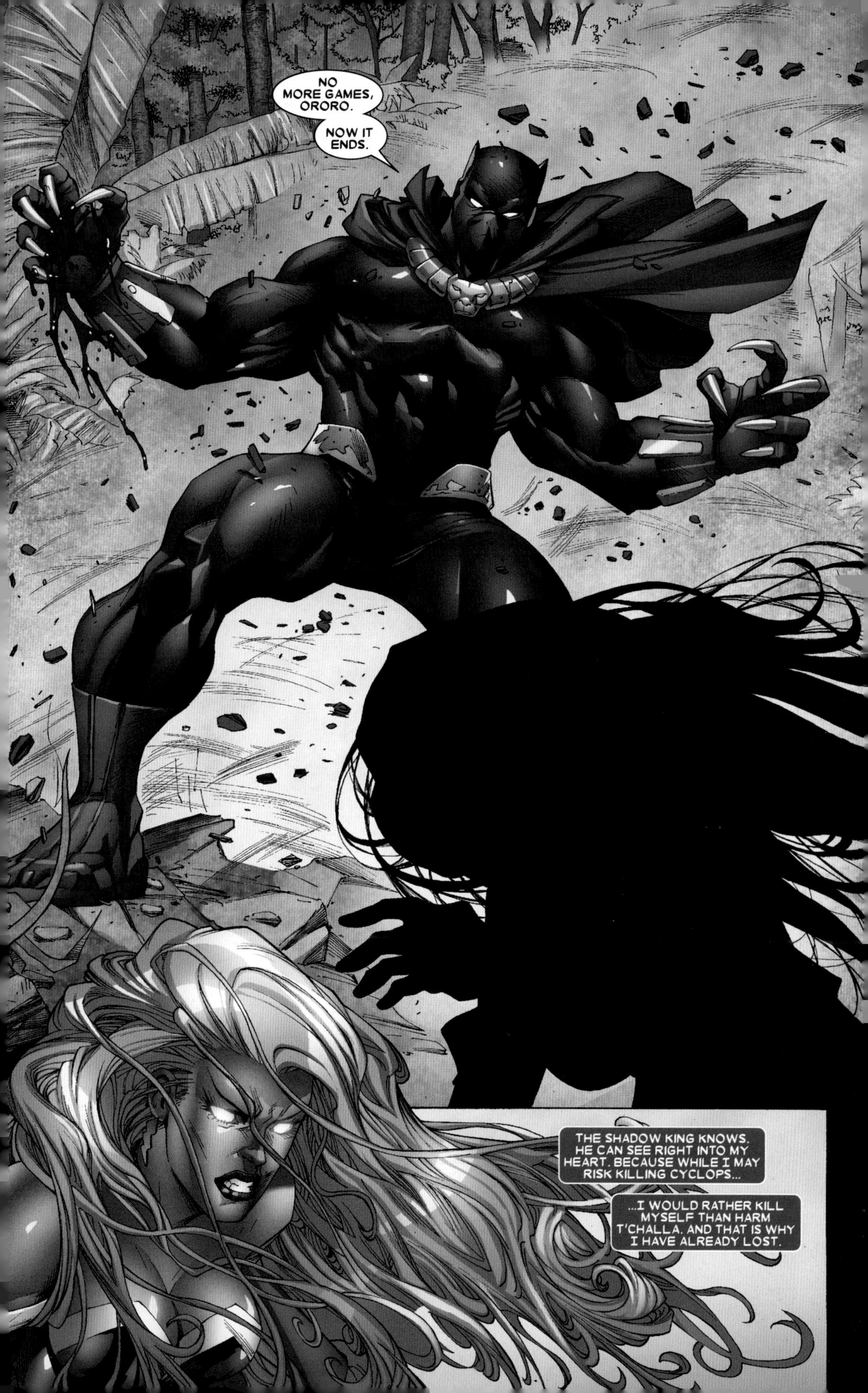
NO MORE GAMES, ORORO.
NOW IT ENDS.
THE SHADOW KING KNOWS. HE CAN SEE RIGHT INTO MY HEART. BECAUSE WHILE I MAY RISK KILLING CYCLOPS...
...I WOULD RATHER KILL MYSELF THAN HARM T'CHALLA. AND THAT IS WHY I HAVE ALREADY LOST.

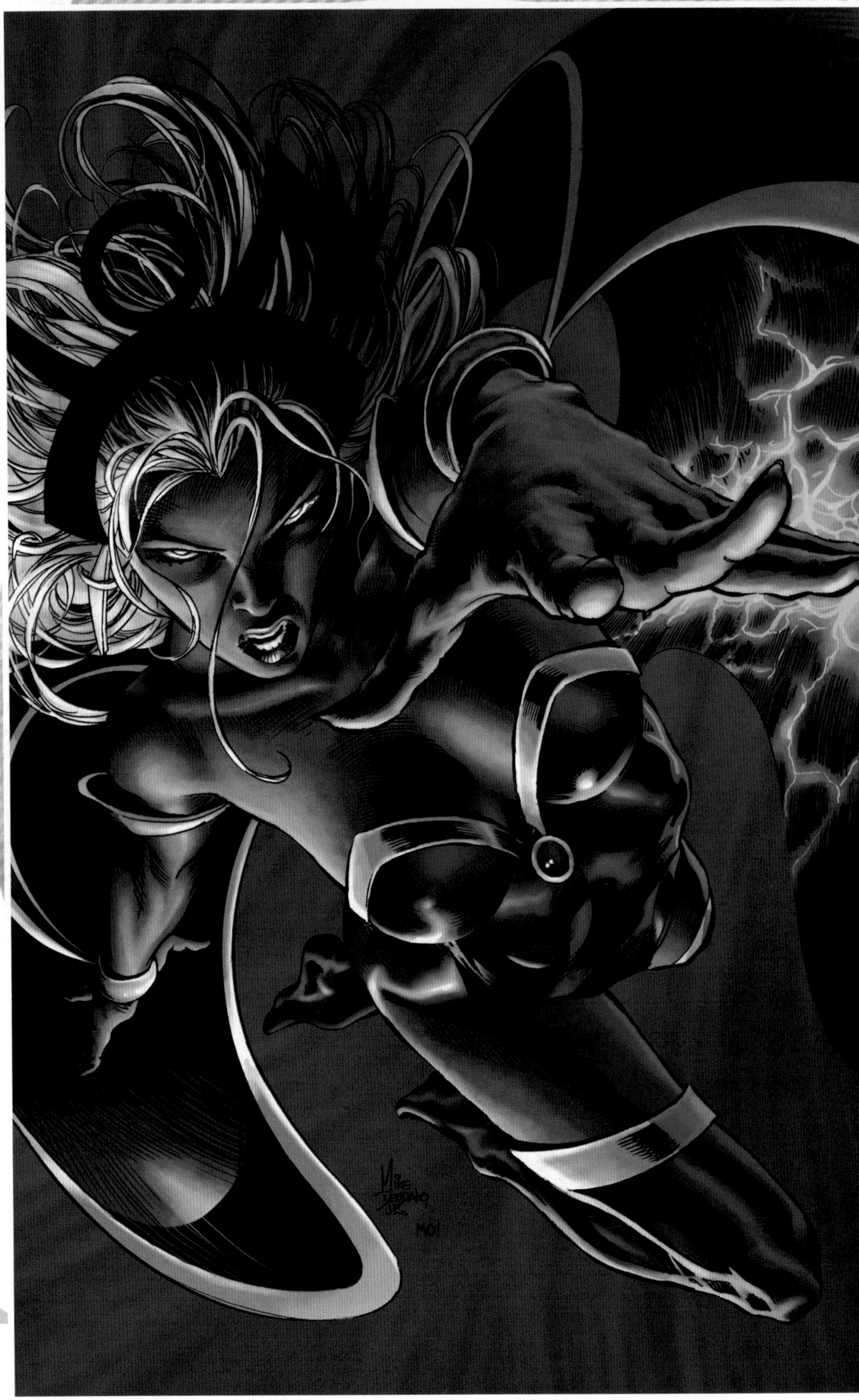

X-MEN: WORLDS APART #3

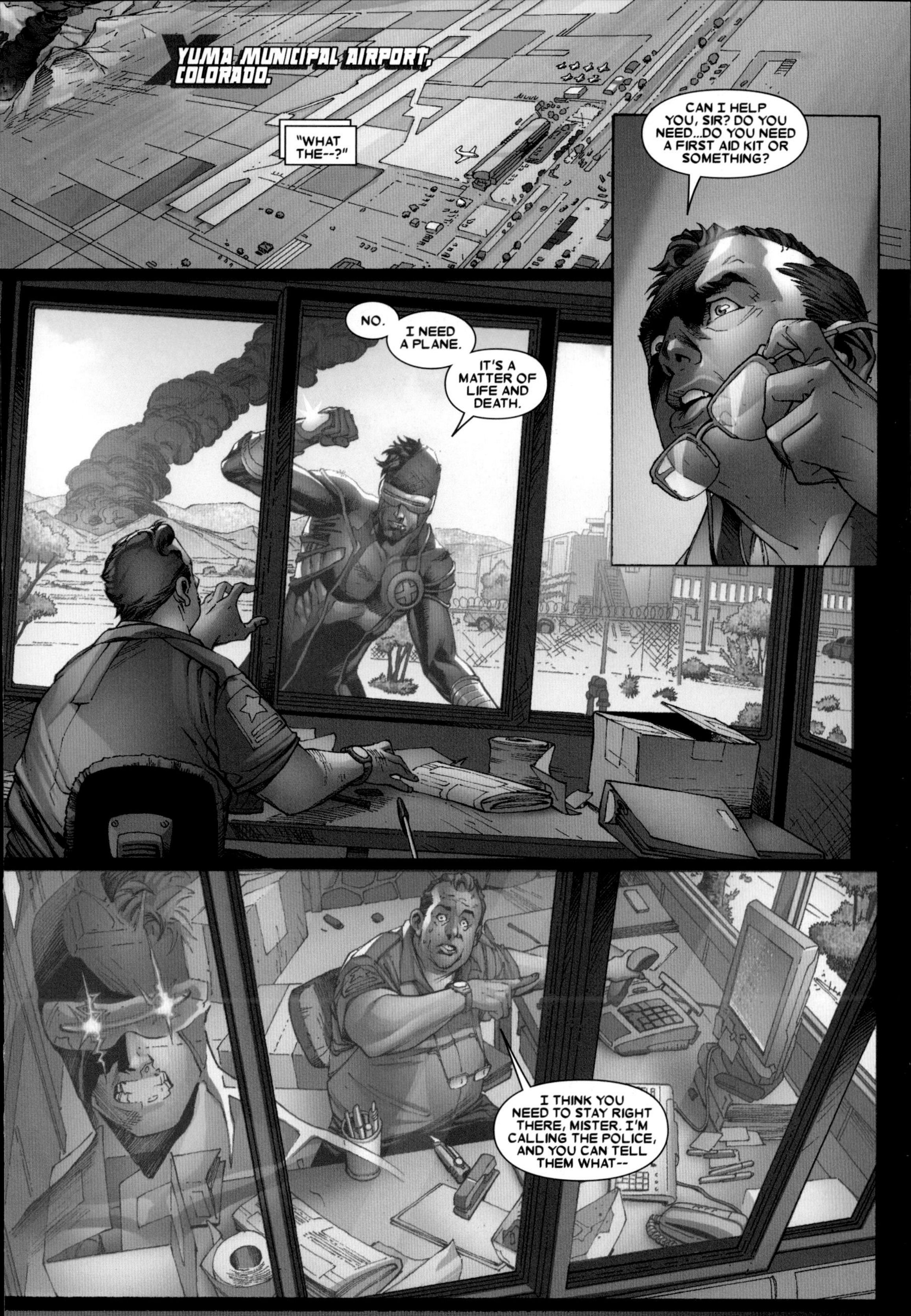
YUMA MUNICIPAL AIRPORT, COLORADO.
"WHAT THE--?"
CAN I HELP YOU, SIR? DO YOU NEED...DO YOU NEED A FIRST AID KIT OR SOMETHING?
NO.
I NEED A PLANE.
IT'S A MATTER OF LIFE AND DEATH.
I THINK YOU NEED TO STAY RIGHT THERE, MISTER. I'M CALLING THE POLICE, AND YOU CAN TELL THEM WHAT--

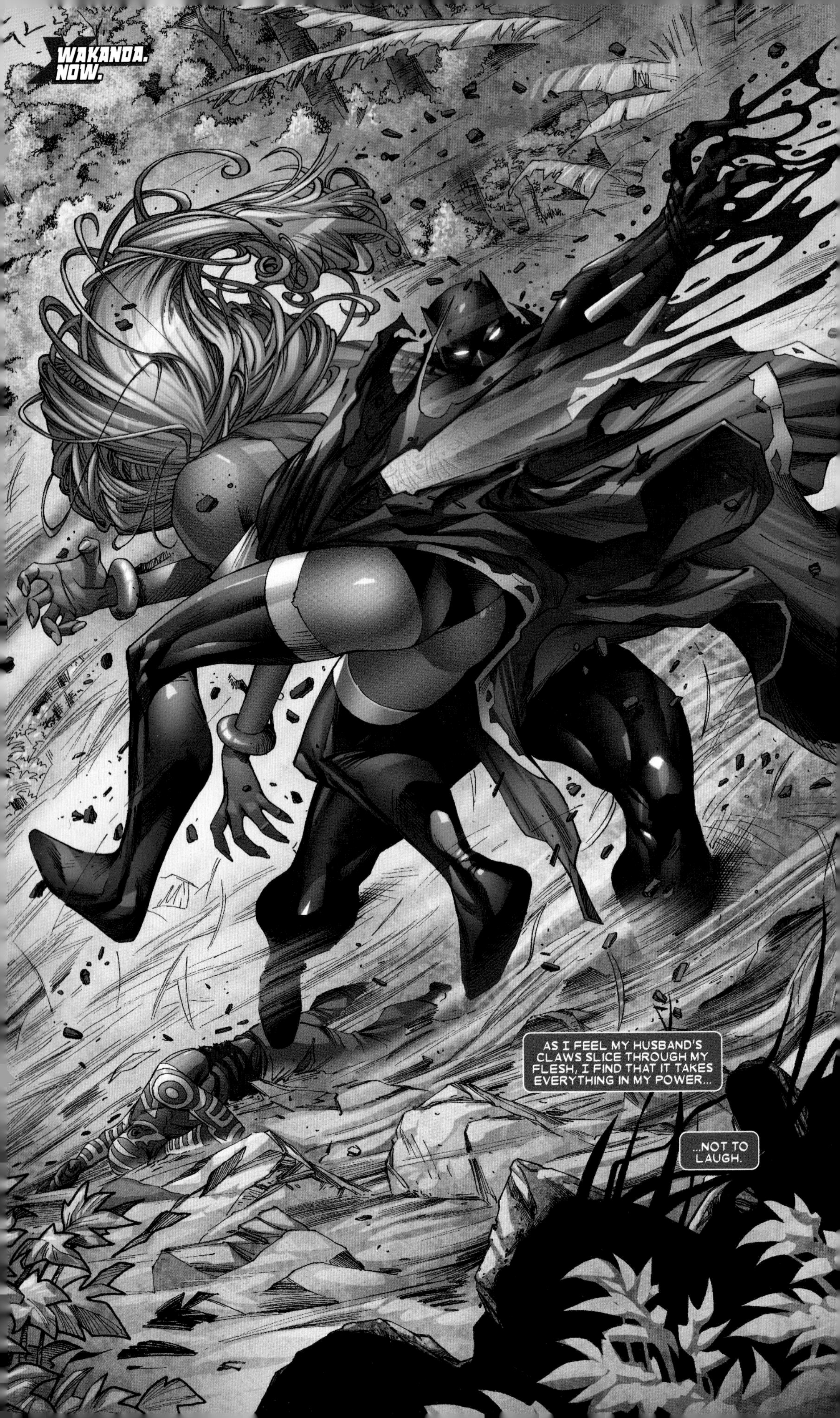
WAKANDA. NOW.
AS I FEEL MY HUSBAND'S CLAWS SLICE THROUGH MY FLESH, I FIND THAT IT TAKES EVERYTHING IN MY POWER...
...NOT TO LAUGH.

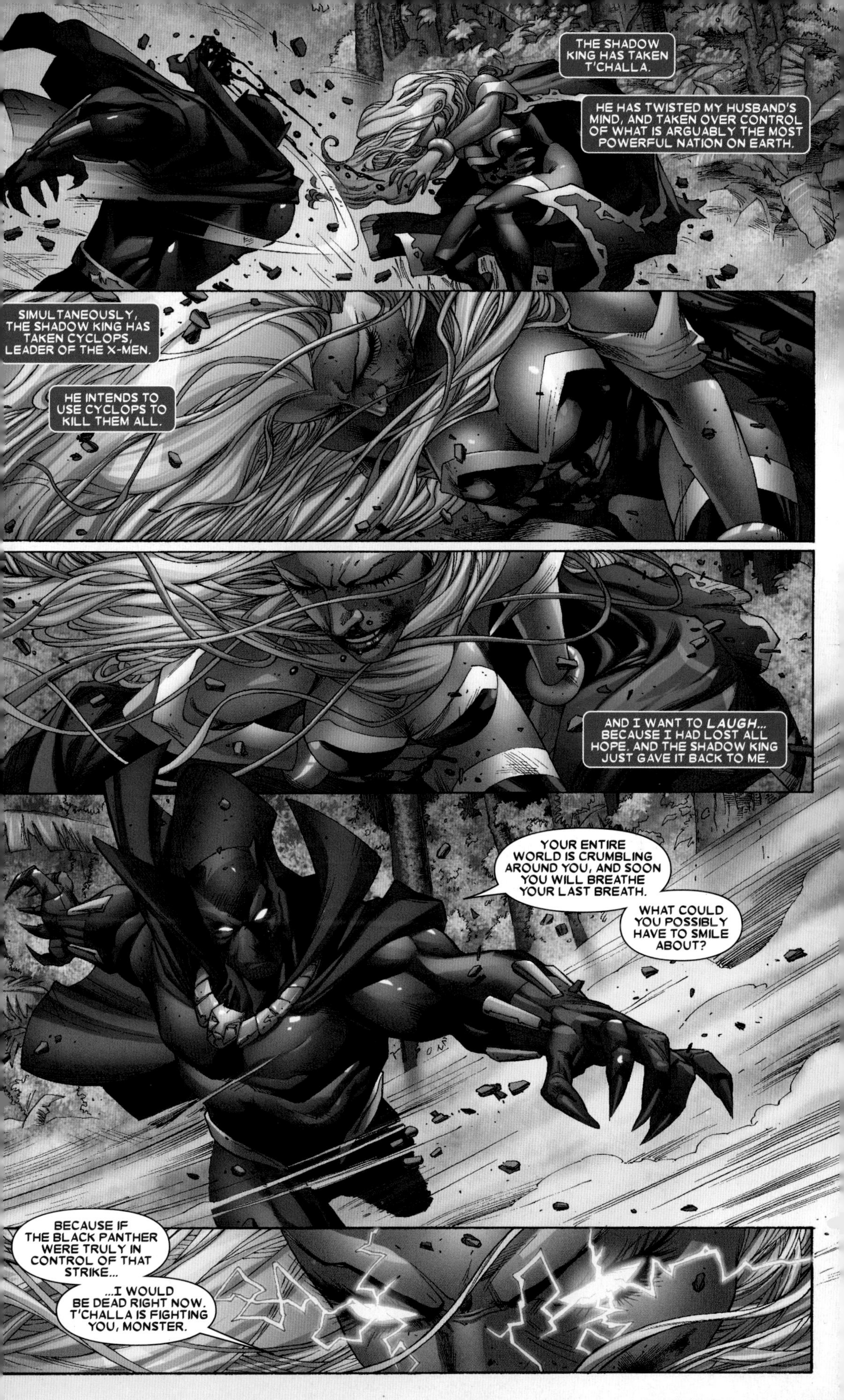
THE SHADOW KING HAS TAKEN T'CHALLA.
HE HAS TWISTED MY HUSBAND'S MIND, AND TAKEN OVER CONTROL OF WHAT IS ARGUABLY THE MOST POWERFUL NATION ON EARTH.
SIMULTANEOUSLY, THE SHADOW KING HAS TAKEN CYCLOPS, LEADER OF THE X-MEN.
HE INTENDS TO USE CYCLOPS TO KILL THEM ALL.
AND I WANT TO *LAUGH*... BECAUSE I HAD LOST ALL HOPE. AND THE SHADOW KING JUST GAVE IT BACK TO ME.
YOUR ENTIRE WORLD IS CRUMBLING AROUND YOU, AND SOON YOU WILL BREATHE YOUR LAST BREATH.
WHAT COULD YOU POSSIBLY HAVE TO SMILE ABOUT?
BECAUSE IF THE BLACK PANTHER WERE TRULY IN CONTROL OF THAT STRIKE...
...I WOULD BE DEAD RIGHT NOW. T'CHALLA IS FIGHTING YOU, MONSTER.

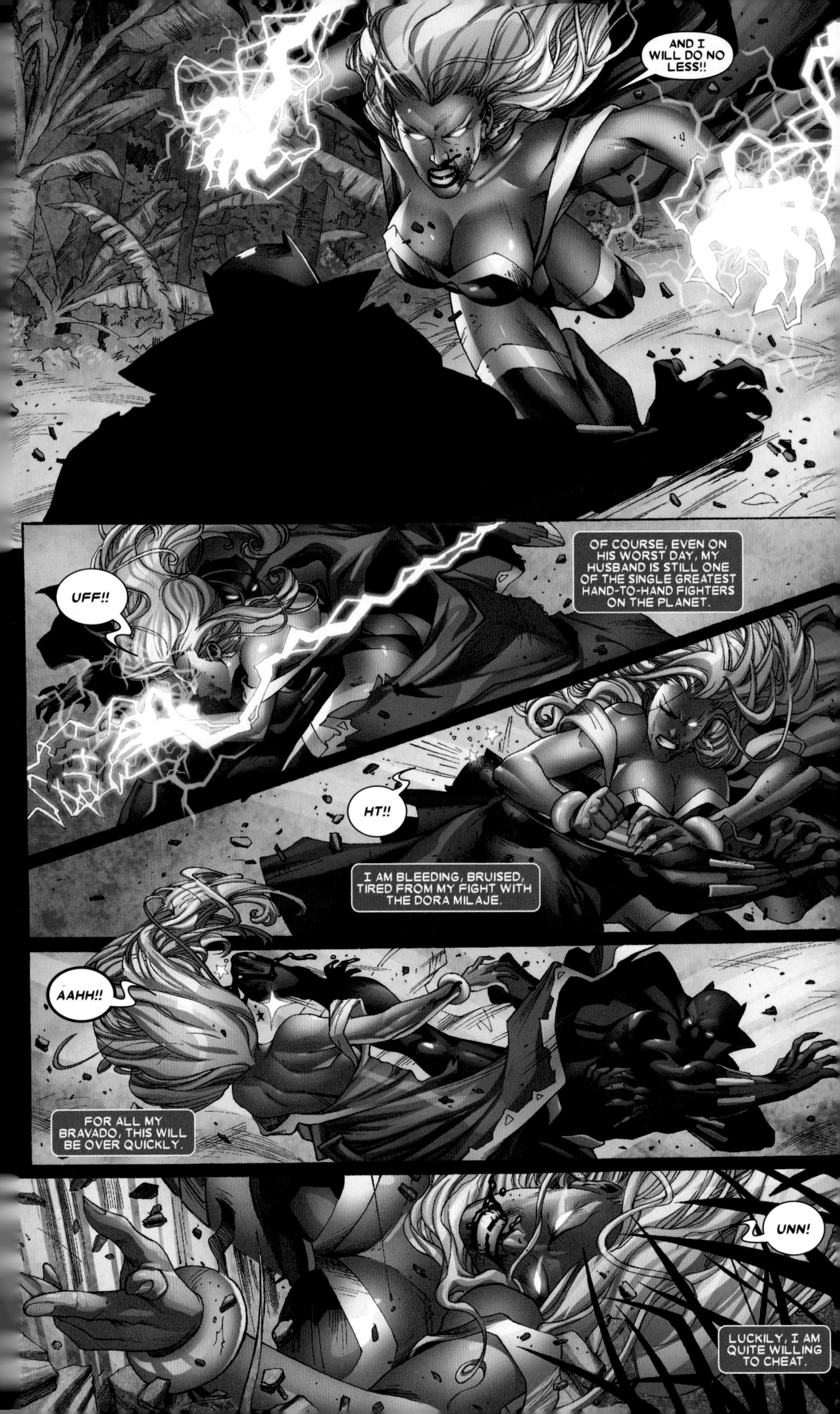
AND I WILL DO NO LESS!!
UFF!!
OF COURSE, EVEN ON HIS WORST DAY, MY HUSBAND IS STILL ONE OF THE SINGLE GREATEST HAND-TO-HAND FIGHTERS ON THE PLANET.
HT!!
I AM BLEEDING, BRUISED, TIRED FROM MY FIGHT WITH THE DORA MILAJE.
AAHH!!
FOR ALL MY BRAVADO, THIS WILL BE OVER QUICKLY.
UNN!
LUCKILY, I AM QUITE WILLING TO CHEAT.

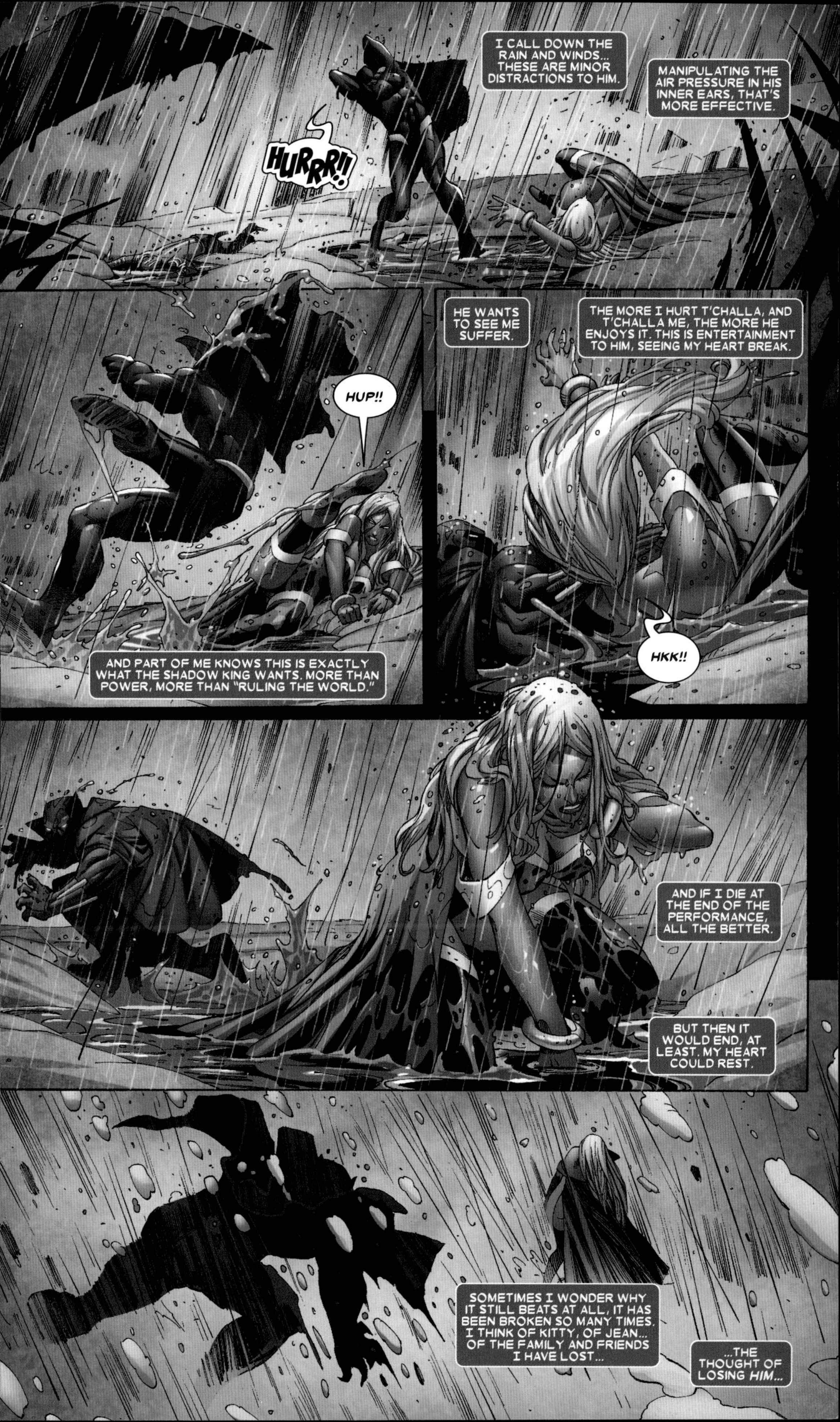

I CALL DOWN THE RAIN AND WINDS... THESE ARE MINOR DISTRACTIONS TO HIM.
MANIPULATING THE AIR PRESSURE IN HIS INNER EARS, THAT'S MORE EFFECTIVE.
HURRR!!
HUP!!
AND PART OF ME KNOWS THIS IS EXACTLY WHAT THE SHADOW KING WANTS. MORE THAN POWER, MORE THAN "RULING THE WORLD."
HE WANTS TO SEE ME SUFFER.
THE MORE I HURT T'CHALLA, AND T'CHALLA ME, THE MORE HE ENJOYS IT. THIS IS ENTERTAINMENT TO HIM, SEEING MY HEART BREAK.
HKK!!
AND IF I DIE AT THE END OF THE PERFORMANCE, ALL THE BETTER.
BUT THEN IT WOULD END, AT LEAST. MY HEART COULD REST.
SOMETIMES I WONDER WHY IT STILL BEATS AT ALL. IT HAS BEEN BROKEN SO MANY TIMES. I THINK OF KITTY, OF JEAN... OF THE FAMILY AND FRIENDS I HAVE LOST...
...THE THOUGHT OF LOSING *HIM*...

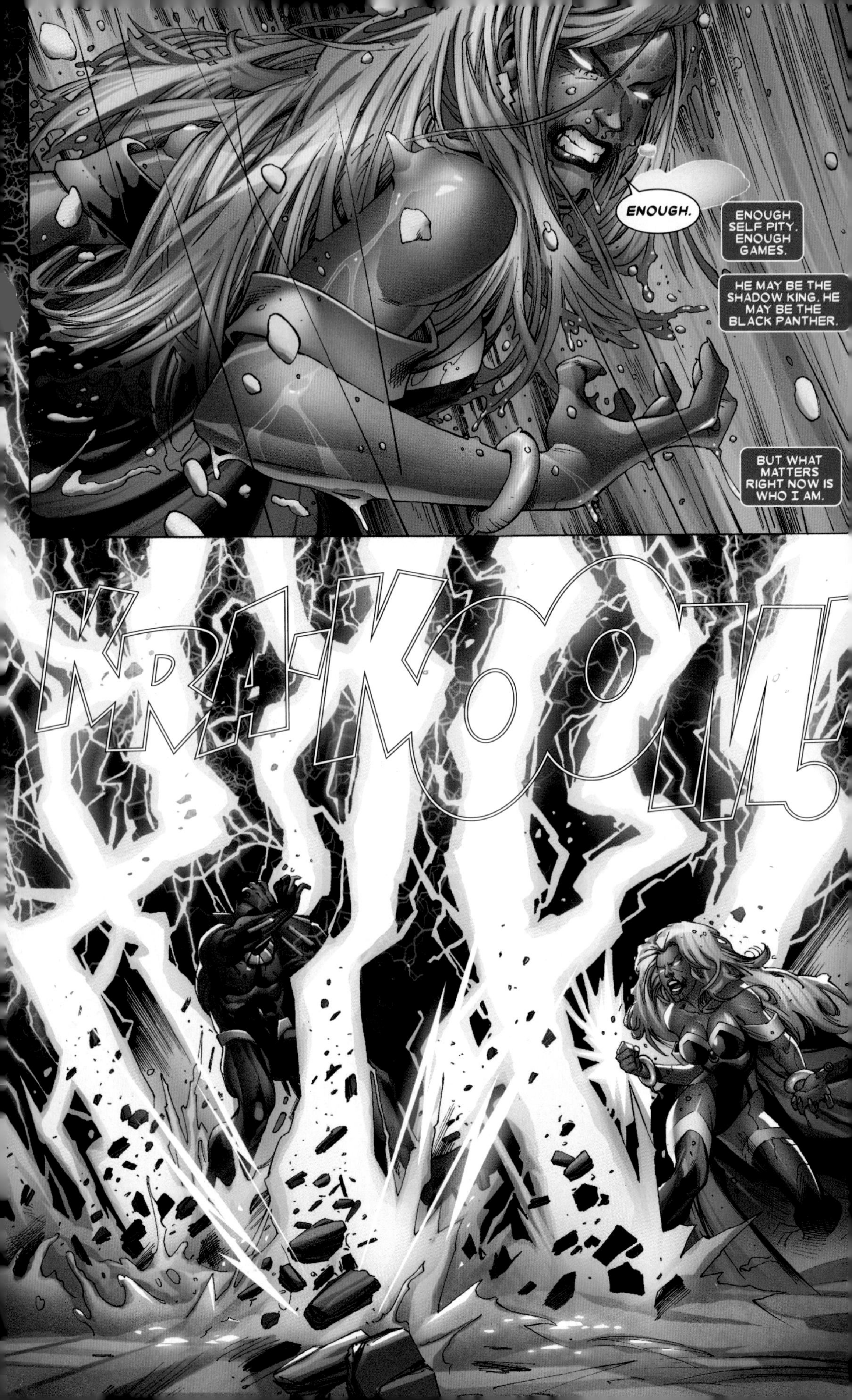

ENOUGH.
ENOUGH SELF PITY. ENOUGH GAMES.
HE MAY BE THE SHADOW KING. HE MAY BE THE BLACK PANTHER.
BUT WHAT MATTERS RIGHT NOW IS WHO I AM.
KRAKOOM!

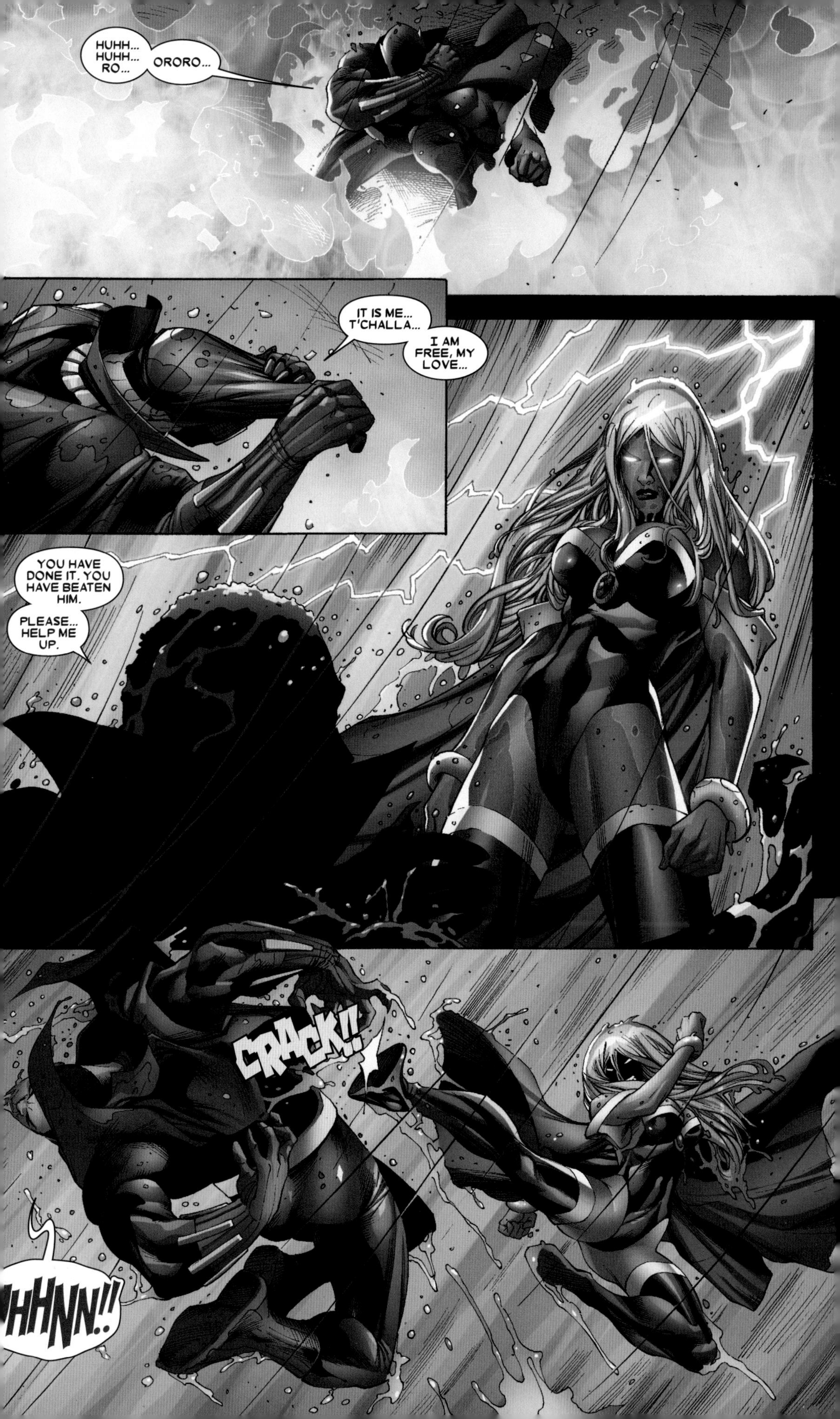
HUHH... HUHH... RO...
ORORO...
IT IS ME... T'CHALLA...
I AM FREE, MY LOVE...
YOU HAVE DONE IT. YOU HAVE BEATEN HIM.
PLEASE... HELP ME UP.
CRACK!!
HHNN!!

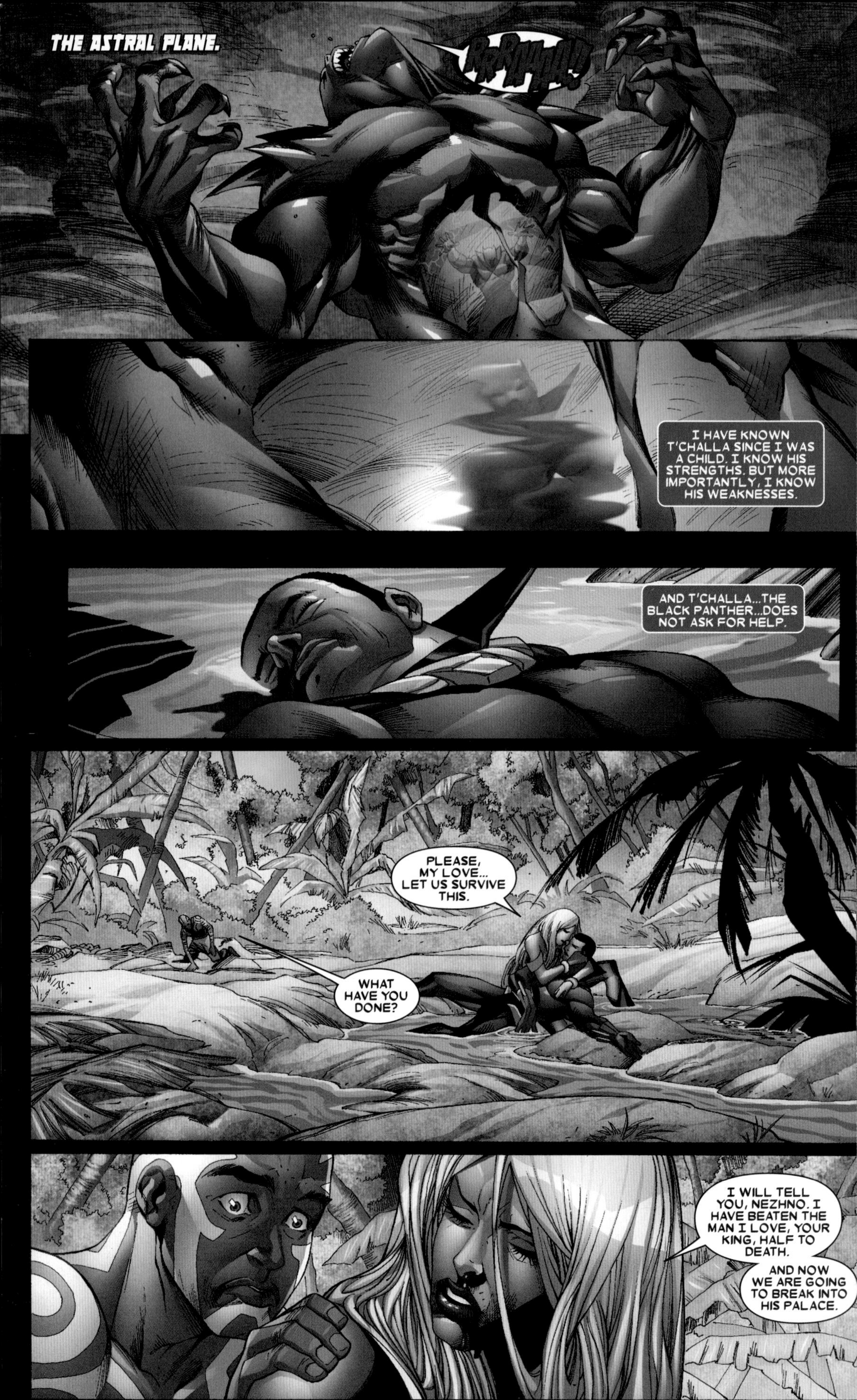
THE ASTRAL PLANE.
I HAVE KNOWN T'CHALLA SINCE I WAS A CHILD. I KNOW HIS STRENGTHS. BUT MORE IMPORTANTLY, I KNOW HIS WEAKNESSES.
AND T'CHALLA...THE BLACK PANTHER...DOES NOT ASK FOR HELP.
PLEASE, MY LOVE... LET US SURVIVE THIS.
WHAT HAVE YOU DONE?
I WILL TELL YOU, NEZHNO. I HAVE BEATEN THE MAN I LOVE, YOUR KING, HALF TO DEATH.
AND NOW WE ARE GOING TO BREAK INTO HIS PALACE.

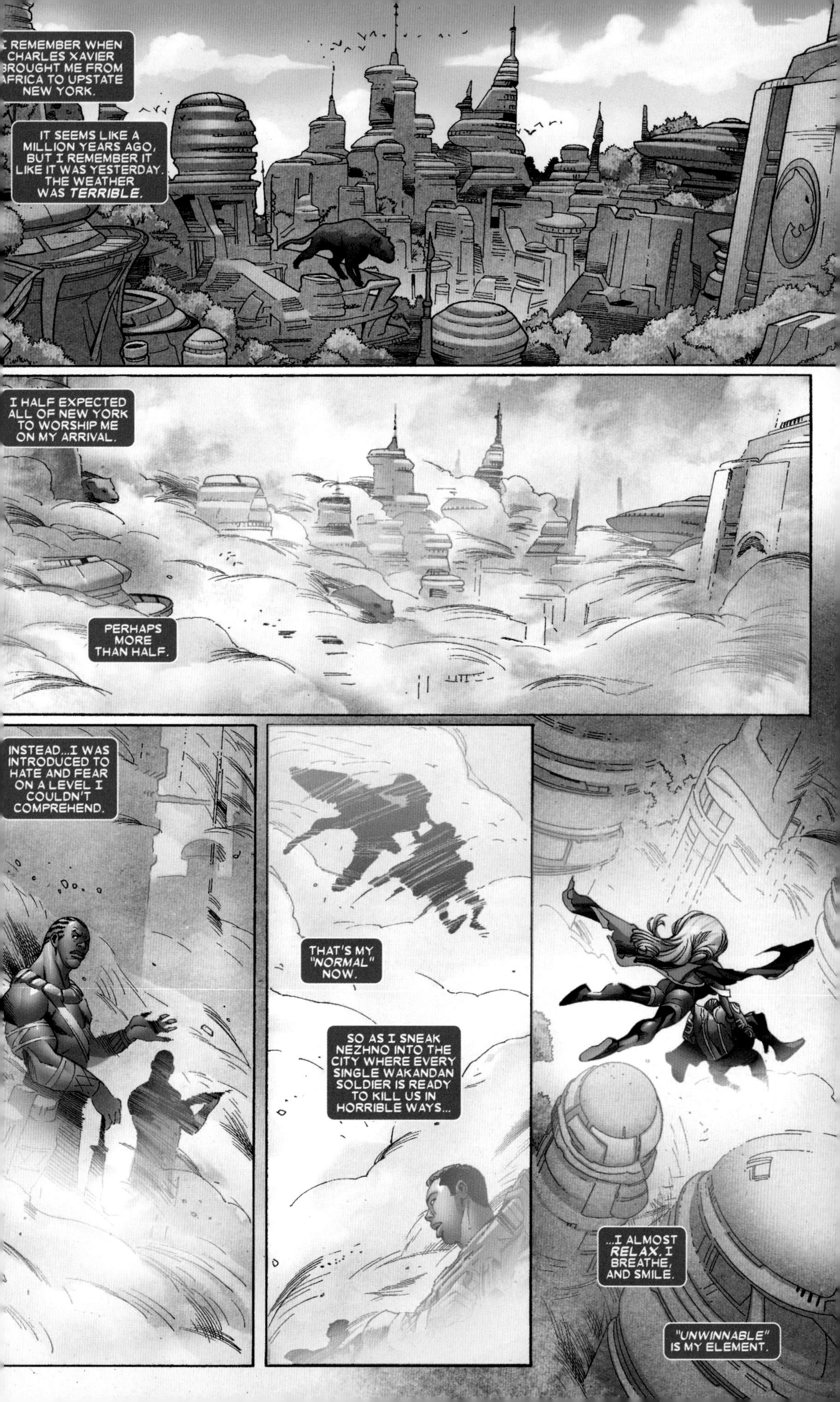
I REMEMBER WHEN CHARLES XAVIER BROUGHT ME FROM AFRICA TO UPSTATE NEW YORK.
IT SEEMS LIKE A MILLION YEARS AGO, BUT I REMEMBER IT LIKE IT WAS YESTERDAY. THE WEATHER WAS *TERRIBLE*.
I HALF EXPECTED ALL OF NEW YORK TO WORSHIP ME ON MY ARRIVAL.
PERHAPS MORE THAN HALF.
INSTEAD...I WAS INTRODUCED TO HATE AND FEAR ON A LEVEL I COULDN'T COMPREHEND.
THAT'S MY "*NORMAL*" NOW.
SO AS I SNEAK NEZHNO INTO THE CITY WHERE EVERY SINGLE WAKANDAN SOLDIER IS READY TO KILL US IN HORRIBLE WAYS...
...I ALMOST *RELAX*. I BREATHE, AND SMILE.
"*UNWINNABLE*" IS MY ELEMENT.

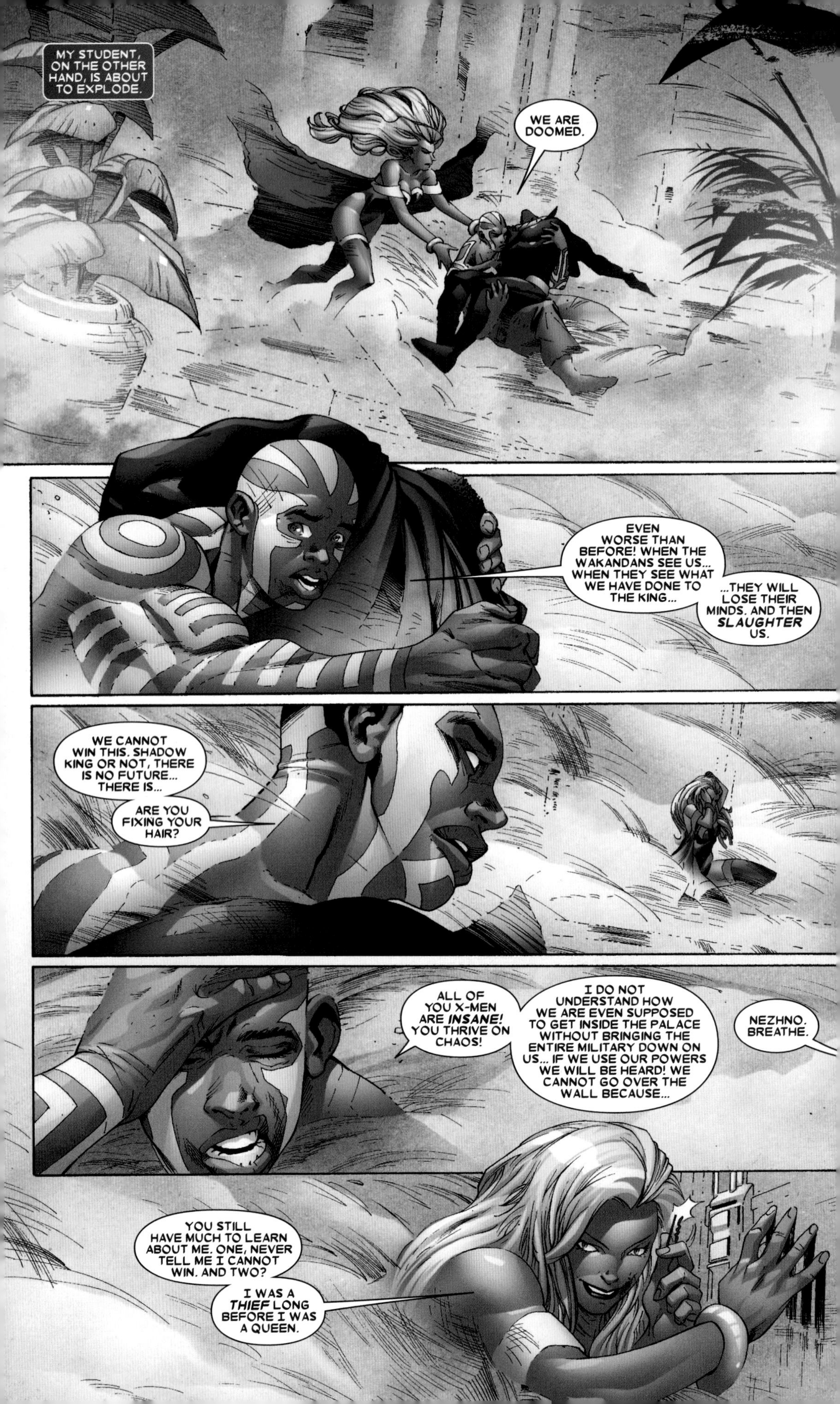

MY STUDENT, ON THE OTHER HAND, IS ABOUT TO EXPLODE.
WE ARE DOOMED.
EVEN WORSE THAN BEFORE! WHEN THE WAKANDANS SEE US... WHEN THEY SEE WHAT WE HAVE DONE TO THE KING...
...THEY WILL LOSE THEIR MINDS. AND THEN *SLAUGHTER* US.
WE CANNOT WIN THIS. SHADOW KING OR NOT, THERE IS NO FUTURE... THERE IS...
ARE YOU FIXING YOUR HAIR?
ALL OF YOU X-MEN ARE *INSANE!* YOU THRIVE ON CHAOS!
I DO NOT UNDERSTAND HOW WE ARE EVEN SUPPOSED TO GET INSIDE THE PALACE WITHOUT BRINGING THE ENTIRE MILITARY DOWN ON US... IF WE USE OUR POWERS WE WILL BE HEARD! WE CANNOT GO OVER THE WALL BECAUSE...
NEZHNO. BREATHE.
YOU STILL HAVE MUCH TO LEARN ABOUT ME. ONE, NEVER TELL ME I CANNOT WIN. AND TWO?
I WAS A *THIEF* LONG BEFORE I WAS A QUEEN.

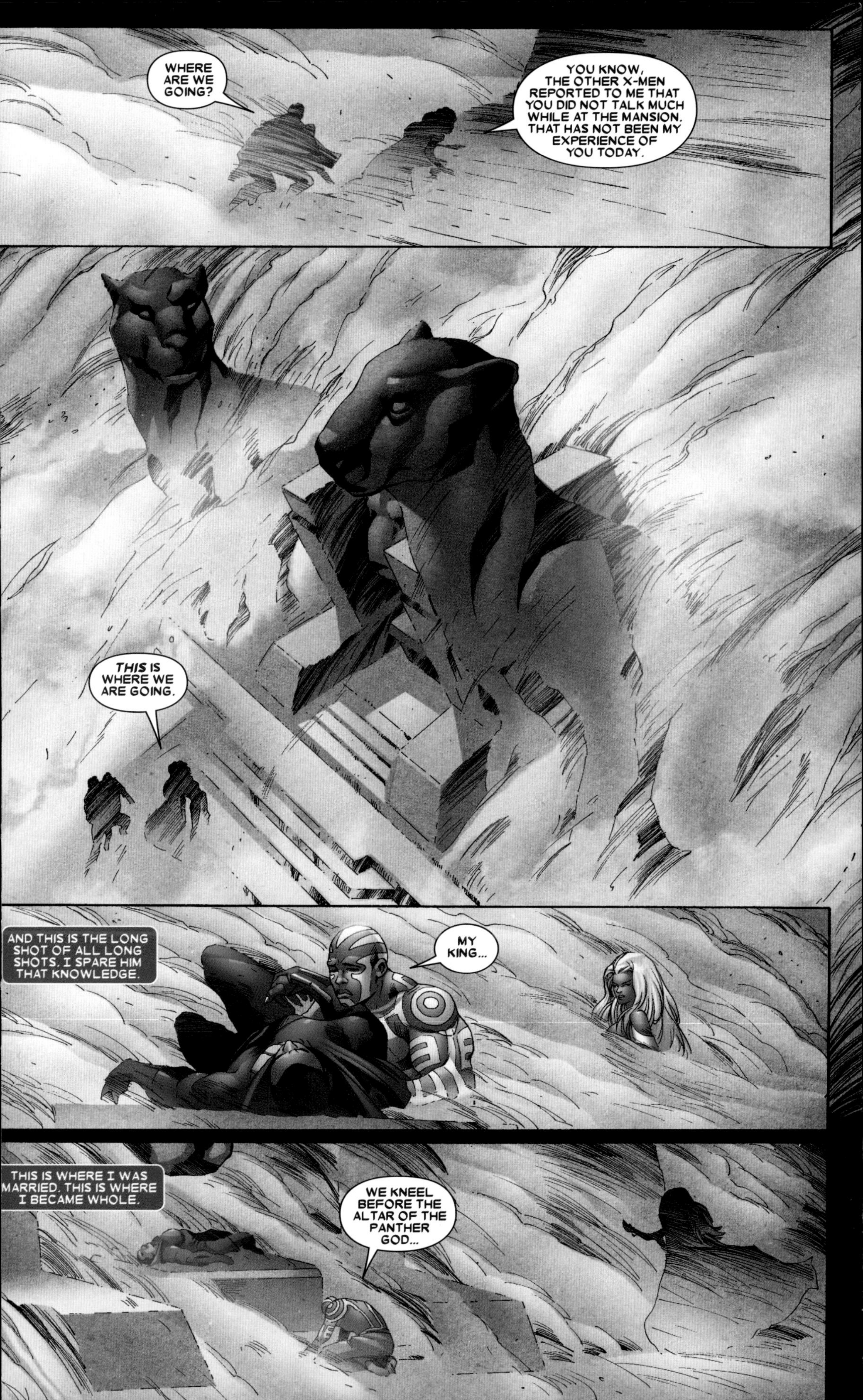
WHERE ARE WE GOING?
YOU KNOW, THE OTHER X-MEN REPORTED TO ME THAT YOU DID NOT TALK MUCH WHILE AT THE MANSION. THAT HAS NOT BEEN MY EXPERIENCE OF YOU TODAY.
THIS IS WHERE WE ARE GOING.
AND THIS IS THE LONG SHOT OF ALL LONG SHOTS. I SPARE HIM THAT KNOWLEDGE.
MY KING...
THIS IS WHERE I WAS MARRIED. THIS IS WHERE I BECAME WHOLE.
WE KNEEL BEFORE THE ALTAR OF THE PANTHER GOD...

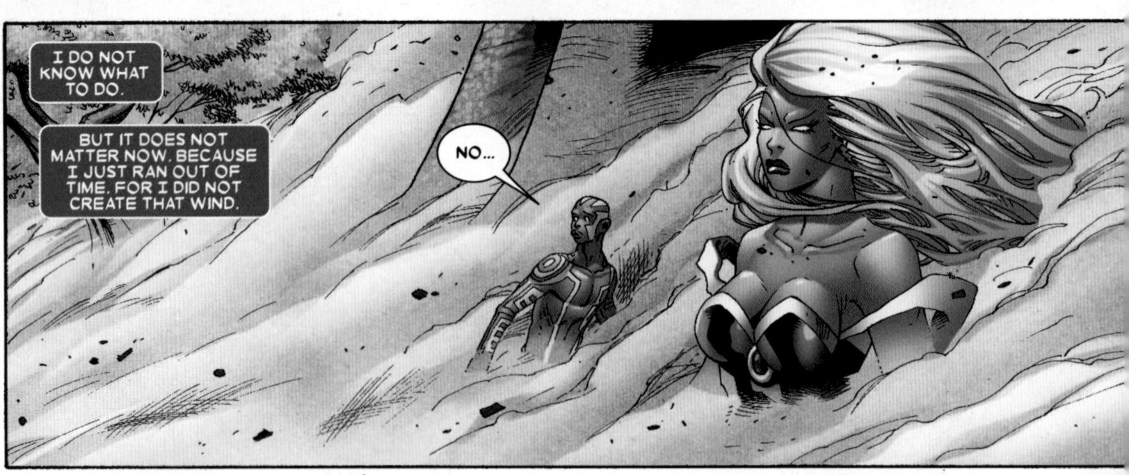
I DO NOT KNOW WHAT TO DO.
BUT IT DOES NOT MATTER NOW. BECAUSE I JUST RAN OUT OF TIME. FOR I DID NOT CREATE THAT WIND.
NO...

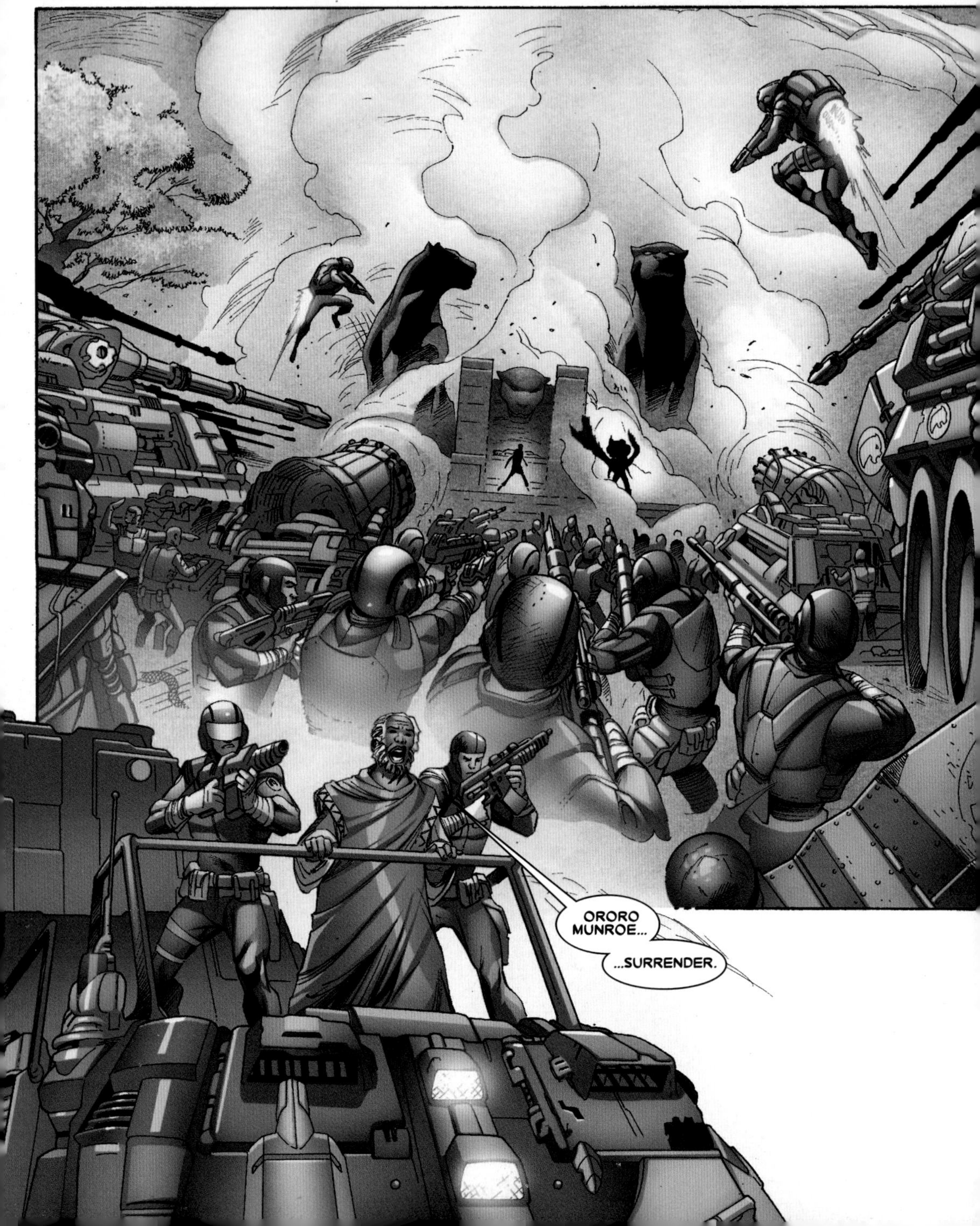
ORORO MUNROE...
...SURRENDER.

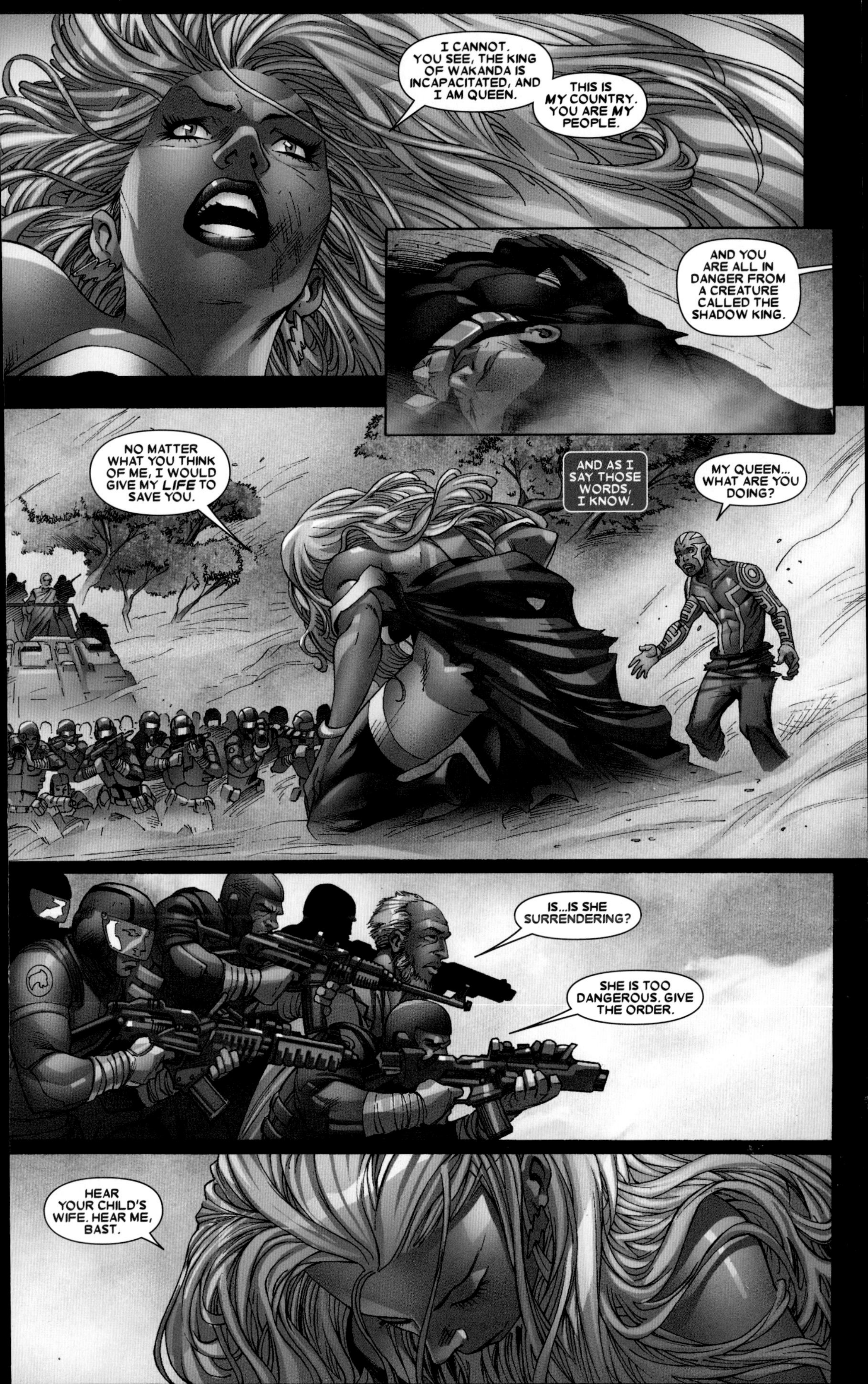
I CANNOT. YOU SEE, THE KING OF WAKANDA IS INCAPACITATED, AND I AM QUEEN.
THIS IS *MY* COUNTRY. YOU ARE *MY* PEOPLE.
AND YOU ARE ALL IN DANGER FROM A CREATURE CALLED THE SHADOW KING.
NO MATTER WHAT YOU THINK OF ME, I WOULD GIVE MY *LIFE* TO SAVE YOU.
AND AS I SAY THOSE WORDS, I KNOW.
MY QUEEN... WHAT ARE YOU DOING?
IS...IS SHE SURRENDERING?
SHE IS TOO DANGEROUS. GIVE THE ORDER.
HEAR YOUR CHILD'S WIFE. HEAR ME, BAST.

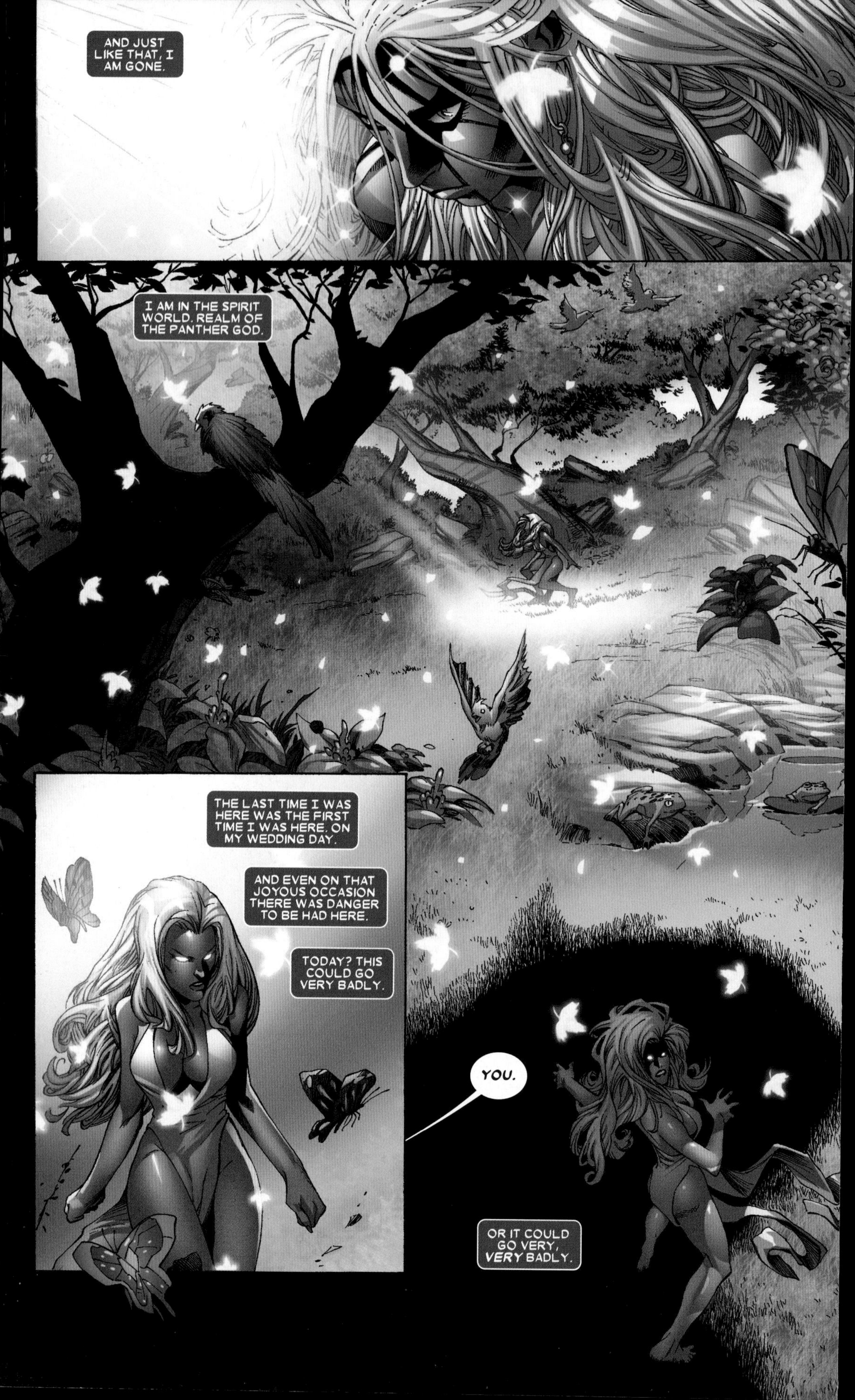
AND JUST LIKE THAT, I AM GONE.
I AM IN THE SPIRIT WORLD. REALM OF THE PANTHER GOD.
THE LAST TIME I WAS HERE WAS THE FIRST TIME I WAS HERE. ON MY WEDDING DAY.
AND EVEN ON THAT JOYOUS OCCASION THERE WAS DANGER TO BE HAD HERE.
TODAY? THIS COULD GO VERY BADLY.
YOU.
OR IT COULD GO VERY, *VERY* BADLY.

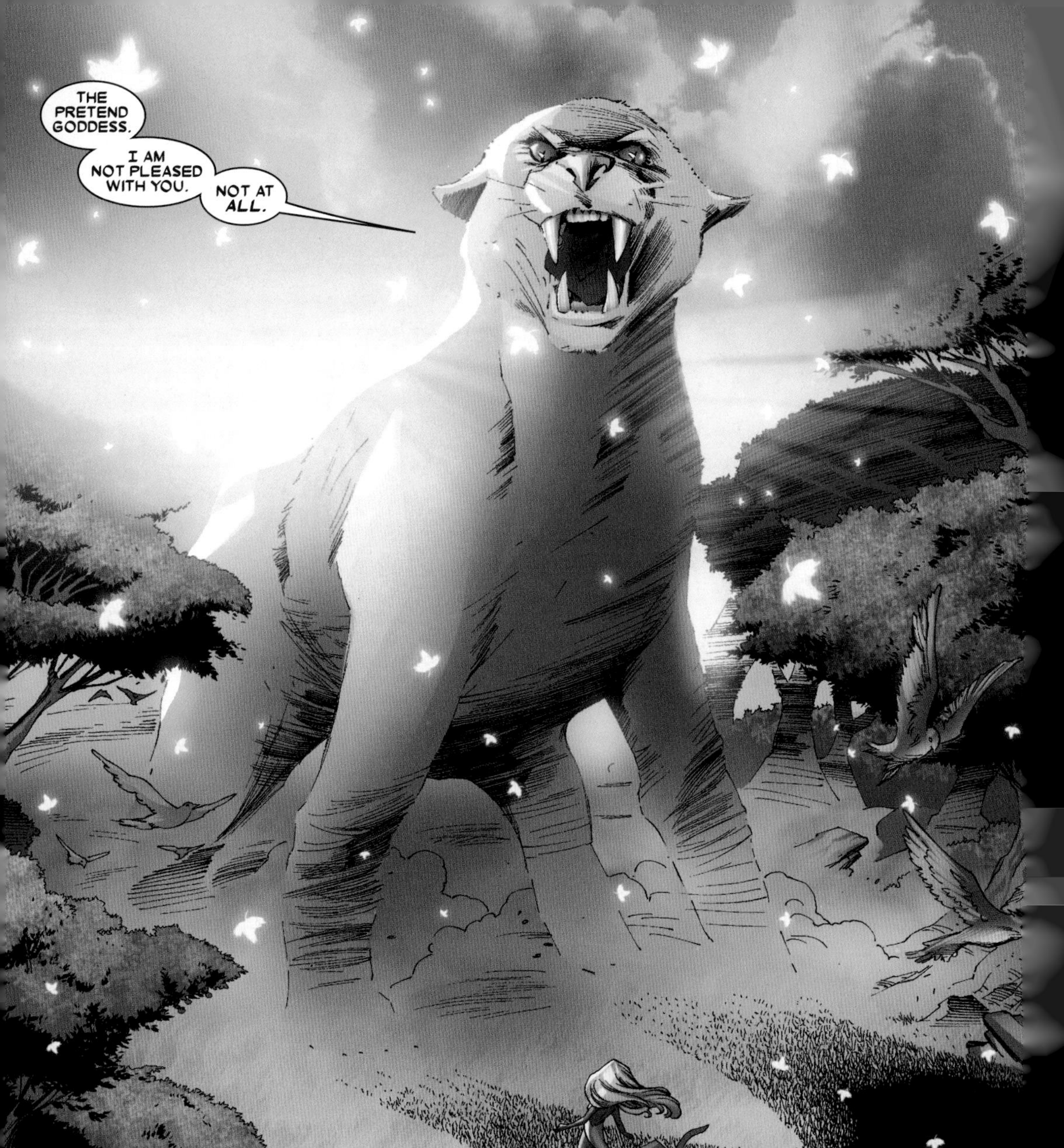
THE PRETEND GODDESS.
I AM NOT PLEASED WITH YOU.
NOT AT ALL.
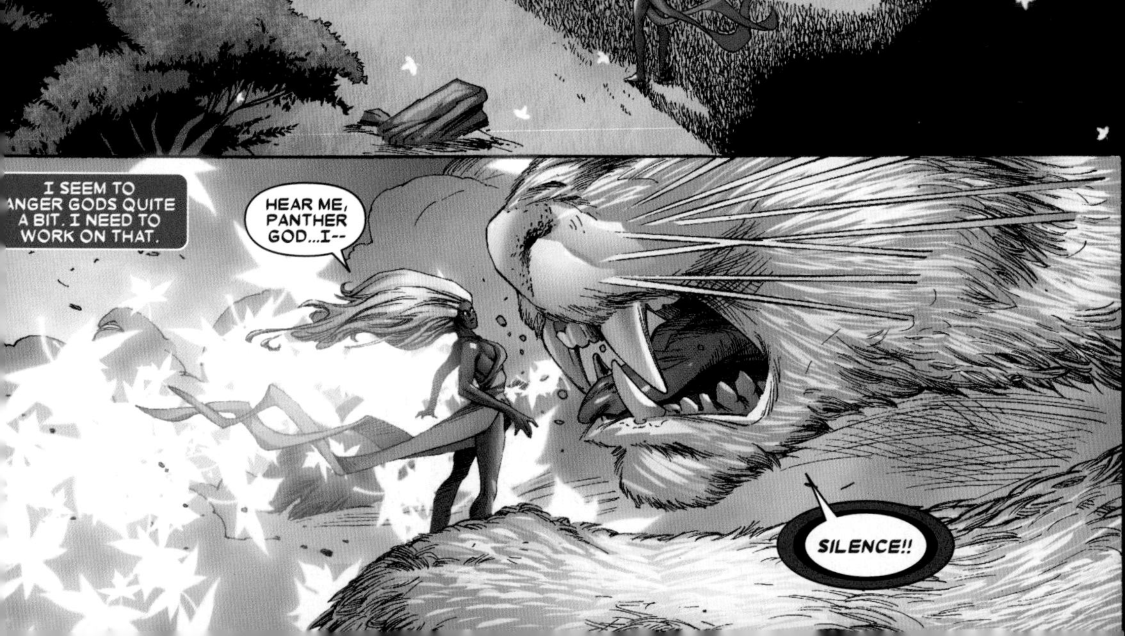
I SEEM TO ANGER GODS QUITE A BIT. I NEED TO WORK ON THAT.
HEAR ME, PANTHER GOD...I--
SILENCE!!

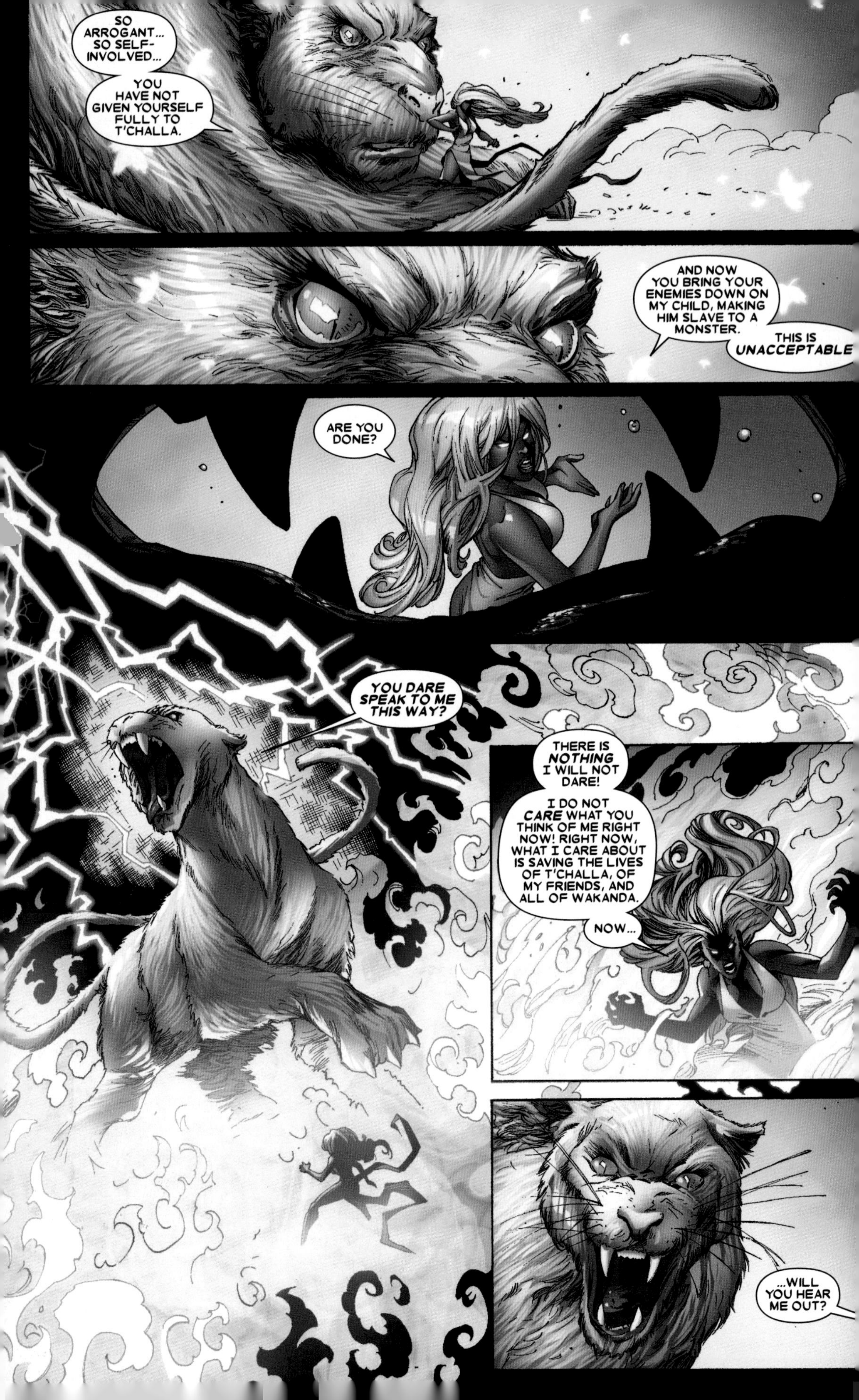
SO ARROGANT... SO SELF-INVOLVED...
YOU HAVE NOT GIVEN YOURSELF FULLY TO T'CHALLA.
AND NOW YOU BRING YOUR ENEMIES DOWN ON MY CHILD, MAKING HIM SLAVE TO A MONSTER.
THIS IS *UNACCEPTABLE*
ARE YOU DONE?
YOU DARE SPEAK TO ME THIS WAY?
THERE IS *NOTHING* I WILL NOT DARE!
I DO NOT *CARE* WHAT YOU THINK OF ME RIGHT NOW! RIGHT NOW, WHAT I CARE ABOUT IS SAVING THE LIVES OF T'CHALLA, OF MY FRIENDS, AND ALL OF WAKANDA.
NOW...
...WILL YOU HEAR ME OUT?

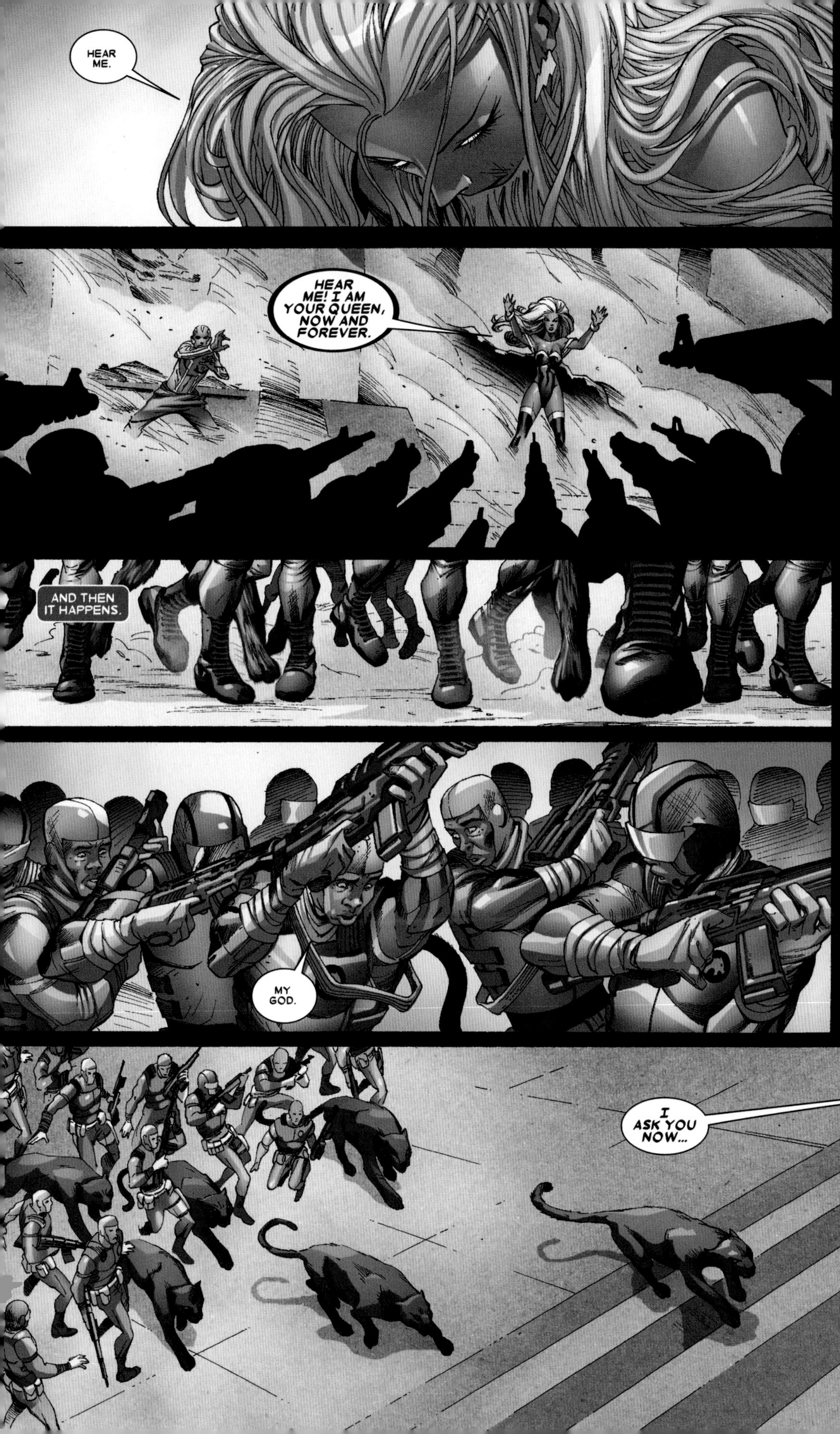
HEAR ME.
HEAR ME! I AM YOUR QUEEN, NOW AND FOREVER.
AND THEN IT HAPPENS.
MY GOD.
I ASK YOU NOW...

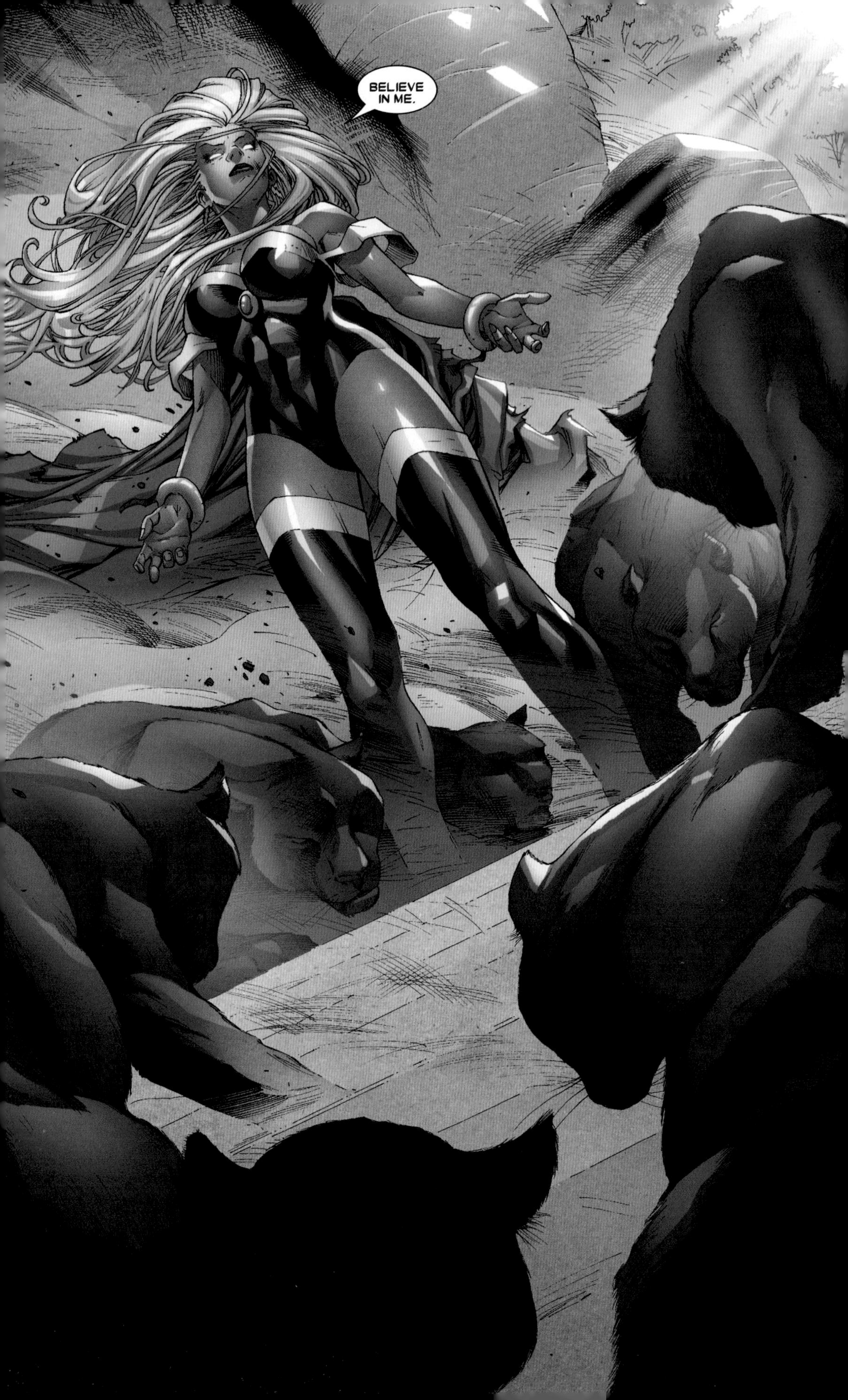
BELIEVE IN ME.

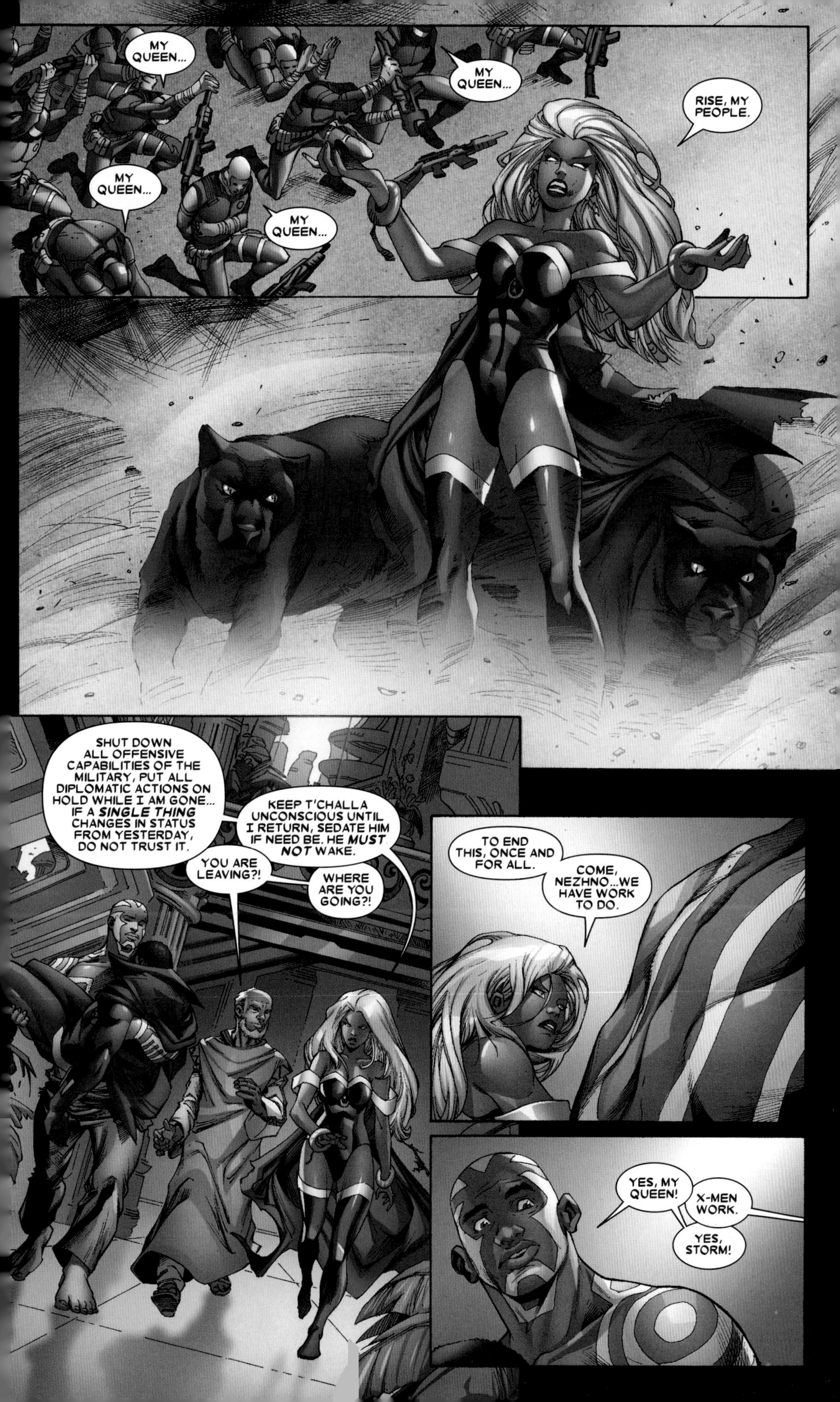
MY QUEEN...
MY QUEEN...
RISE, MY PEOPLE.
MY QUEEN...
MY QUEEN...
SHUT DOWN ALL OFFENSIVE CAPABILITIES OF THE MILITARY, PUT ALL DIPLOMATIC ACTIONS ON HOLD WHILE I AM GONE... IF A SINGLE THING CHANGES IN STATUS FROM YESTERDAY, DO NOT TRUST IT.
KEEP T'CHALLA UNCONSCIOUS UNTIL I RETURN, SEDATE HIM IF NEED BE. HE MUST NOT WAKE.
YOU ARE LEAVING?!
WHERE ARE YOU GOING?!
TO END THIS, ONCE AND FOR ALL.
COME, NEZHNO...WE HAVE WORK TO DO.
YES, MY QUEEN!
X-MEN WORK.
YES, STORM!

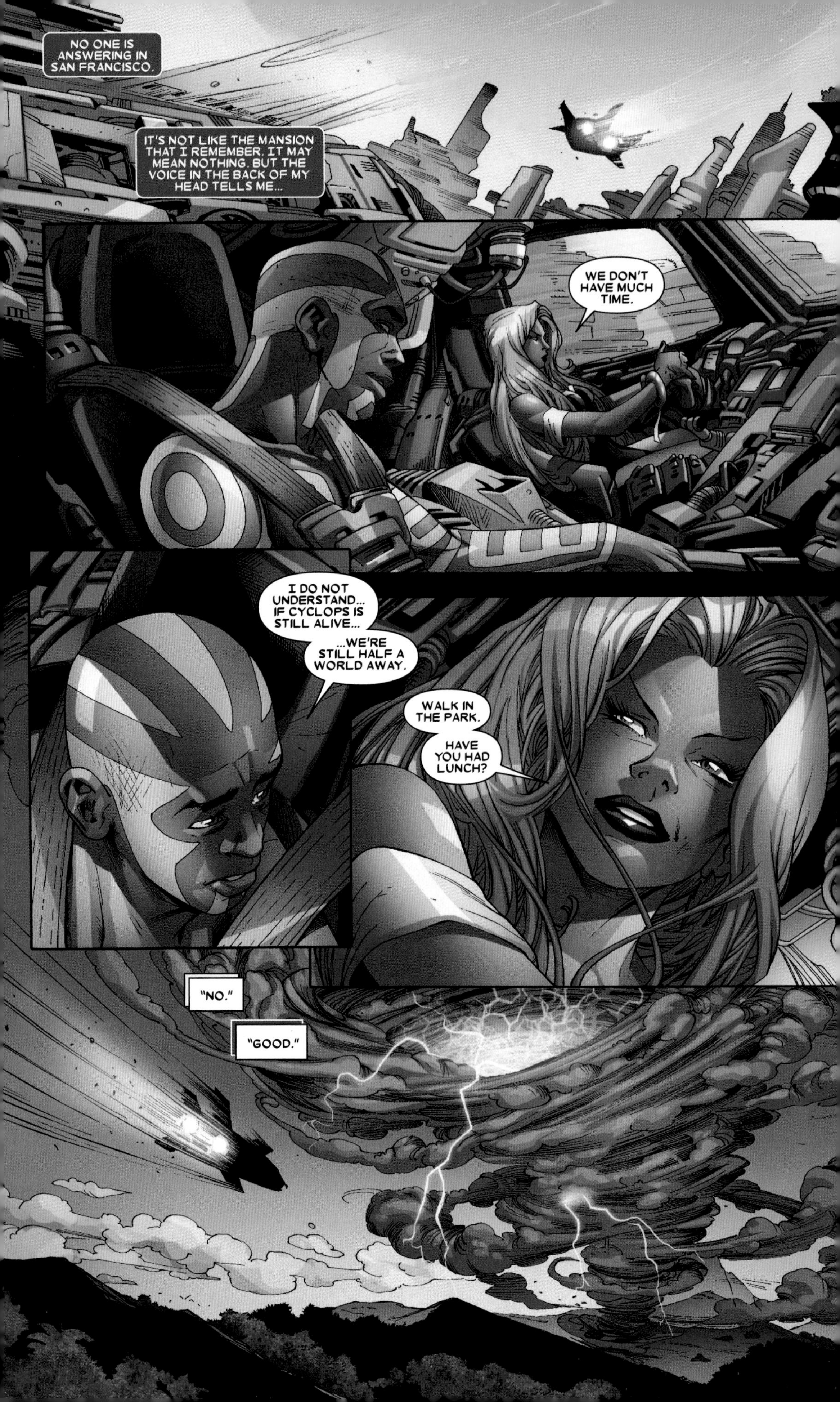
NO ONE IS ANSWERING IN SAN FRANCISCO.
IT'S NOT LIKE THE MANSION THAT I REMEMBER. IT MAY MEAN NOTHING. BUT THE VOICE IN THE BACK OF MY HEAD TELLS ME...
WE DON'T HAVE MUCH TIME.
I DO NOT UNDERSTAND... IF CYCLOPS IS STILL ALIVE...
...WE'RE STILL HALF A WORLD AWAY.
WALK IN THE PARK.
HAVE YOU HAD LUNCH?
"NO."
"GOOD."

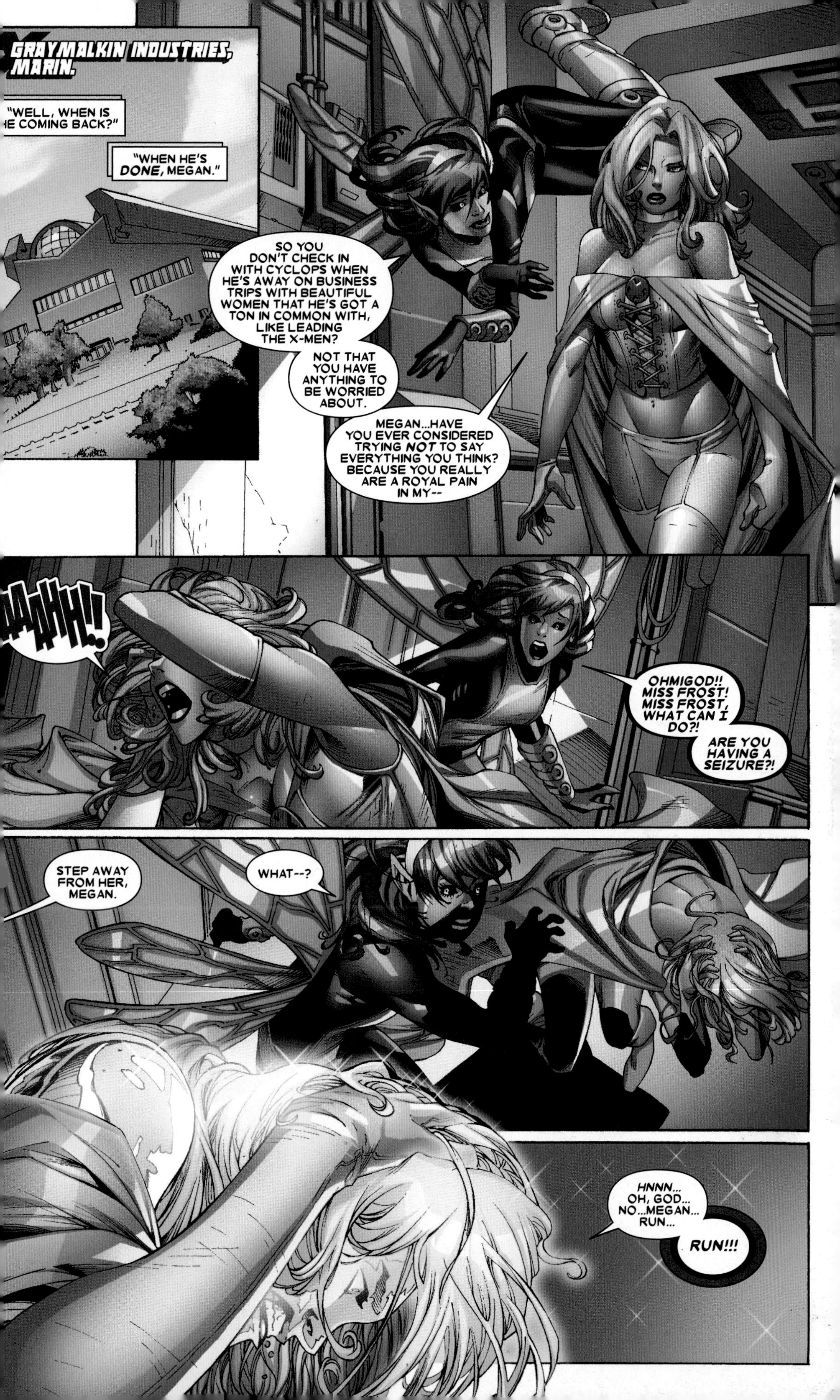

GRAYMALKIN INDUSTRIES, MARIN.
"WELL, WHEN IS HE COMING BACK?"
"WHEN HE'S DONE, MEGAN."
SO YOU DON'T CHECK IN WITH CYCLOPS WHEN HE'S AWAY ON BUSINESS TRIPS WITH BEAUTIFUL WOMEN THAT HE'S GOT A TON IN COMMON WITH, LIKE LEADING THE X-MEN?
NOT THAT YOU HAVE ANYTHING TO BE WORRIED ABOUT.
MEGAN...HAVE YOU EVER CONSIDERED TRYING NOT TO SAY EVERYTHING YOU THINK? BECAUSE YOU REALLY ARE A ROYAL PAIN IN MY--
AAAHH!!
OHMIGOD!! MISS FROST! MISS FROST, WHAT CAN I DO?!
ARE YOU HAVING A SEIZURE?!
STEP AWAY FROM HER, MEGAN.
WHAT--?
HNNN... OH, GOD... NO...MEGAN... RUN...
RUN!!!

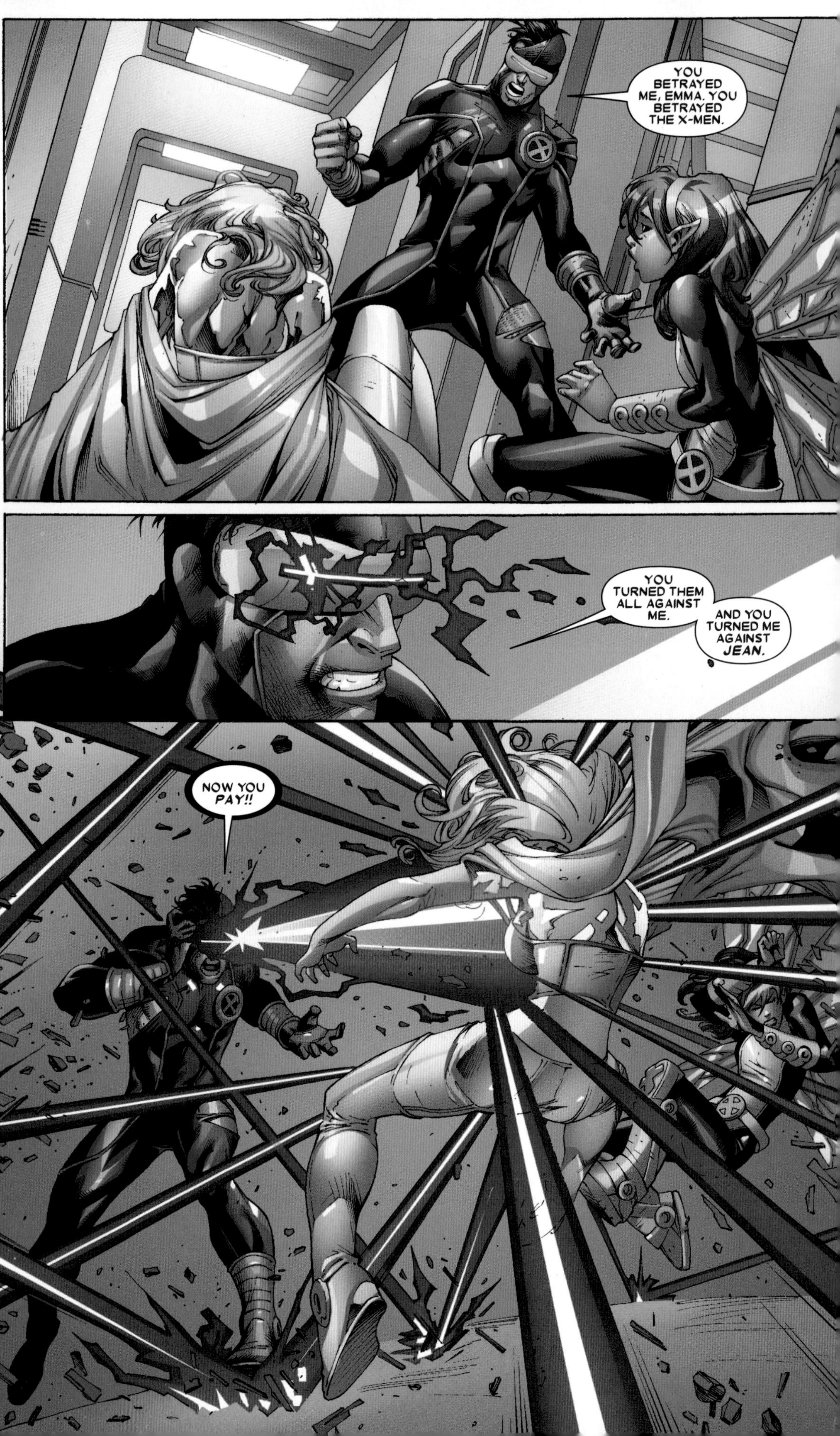
YOU BETRAYED ME, EMMA. YOU BETRAYED THE X-MEN.
YOU TURNED THEM ALL AGAINST ME.
AND YOU TURNED ME AGAINST JEAN.
NOW YOU PAY!!

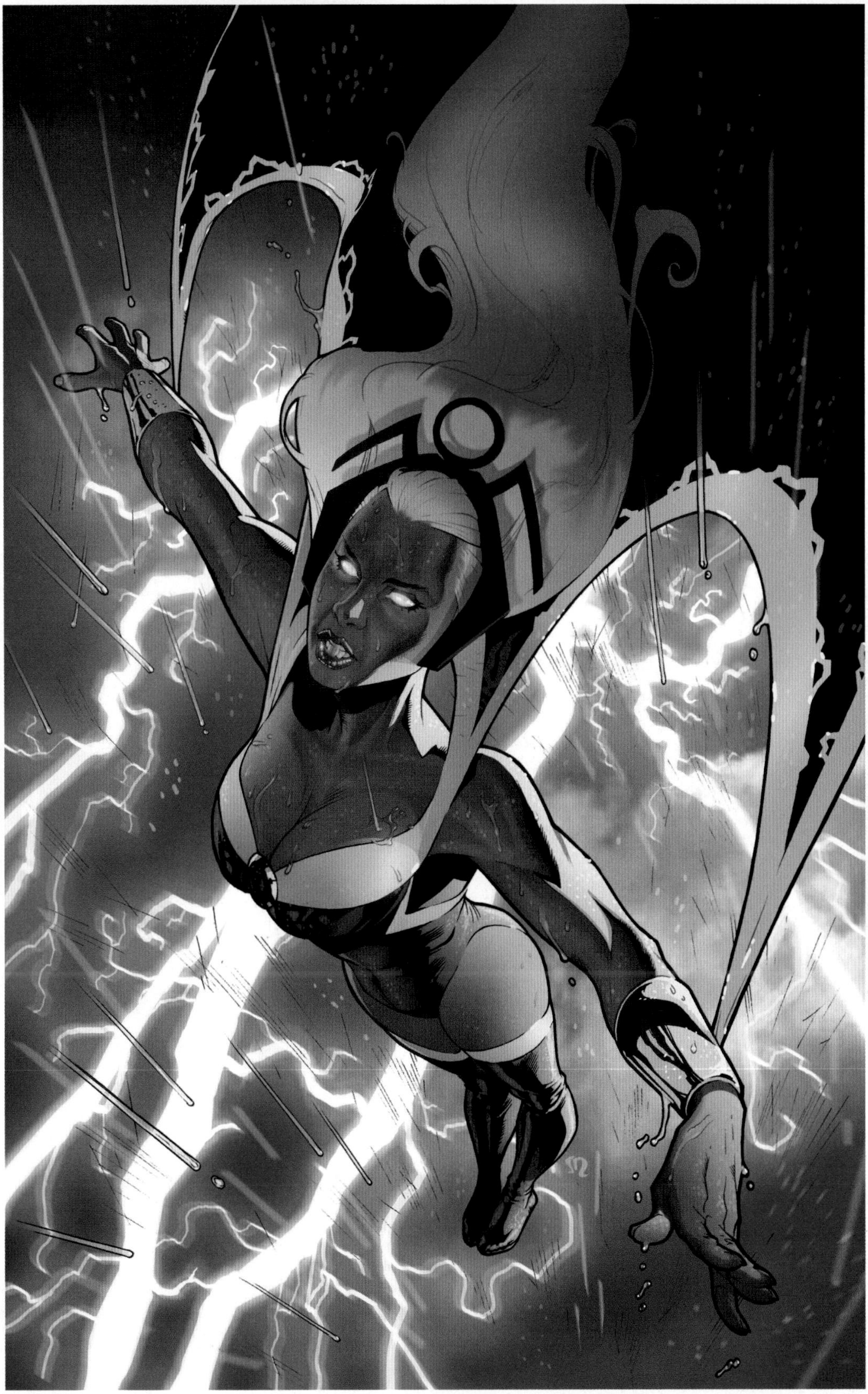

X-MEN: WORLDS APART #4

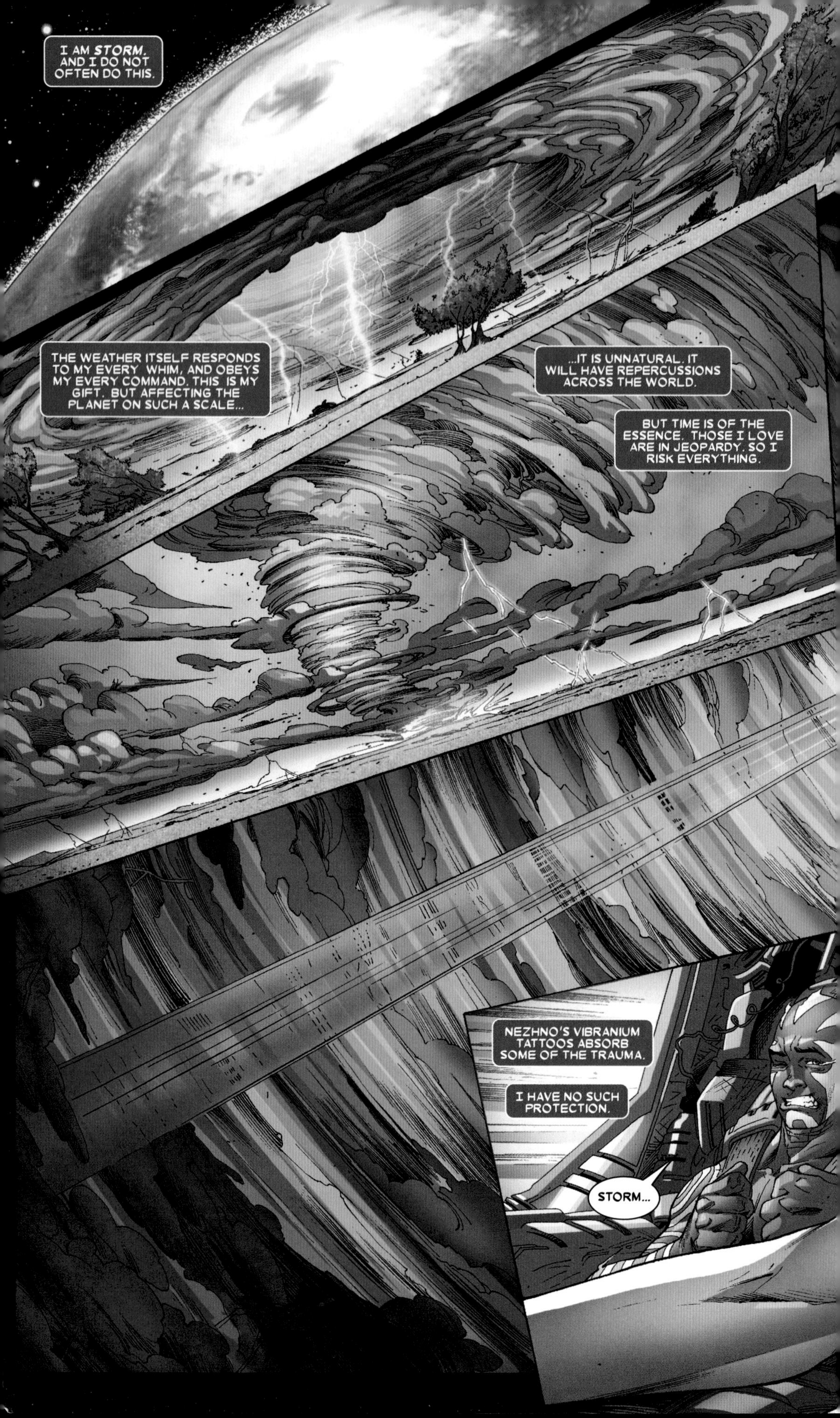
I AM STORM. AND I DO NOT OFTEN DO THIS.
THE WEATHER ITSELF RESPONDS TO MY EVERY WHIM, AND OBEYS MY EVERY COMMAND. THIS IS MY GIFT. BUT AFFECTING THE PLANET ON SUCH A SCALE...
...IT IS UNNATURAL. IT WILL HAVE REPERCUSSIONS ACROSS THE WORLD.
BUT TIME IS OF THE ESSENCE. THOSE I LOVE ARE IN JEOPARDY. SO I RISK EVERYTHING.
NEZHNO'S VIBRANIUM TATTOOS ABSORB SOME OF THE TRAUMA.
I HAVE NO SUCH PROTECTION.
STORM...

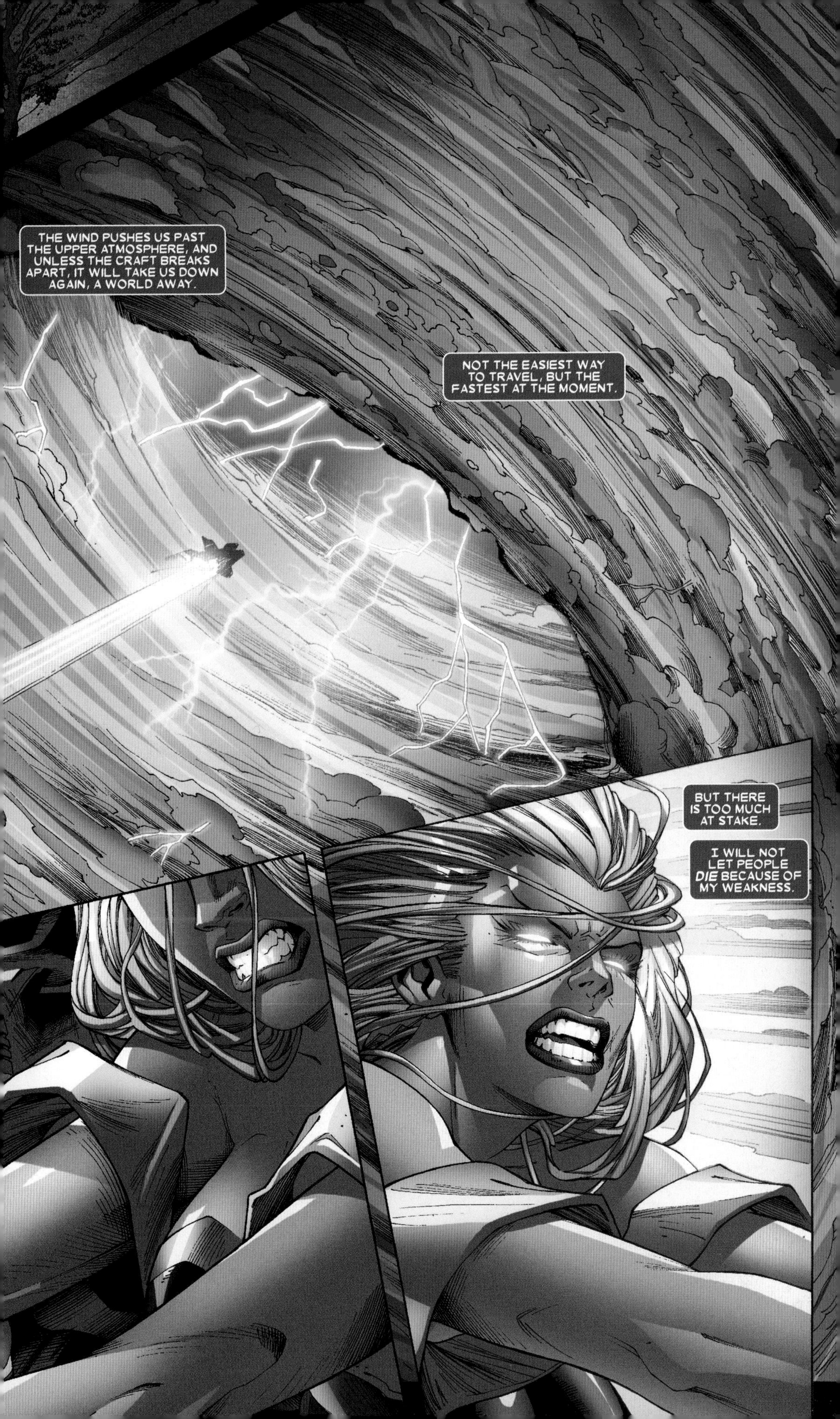

THE WIND PUSHES US PAST THE UPPER ATMOSPHERE, AND UNLESS THE CRAFT BREAKS APART, IT WILL TAKE US DOWN AGAIN, A WORLD AWAY.
NOT THE EASIEST WAY TO TRAVEL, BUT THE FASTEST AT THE MOMENT.
BUT THERE IS TOO MUCH AT STAKE.
I WILL NOT LET PEOPLE DIE BECAUSE OF MY WEAKNESS.

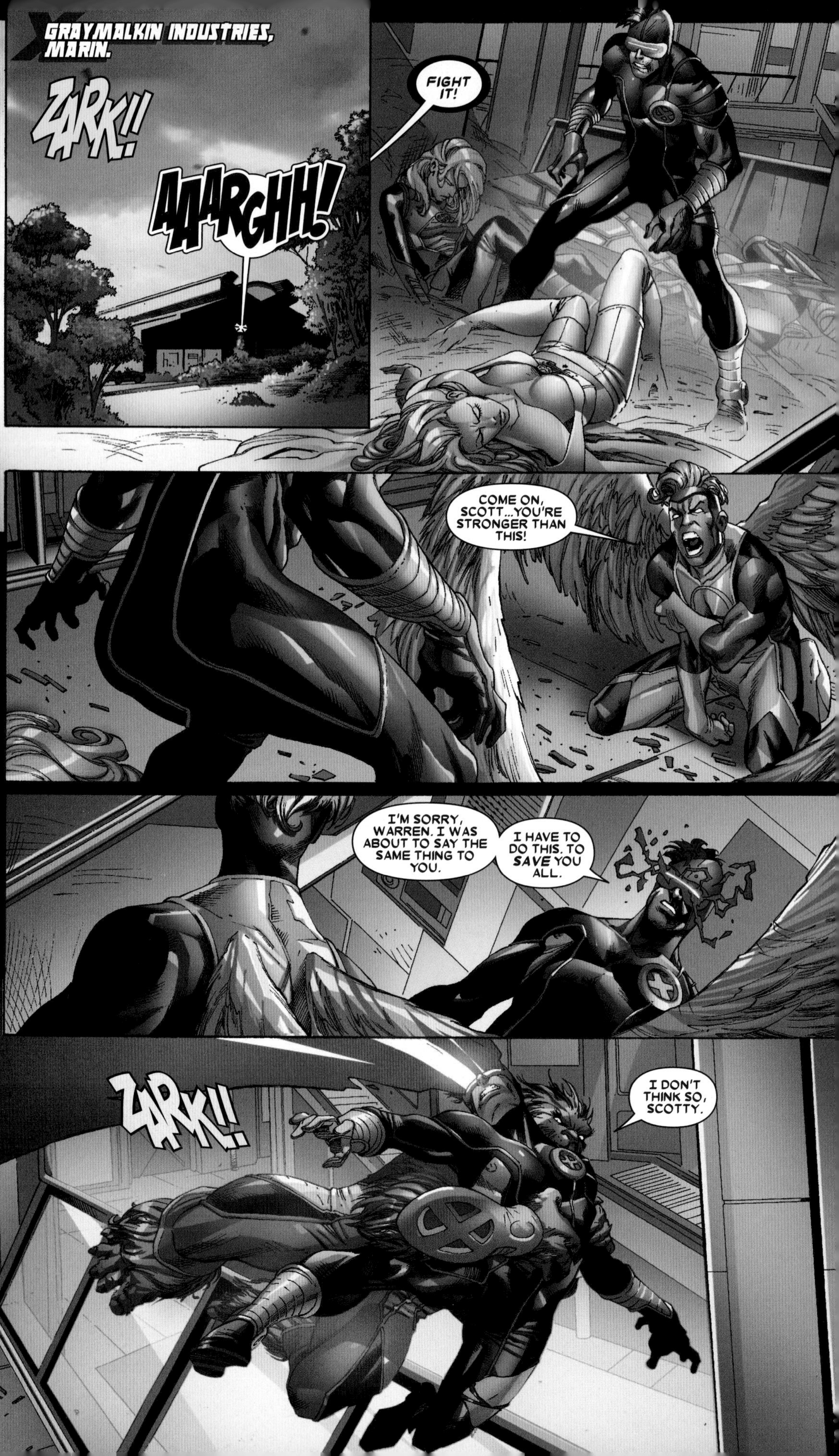
GRAYMALKIN INDUSTRIES, MARIN.
ZARK!!
AAARGHH!
FIGHT IT!
COME ON, SCOTT...YOU'RE STRONGER THAN THIS!
I'M SORRY, WARREN. I WAS ABOUT TO SAY THE SAME THING TO YOU.
I HAVE TO DO THIS. TO SAVE YOU ALL.
ZARK!!
I DON'T THINK SO, SCOTTY.

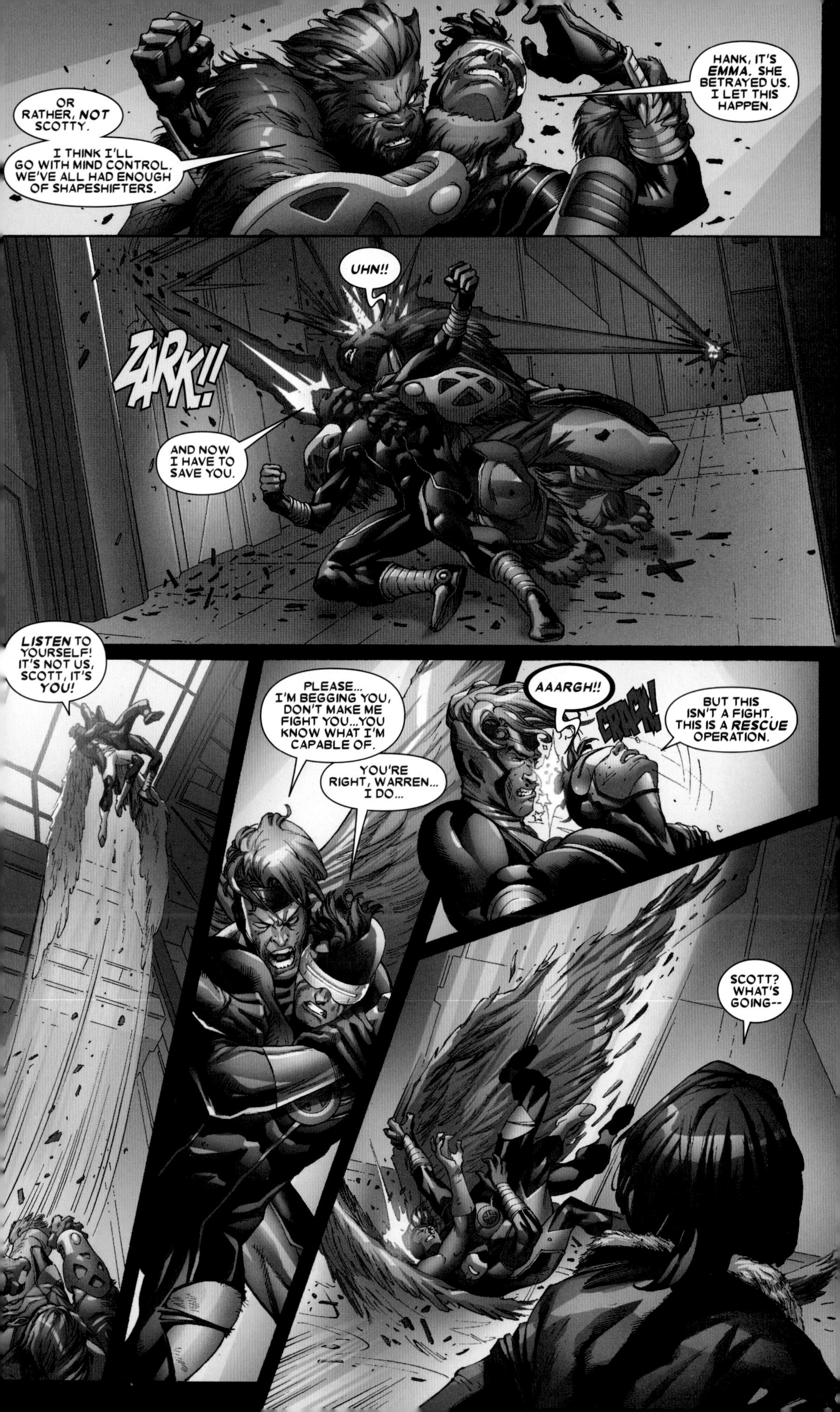

OR RATHER, NOT SCOTTY.
I THINK I'LL GO WITH MIND CONTROL. WE'VE ALL HAD ENOUGH OF SHAPESHIFTERS.
HANK, IT'S EMMA. SHE BETRAYED US. I LET THIS HAPPEN.
UHN!!
ZARK!!
AND NOW I HAVE TO SAVE YOU.
LISTEN TO YOURSELF! IT'S NOT US, SCOTT, IT'S YOU!
PLEASE... I'M BEGGING YOU, DON'T MAKE ME FIGHT YOU...YOU KNOW WHAT I'M CAPABLE OF.
YOU'RE RIGHT, WARREN... I DO...
AAARGH!!
CRACK!
BUT THIS ISN'T A FIGHT. THIS IS A RESCUE OPERATION.
SCOTT? WHAT'S GOING--

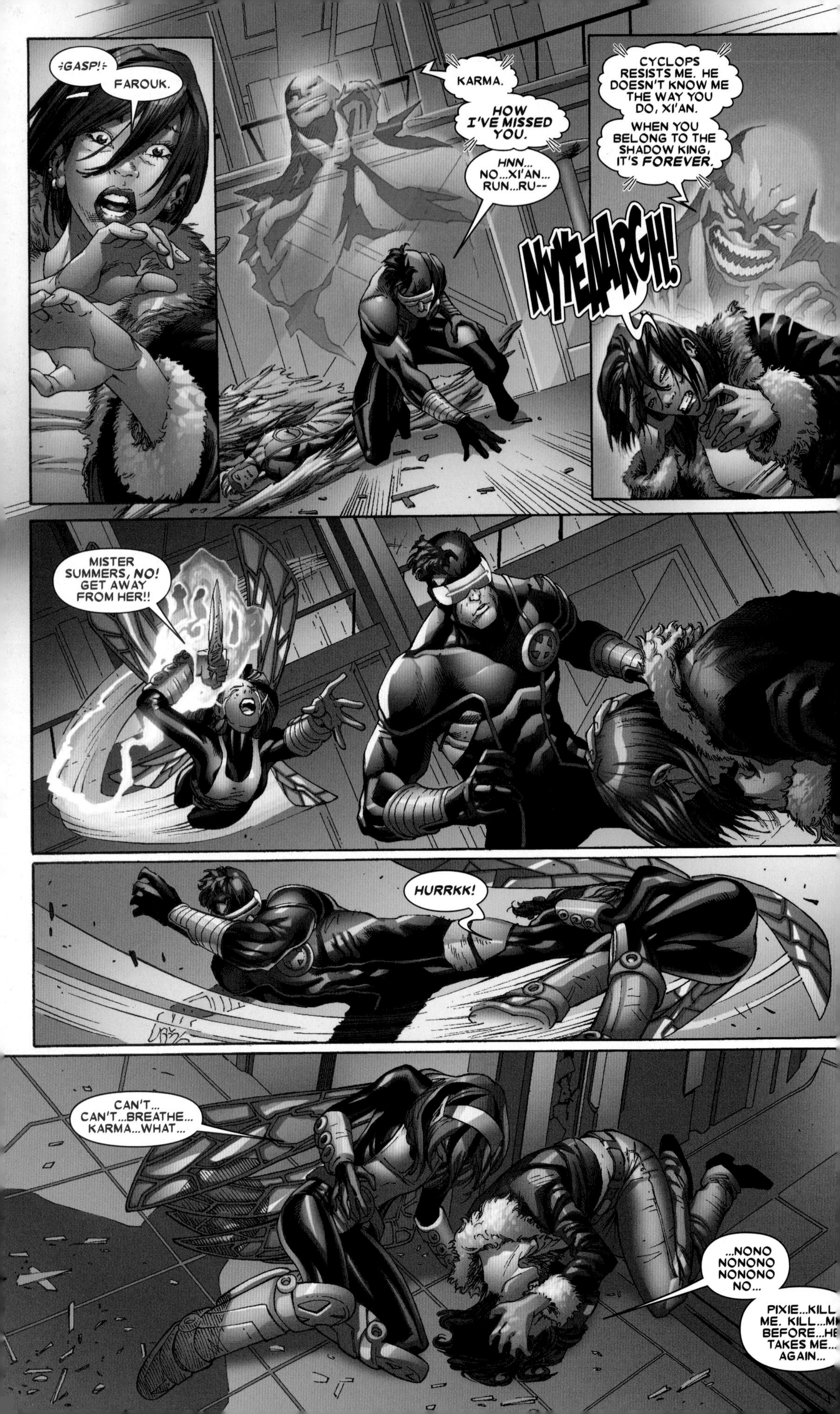

¡GASP!¡
FAROUK.
KARMA.
HOW I'VE MISSED YOU.
HNN... NO...XI'AN... RUN...RU--
CYCLOPS RESISTS ME. HE DOESN'T KNOW ME THE WAY YOU DO, XI'AN.
WHEN YOU BELONG TO THE SHADOW KING, IT'S FOREVER.
NYYEAARGH!
MISTER SUMMERS, NO! GET AWAY FROM HER!!
HURRKK!
CAN'T... CAN'T...BREATHE... KARMA...WHAT...
...NONO NONONO NONONO NO...
PIXIE...KILL ME. KILL...M BEFORE...HE TAKES ME... AGAIN...

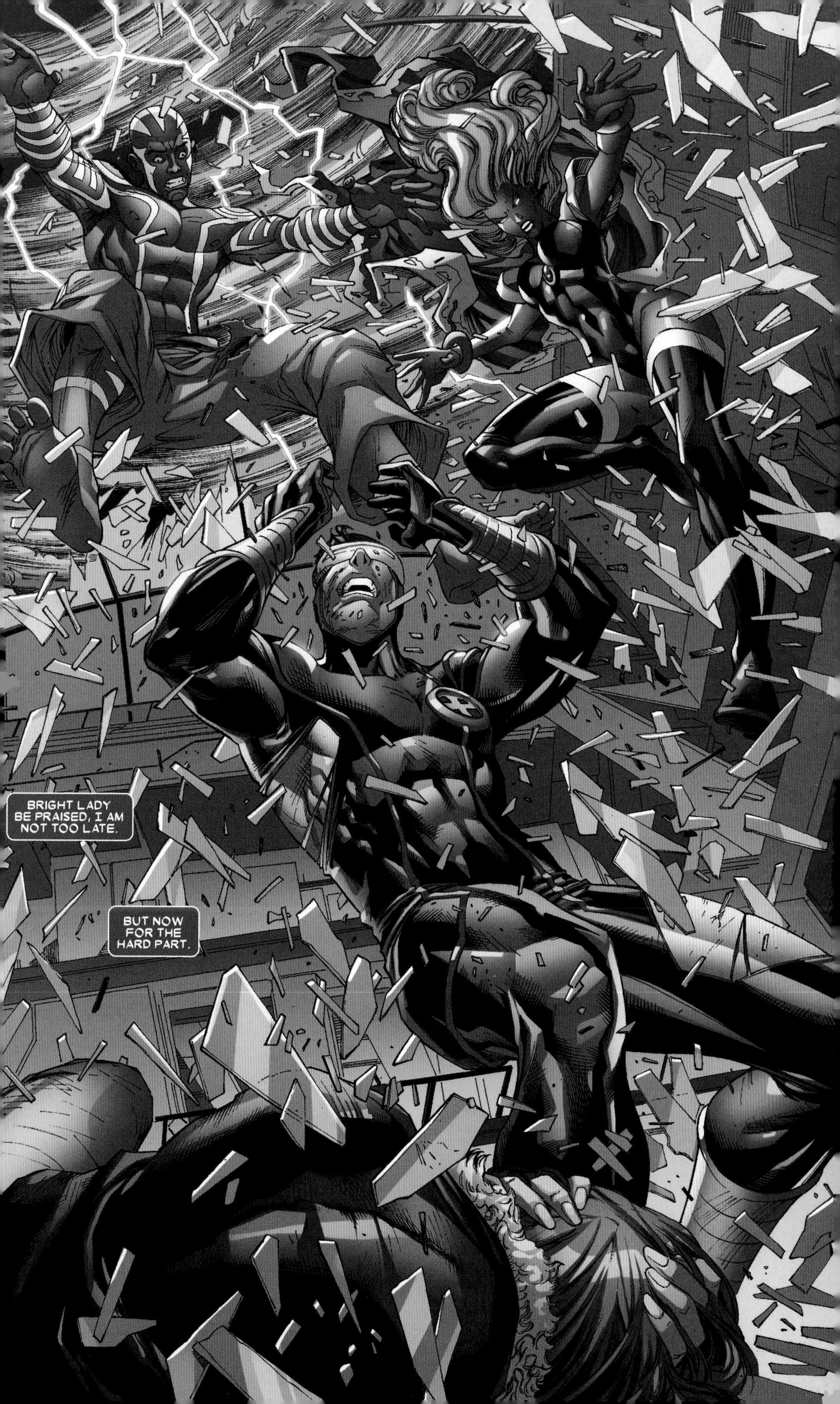
BRIGHT LADY
BE PRAISED, I AM
NOT TOO LATE.
BUT NOW
FOR THE
HARD PART.

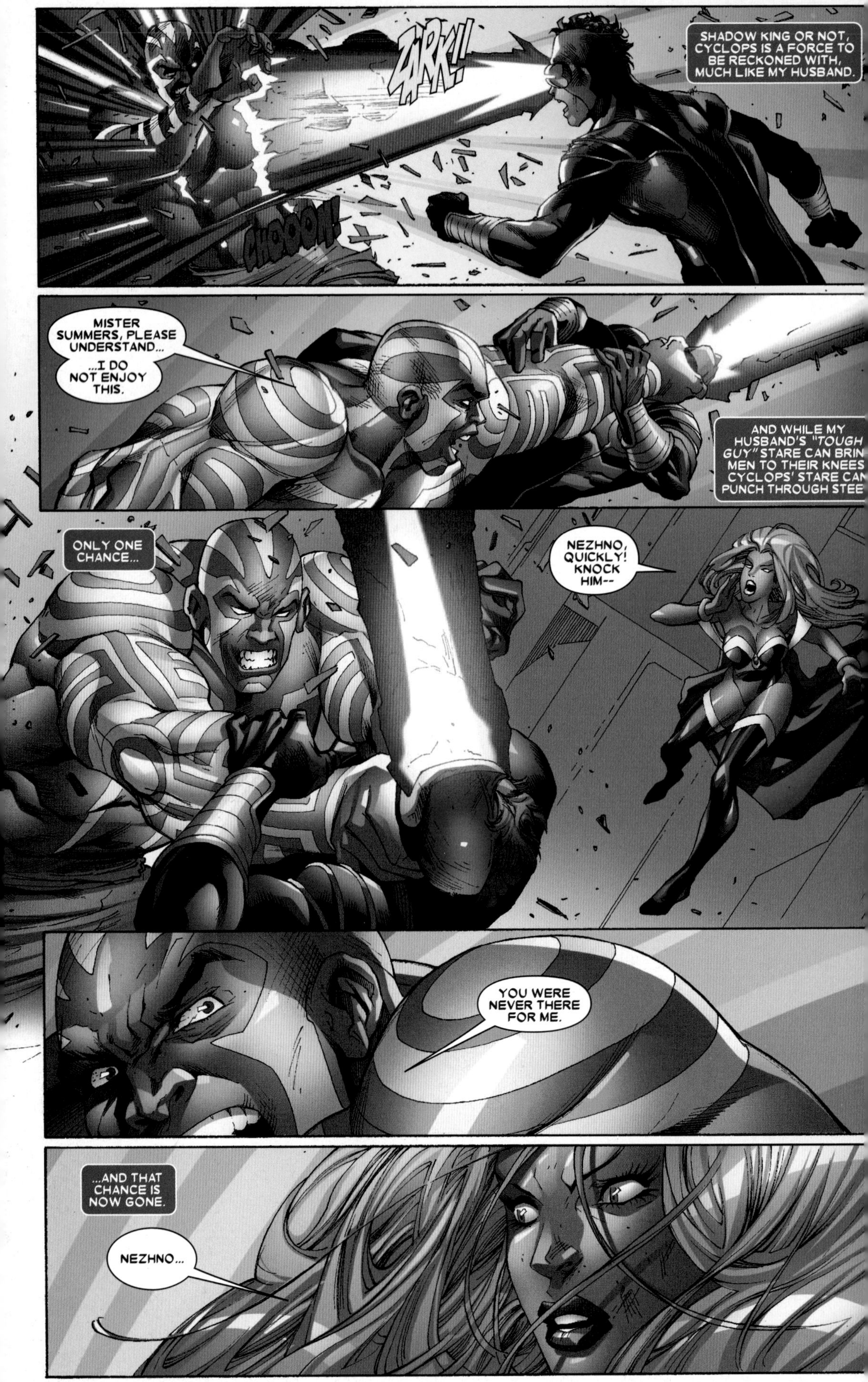
ZARK!!
SHADOW KING OR NOT, CYCLOPS IS A FORCE TO BE RECKONED WITH, MUCH LIKE MY HUSBAND.
CHOOOM!
MISTER SUMMERS, PLEASE UNDERSTAND...
...I DO NOT ENJOY THIS.
AND WHILE MY HUSBAND'S "TOUGH GUY" STARE CAN BRIN MEN TO THEIR KNEES CYCLOPS' STARE CAN PUNCH THROUGH STEE
ONLY ONE CHANCE...
NEZHNO, QUICKLY! KNOCK HIM--
YOU WERE NEVER THERE FOR ME.
...AND THAT CHANCE IS NOW GONE.
NEZHNO...

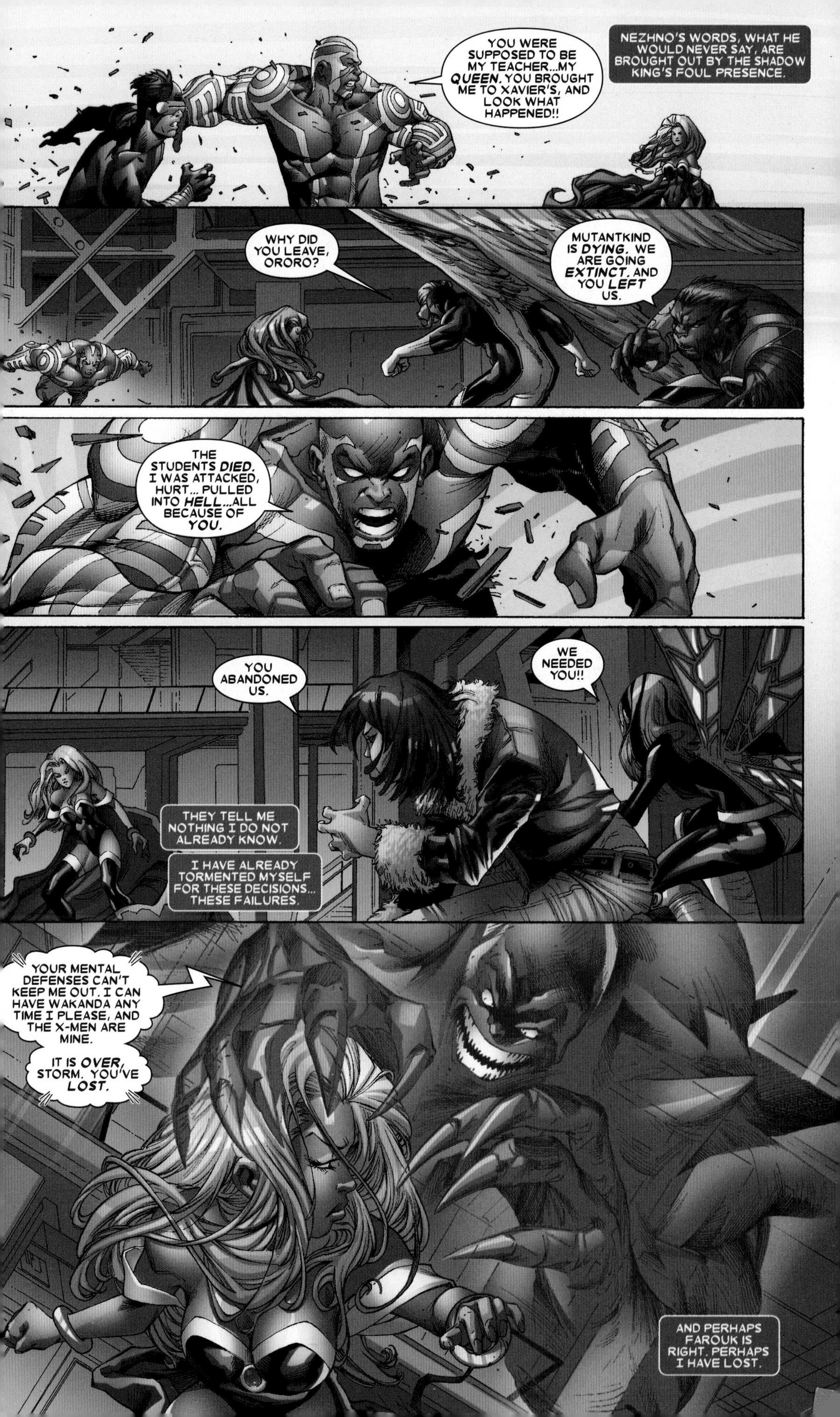
YOU WERE SUPPOSED TO BE MY TEACHER...MY QUEEN. YOU BROUGHT ME TO XAVIER'S, AND LOOK WHAT HAPPENED!!
NEZHNO'S WORDS, WHAT HE WOULD NEVER SAY, ARE BROUGHT OUT BY THE SHADOW KING'S FOUL PRESENCE.
WHY DID YOU LEAVE, ORORO?
MUTANTKIND IS DYING. WE ARE GOING EXTINCT. AND YOU LEFT US.
THE STUDENTS DIED. I WAS ATTACKED, HURT... PULLED INTO HELL...ALL BECAUSE OF YOU.
YOU ABANDONED US.
WE NEEDED YOU!!
THEY TELL ME NOTHING I DO NOT ALREADY KNOW.
I HAVE ALREADY TORMENTED MYSELF FOR THESE DECISIONS... THESE FAILURES.
YOUR MENTAL DEFENSES CAN'T KEEP ME OUT. I CAN HAVE WAKANDA ANY TIME I PLEASE, AND THE X-MEN ARE MINE.
IT IS OVER, STORM. YOU'VE LOST.
AND PERHAPS FAROUK IS RIGHT. PERHAPS I HAVE LOST.

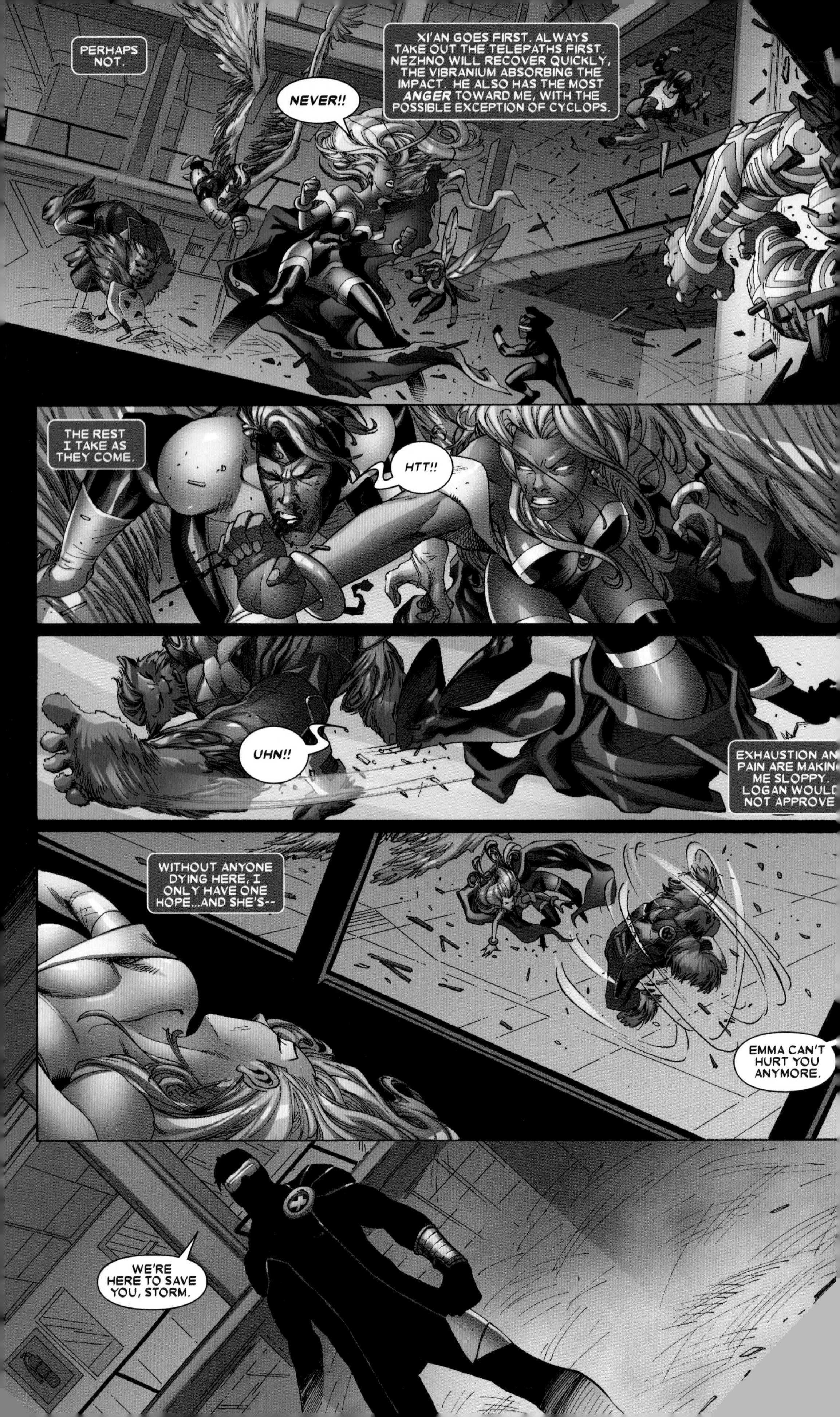

PERHAPS NOT.
XI'AN GOES FIRST. ALWAYS TAKE OUT THE TELEPATHS FIRST. NEZHNO WILL RECOVER QUICKLY, THE VIBRANIUM ABSORBING THE IMPACT. HE ALSO HAS THE MOST ANGER TOWARD ME, WITH THE POSSIBLE EXCEPTION OF CYCLOPS.
NEVER!!
THE REST I TAKE AS THEY COME.
HTT!!
UHN!!
EXHAUSTION AN PAIN ARE MAKIN ME SLOPPY. LOGAN WOULD NOT APPROVE
WITHOUT ANYONE DYING HERE, I ONLY HAVE ONE HOPE...AND SHE'S--
EMMA CAN'T HURT YOU ANYMORE.
WE'RE HERE TO SAVE YOU, STORM.

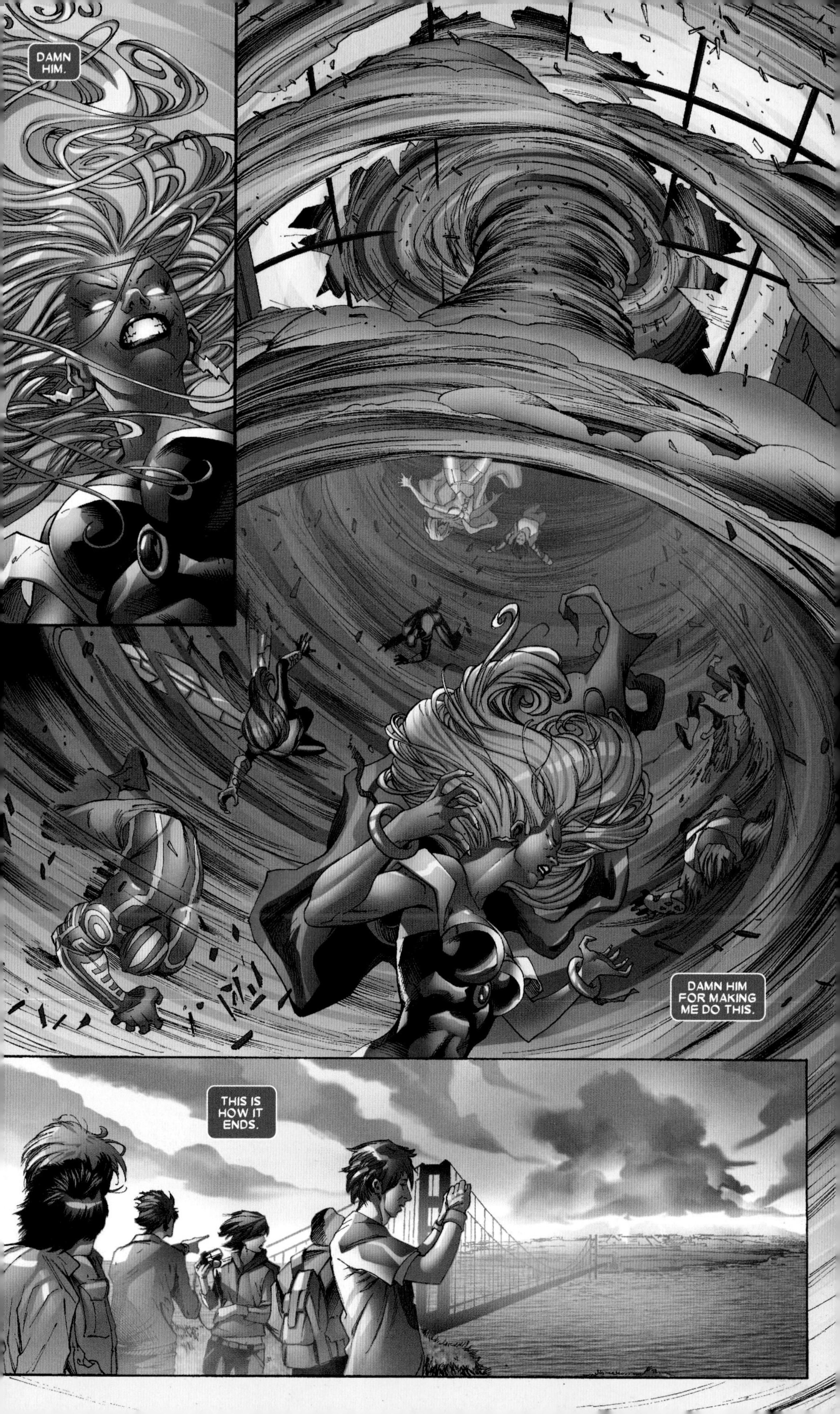
DAMN HIM.
DAMN HIM FOR MAKING ME DO THIS.
THIS IS HOW IT ENDS.

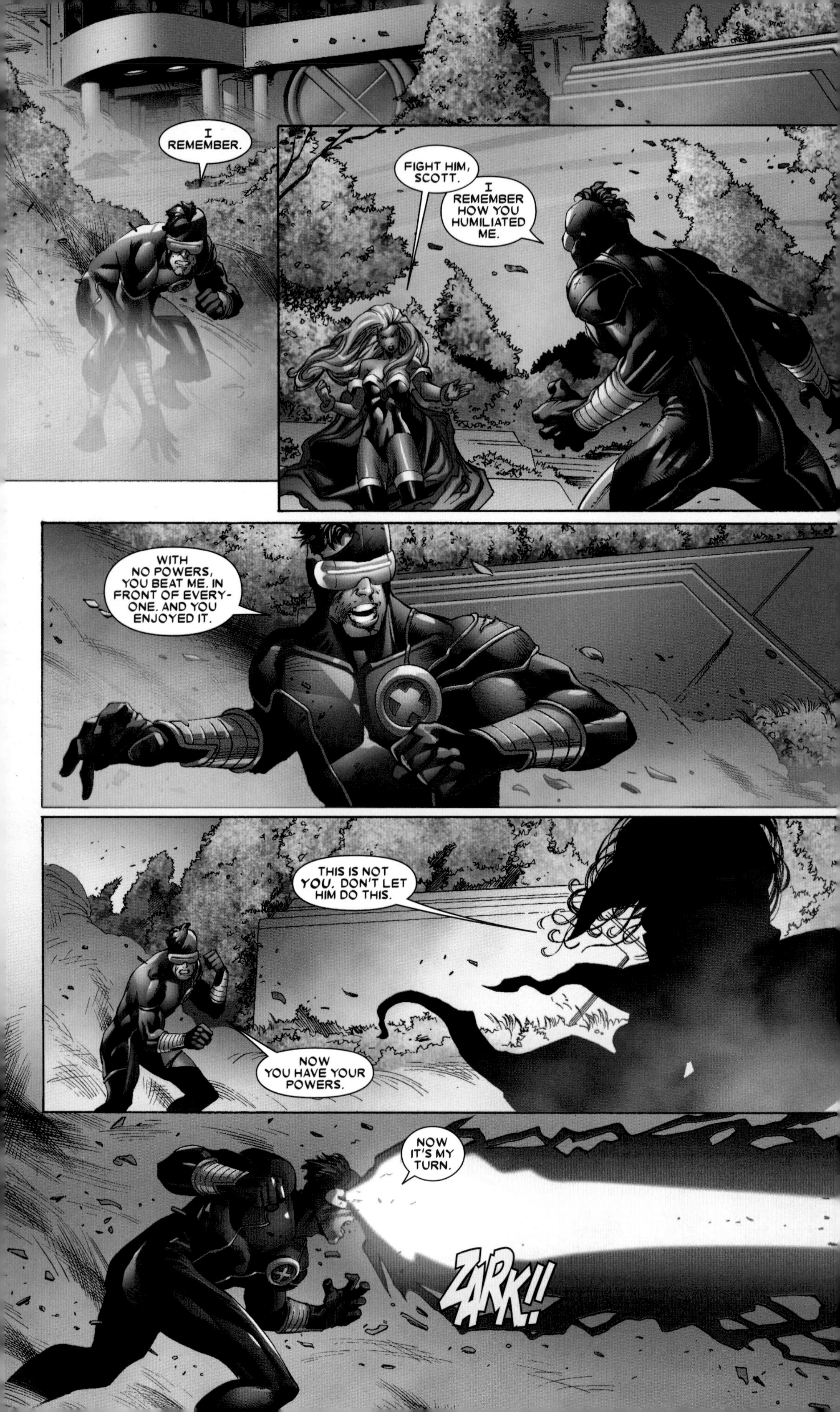

I REMEMBER.
FIGHT HIM, SCOTT.
I REMEMBER HOW YOU HUMILIATED ME.
WITH NO POWERS, YOU BEAT ME. IN FRONT OF EVERY-ONE. AND YOU ENJOYED IT.
THIS IS NOT YOU. DON'T LET HIM DO THIS.
NOW YOU HAVE YOUR POWERS.
NOW IT'S MY TURN.
ZARK!!

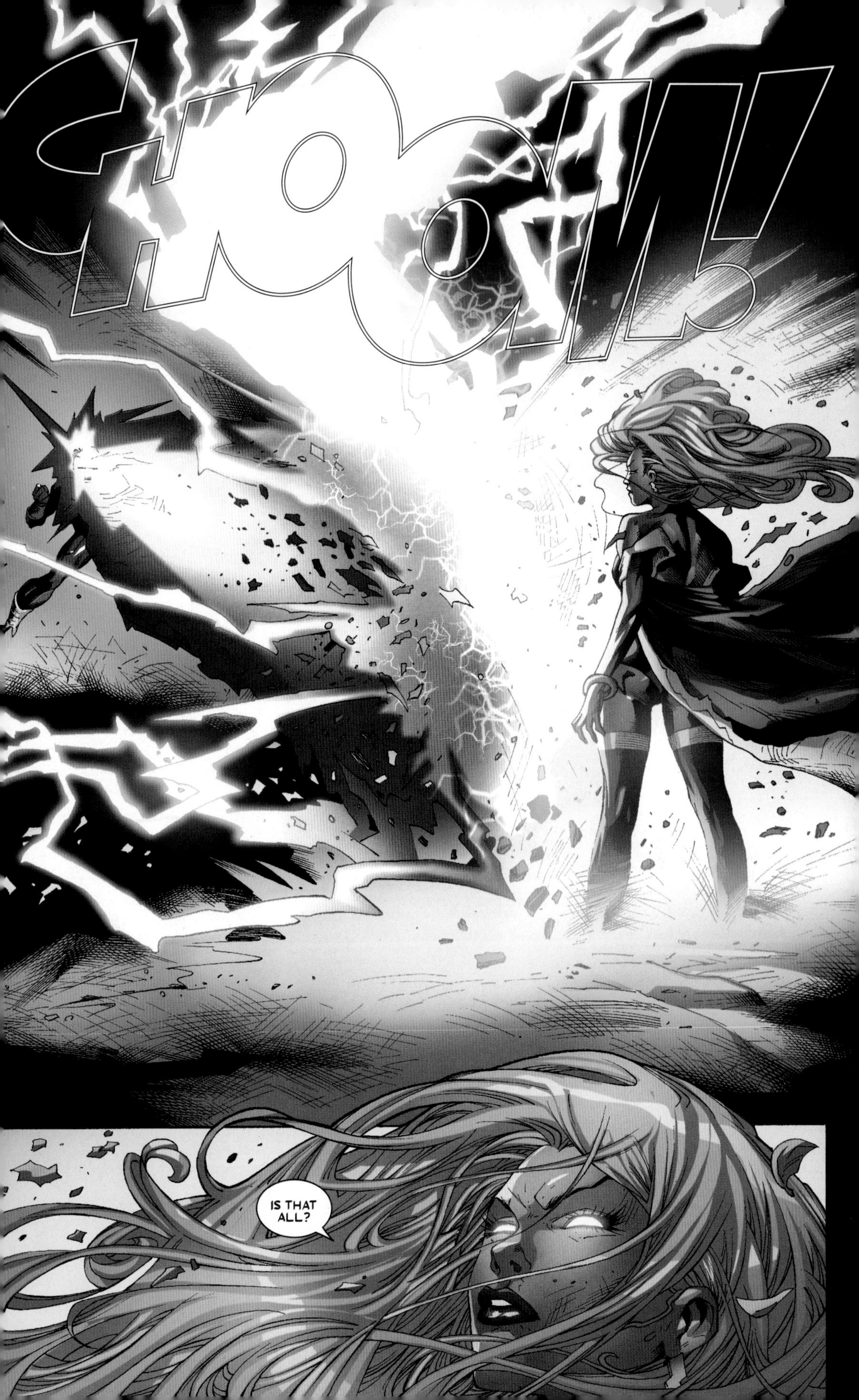
CHOOM!
IS THAT ALL?

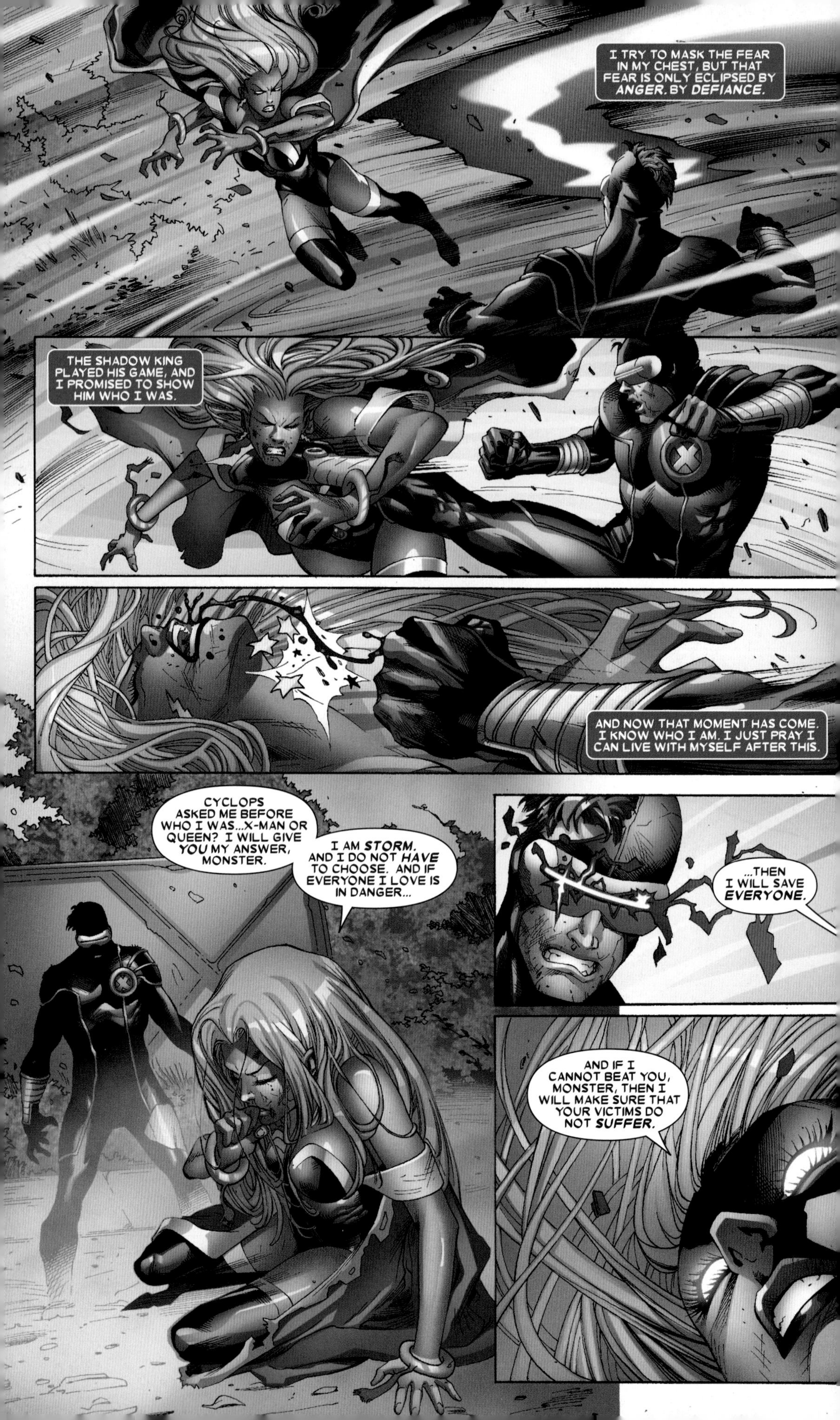

I TRY TO MASK THE FEAR IN MY CHEST, BUT THAT FEAR IS ONLY ECLIPSED BY ANGER. BY DEFIANCE.
THE SHADOW KING PLAYED HIS GAME, AND I PROMISED TO SHOW HIM WHO I WAS.
AND NOW THAT MOMENT HAS COME. I KNOW WHO I AM. I JUST PRAY I CAN LIVE WITH MYSELF AFTER THIS.
CYCLOPS ASKED ME BEFORE WHO I WAS...X-MAN OR QUEEN? I WILL GIVE YOU MY ANSWER, MONSTER.
I AM STORM. AND I DO NOT HAVE TO CHOOSE. AND IF EVERYONE I LOVE IS IN DANGER...
...THEN I WILL SAVE EVERYONE.
AND IF I CANNOT BEAT YOU, MONSTER, THEN I WILL MAKE SURE THAT YOUR VICTIMS DO NOT SUFFER.

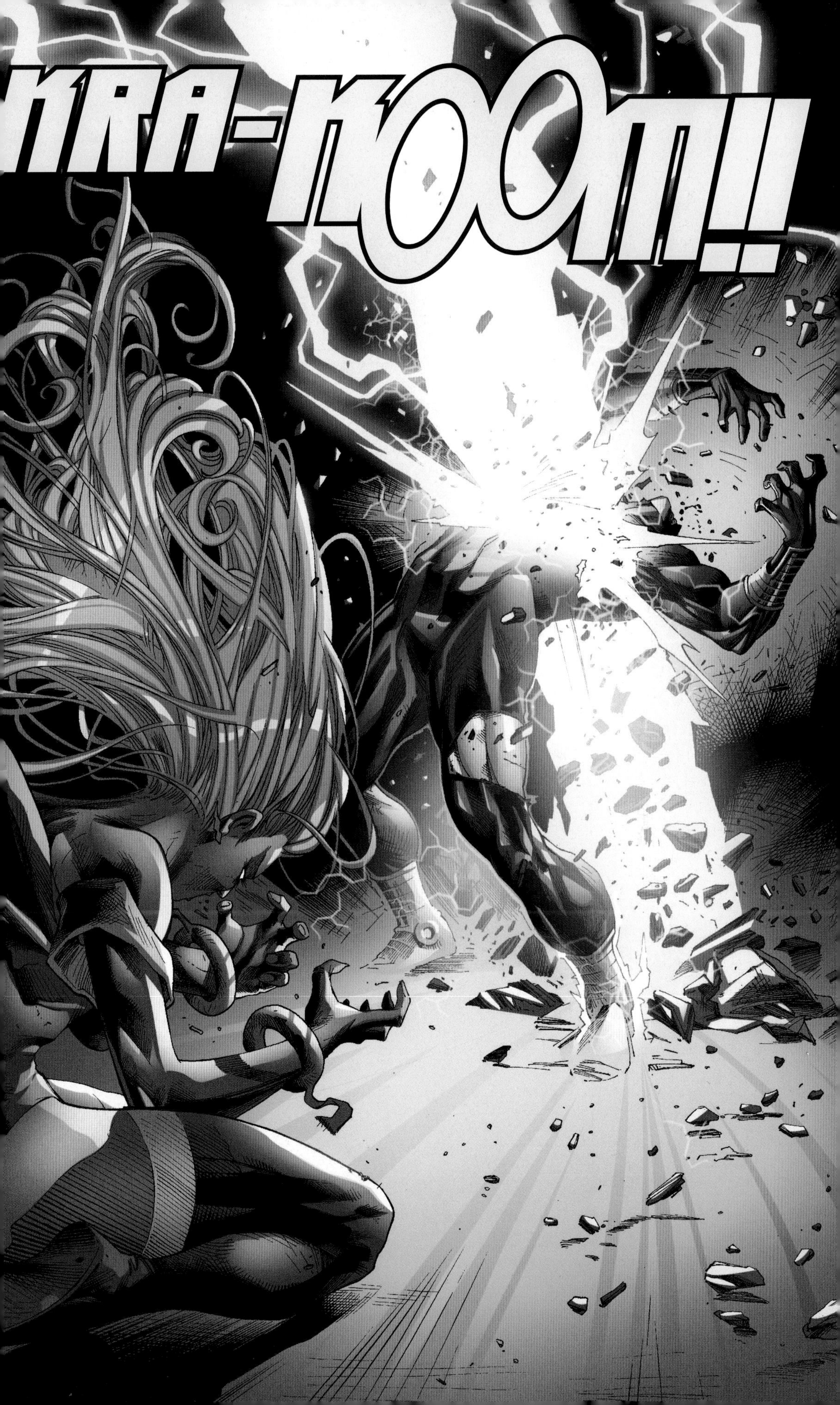
KRA-KOOM!!

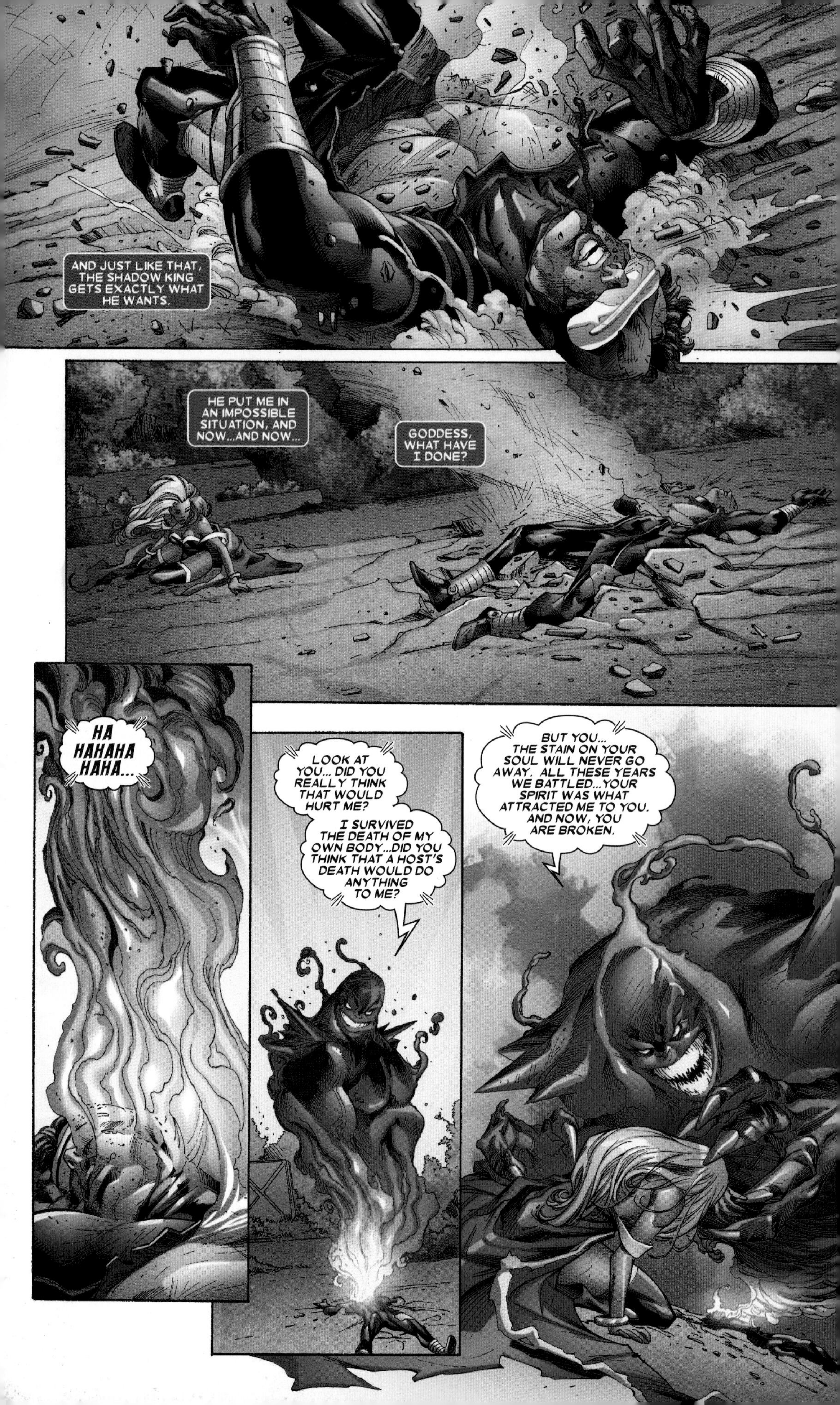
AND JUST LIKE THAT, THE SHADOW KING GETS EXACTLY WHAT HE WANTS.
HE PUT ME IN AN IMPOSSIBLE SITUATION, AND NOW...AND NOW...
GODDESS, WHAT HAVE I DONE?
HA HAHAHA HAHA...
LOOK AT YOU... DID YOU REALLY THINK THAT WOULD HURT ME?
I SURVIVED THE DEATH OF MY OWN BODY...DID YOU THINK THAT A HOST'S DEATH WOULD DO ANYTHING TO ME?
BUT YOU... THE STAIN ON YOUR SOUL WILL NEVER GO AWAY. ALL THESE YEARS WE BATTLED...YOUR SPIRIT WAS WHAT ATTRACTED ME TO YOU. AND NOW, YOU ARE BROKEN.

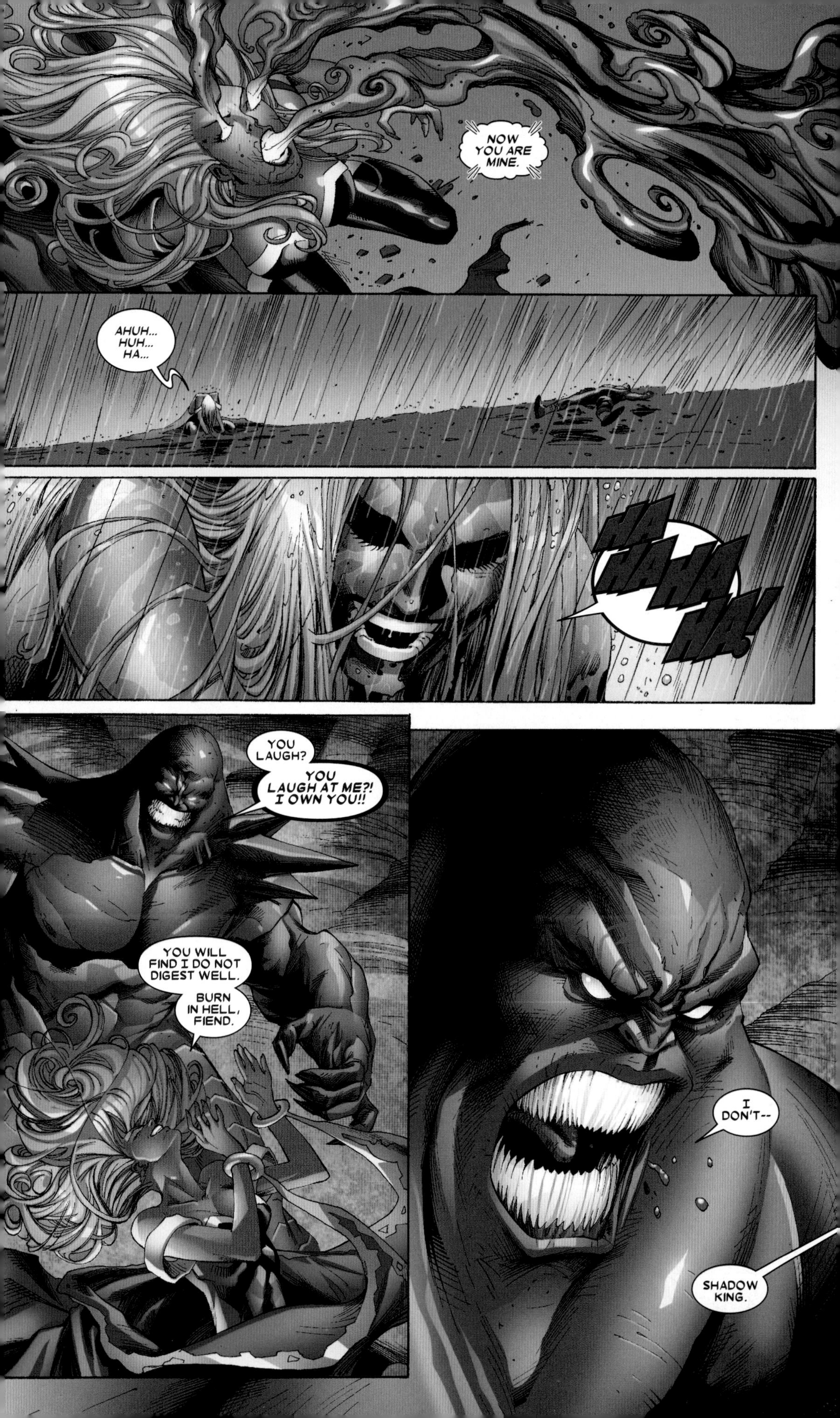
NOW YOU ARE MINE.
AHUH... HUH... HA...
HA HAHAHA HA!
YOU LAUGH?
YOU LAUGH AT ME?! I OWN YOU!!
YOU WILL FIND I DO NOT DIGEST WELL.
BURN IN HELL, FIEND.
I DON'T--
SHADOW KING.

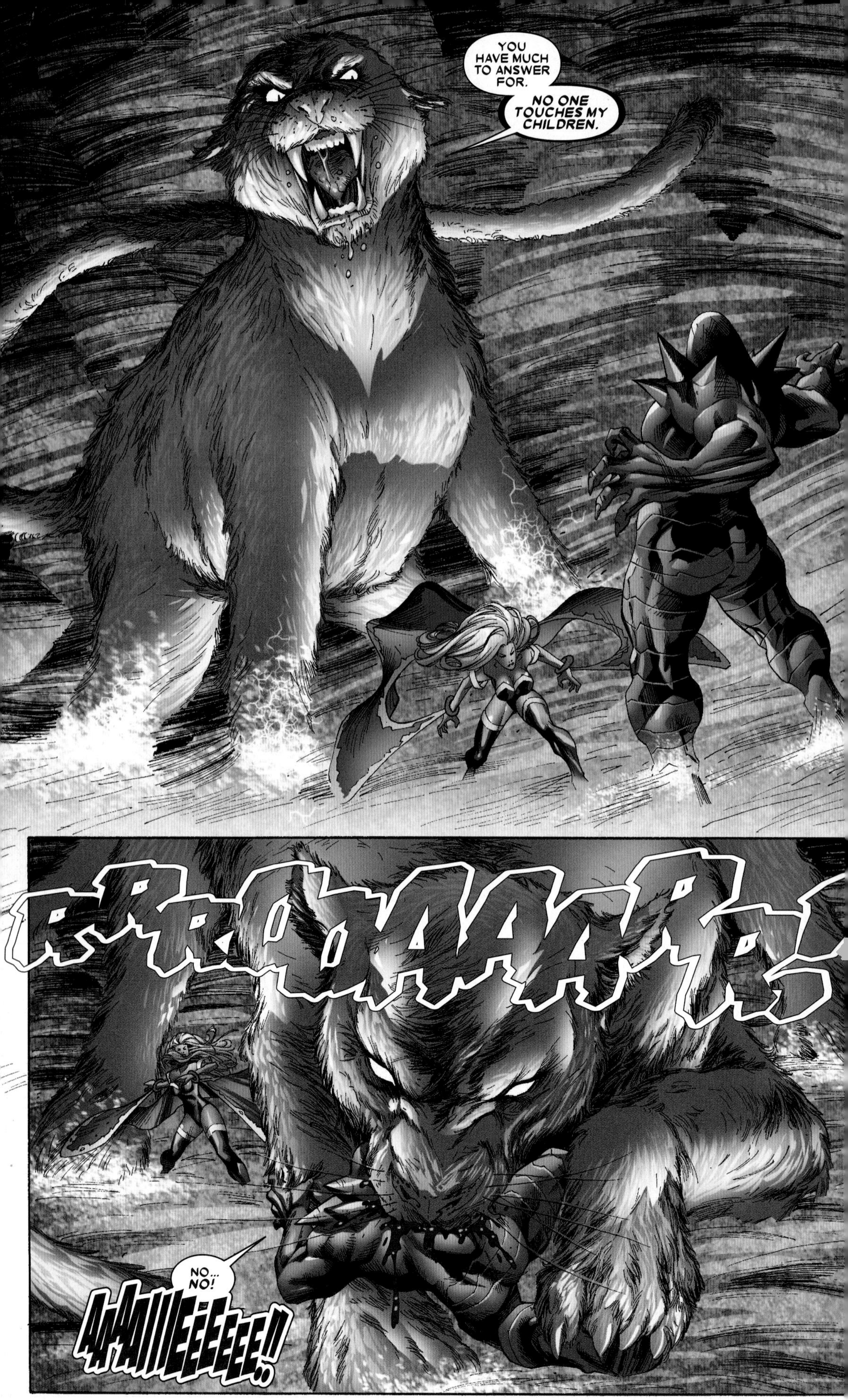
YOU HAVE MUCH TO ANSWER FOR.
NO ONE TOUCHES MY CHILDREN.
NO... NO!
AAAIIIEEEEEE!!

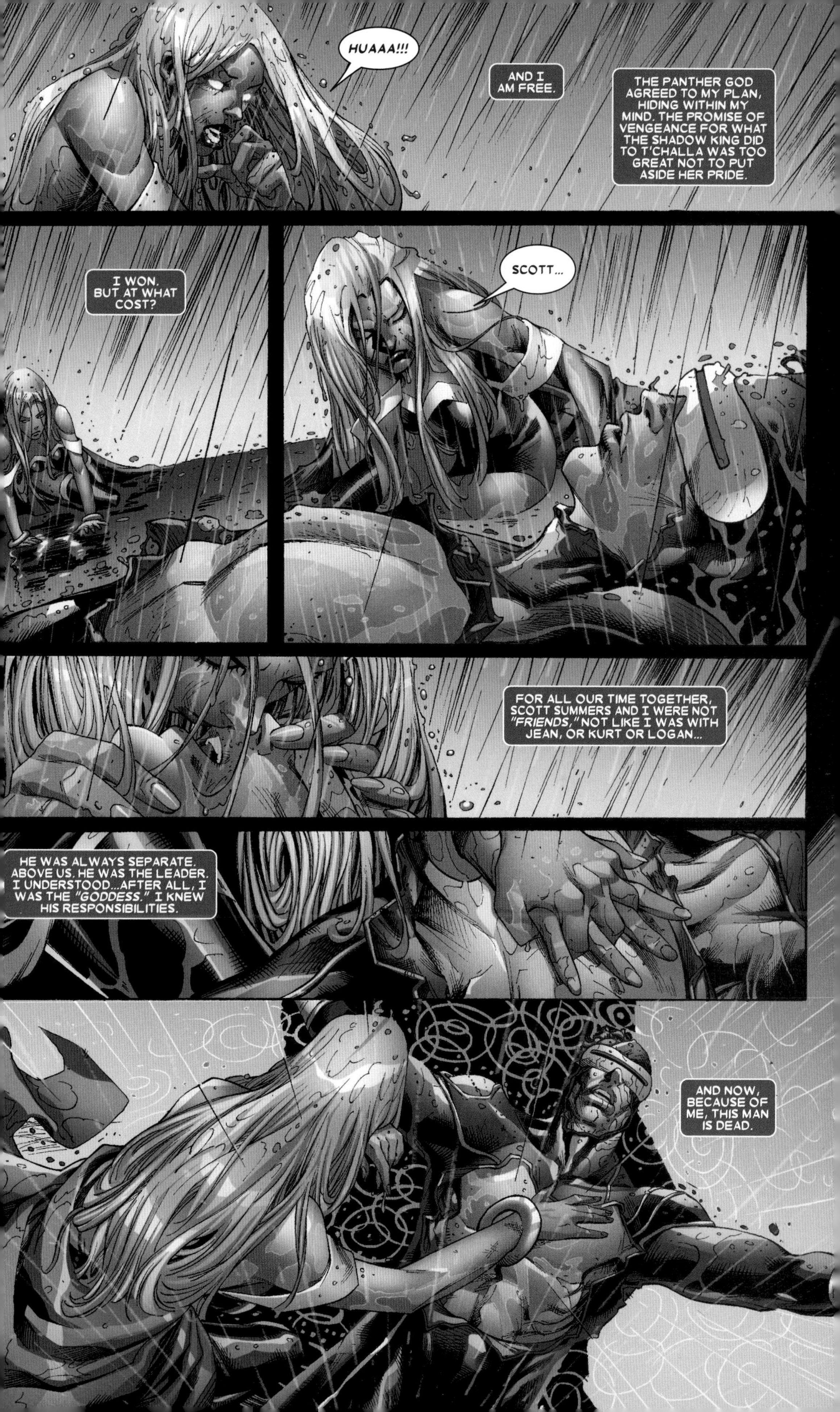
HUAAA!!!
AND I AM FREE.
THE PANTHER GOD AGREED TO MY PLAN, HIDING WITHIN MY MIND. THE PROMISE OF VENGEANCE FOR WHAT THE SHADOW KING DID TO T'CHALLA WAS TOO GREAT NOT TO PUT ASIDE HER PRIDE.
I WON. BUT AT WHAT COST?
SCOTT...
FOR ALL OUR TIME TOGETHER, SCOTT SUMMERS AND I WERE NOT "FRIENDS," NOT LIKE I WAS WITH JEAN, OR KURT OR LOGAN...
HE WAS ALWAYS SEPARATE. ABOVE US. HE WAS THE LEADER. I UNDERSTOOD...AFTER ALL, I WAS THE "GODDESS." I KNEW HIS RESPONSIBILITIES.
AND NOW, BECAUSE OF ME, THIS MAN IS DEAD.

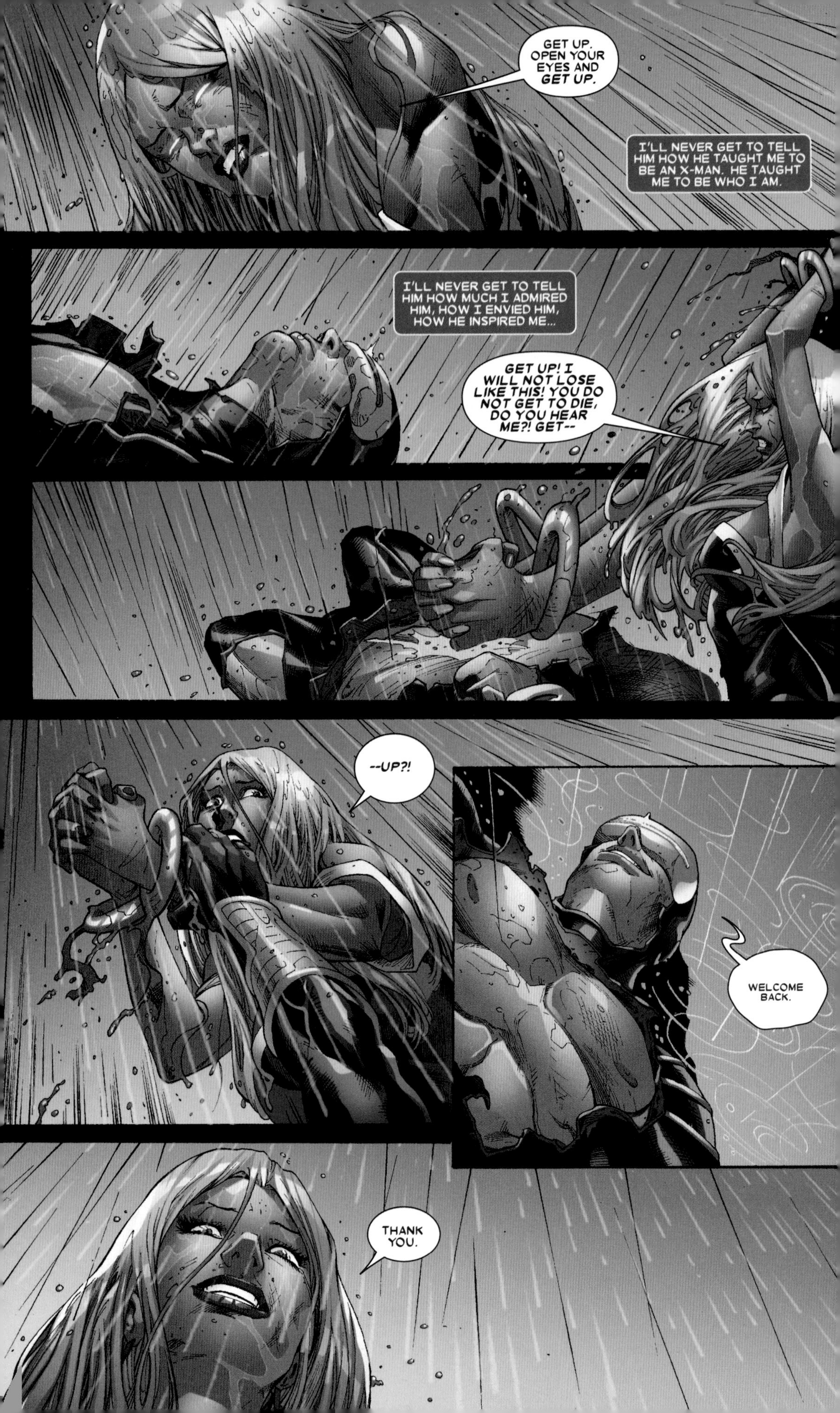
GET UP. OPEN YOUR EYES AND GET UP.
I'LL NEVER GET TO TELL HIM HOW HE TAUGHT ME TO BE AN X-MAN. HE TAUGHT ME TO BE WHO I AM.
I'LL NEVER GET TO TELL HIM HOW MUCH I ADMIRED HIM, HOW I ENVIED HIM, HOW HE INSPIRED ME...
GET UP! I WILL NOT LOSE LIKE THIS! YOU DO NOT GET TO DIE, DO YOU HEAR ME?! GET--
--UP?!
WELCOME BACK.
THANK YOU.

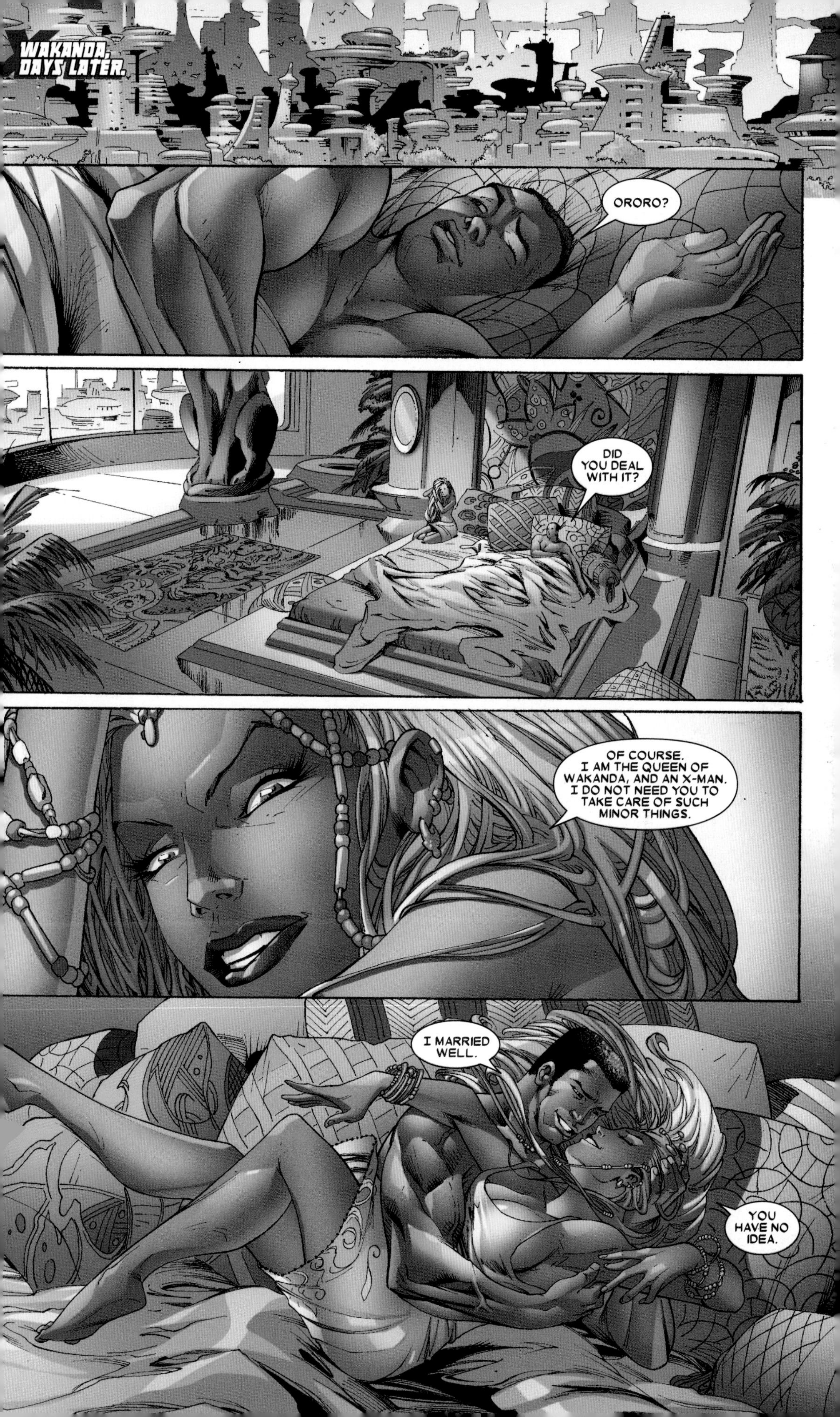
WAKANDA, DAYS LATER.
ORORO?
DID YOU DEAL WITH IT?
OF COURSE. I AM THE QUEEN OF WAKANDA, AND AN X-MAN. I DO NOT NEED YOU TO TAKE CARE OF SUCH MINOR THINGS.
I MARRIED WELL.
YOU HAVE NO IDEA.

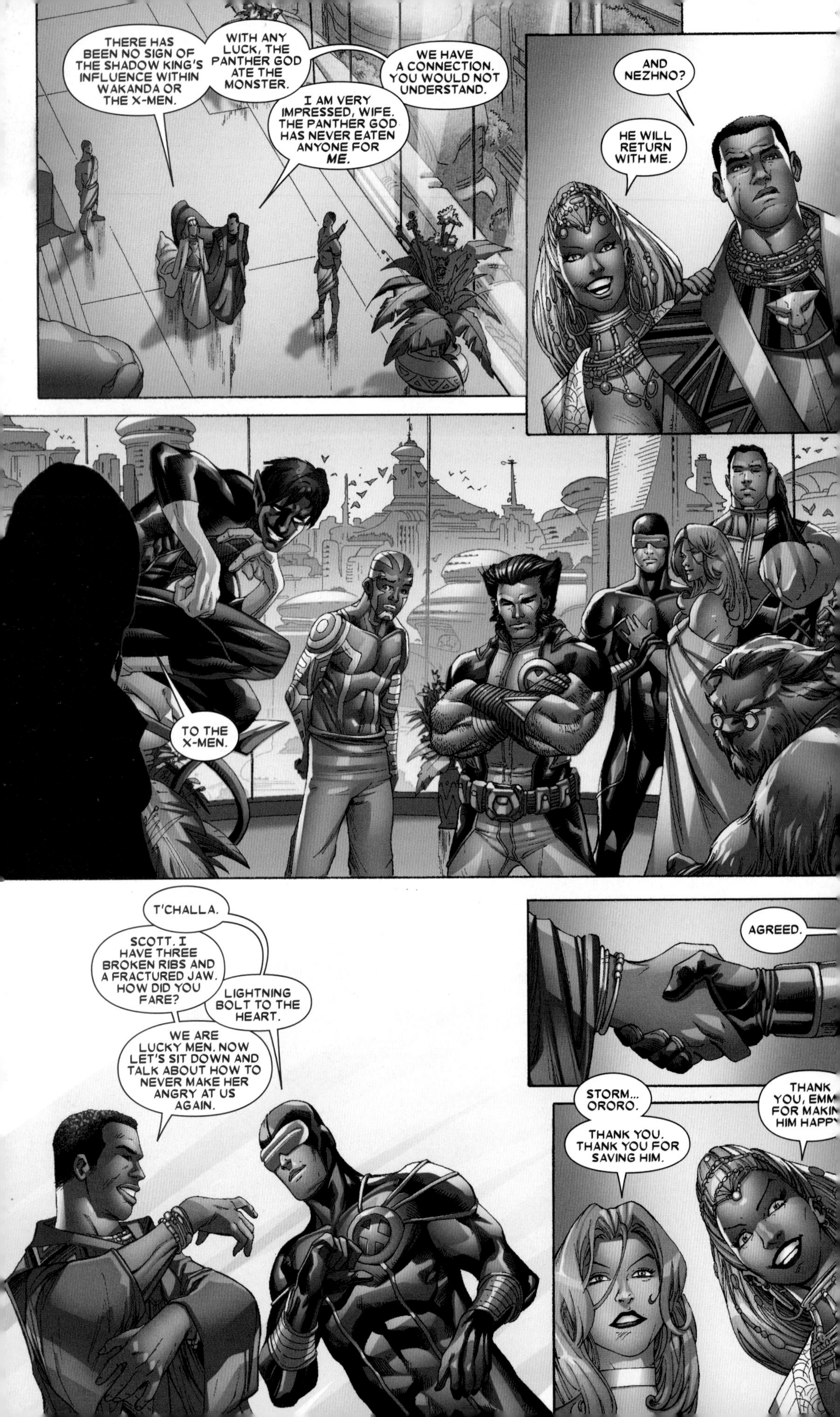
THERE HAS BEEN NO SIGN OF THE SHADOW KING'S INFLUENCE WITHIN WAKANDA OR THE X-MEN.
WITH ANY LUCK, THE PANTHER GOD ATE THE MONSTER.
I AM VERY IMPRESSED, WIFE. THE PANTHER GOD HAS NEVER EATEN ANYONE FOR *ME.*
WE HAVE A CONNECTION. YOU WOULD NOT UNDERSTAND.
AND NEZHNO?
HE WILL RETURN WITH ME.
TO THE X-MEN.
T'CHALLA.
SCOTT. I HAVE THREE BROKEN RIBS AND A FRACTURED JAW. HOW DID YOU FARE?
LIGHTNING BOLT TO THE HEART.
WE ARE LUCKY MEN. NOW LET'S SIT DOWN AND TALK ABOUT HOW TO NEVER MAKE HER ANGRY AT US AGAIN.
AGREED.
STORM... ORORO.
THANK YOU. THANK YOU FOR SAVING HIM.

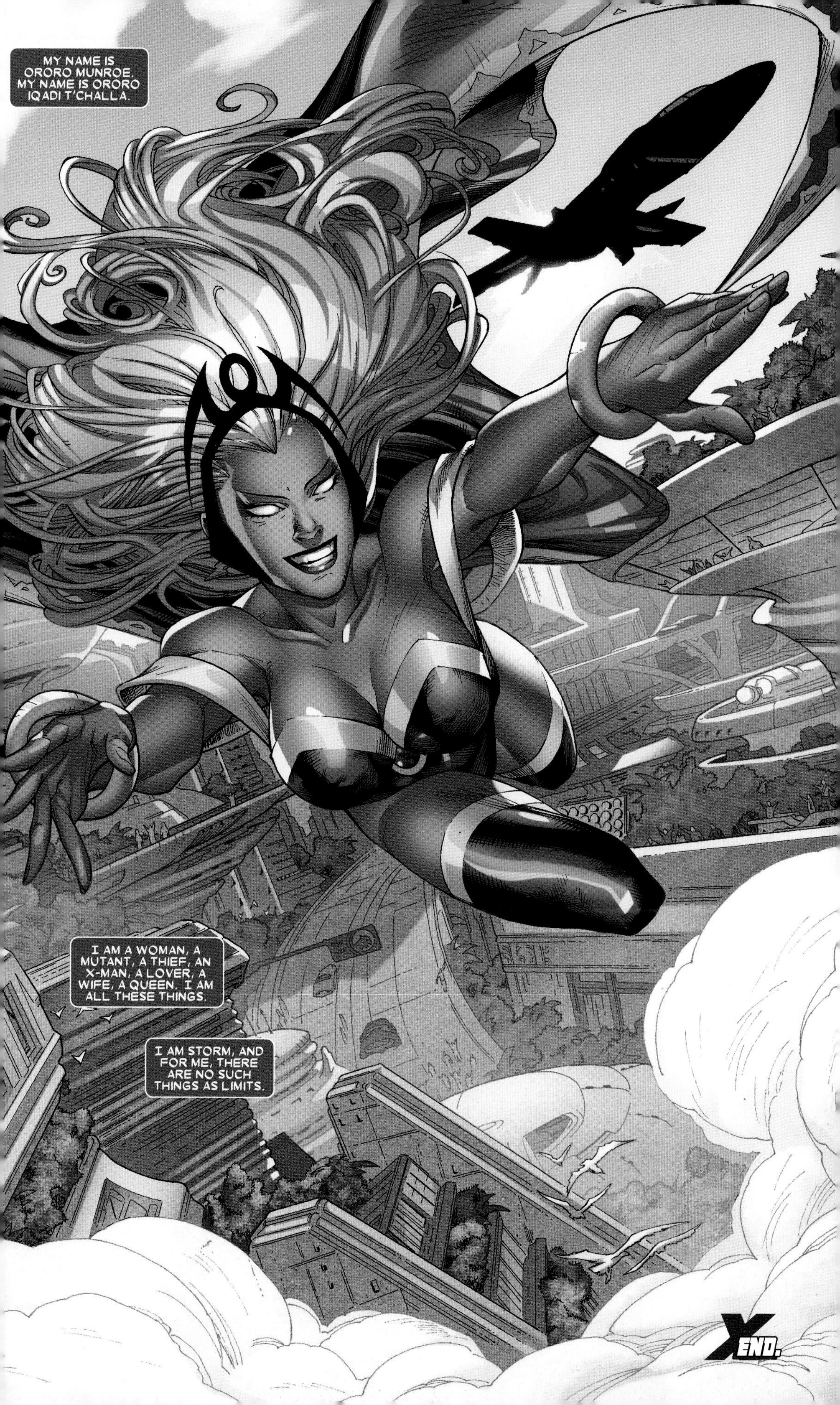
MY NAME IS ORORO MUNROE. MY NAME IS ORORO IQADI T'CHALLA.
I AM A WOMAN, A MUTANT, A THIEF, AN X-MAN, A LOVER, A WIFE, A QUEEN. I AM ALL THESE THINGS.
I AM STORM, AND FOR ME, THERE ARE NO SUCH THINGS AS LIMITS.
END.

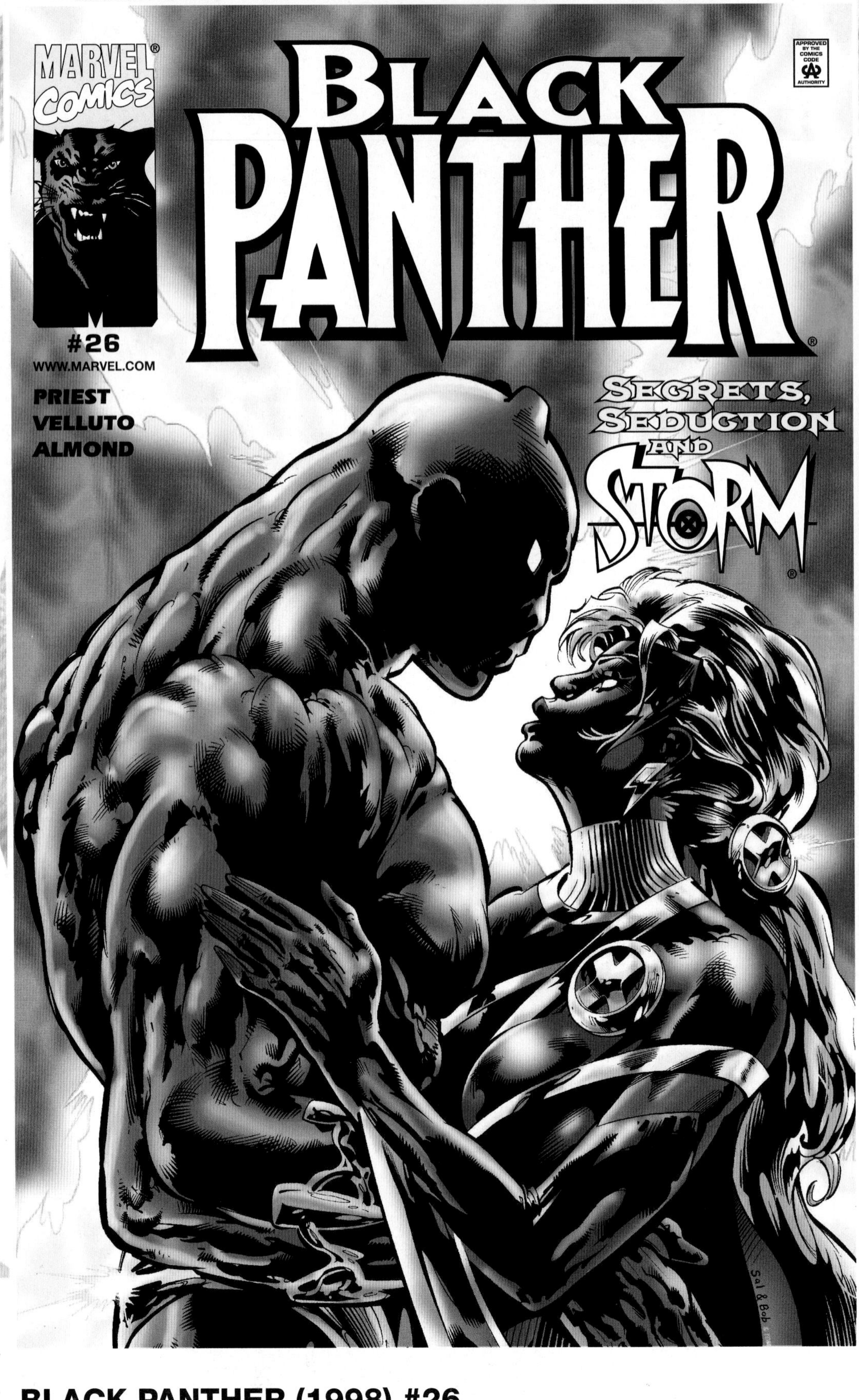
MARVEL COMICS
BLACK PANTHER
APPROVED BY THE COMICS CODE AUTHORITY
#26
WWW.MARVEL.COM
PRIEST
VELLUTO
ALMOND
SECRETS, SEDUCTION AND STORM

BLACK PANTHER (1998) #26

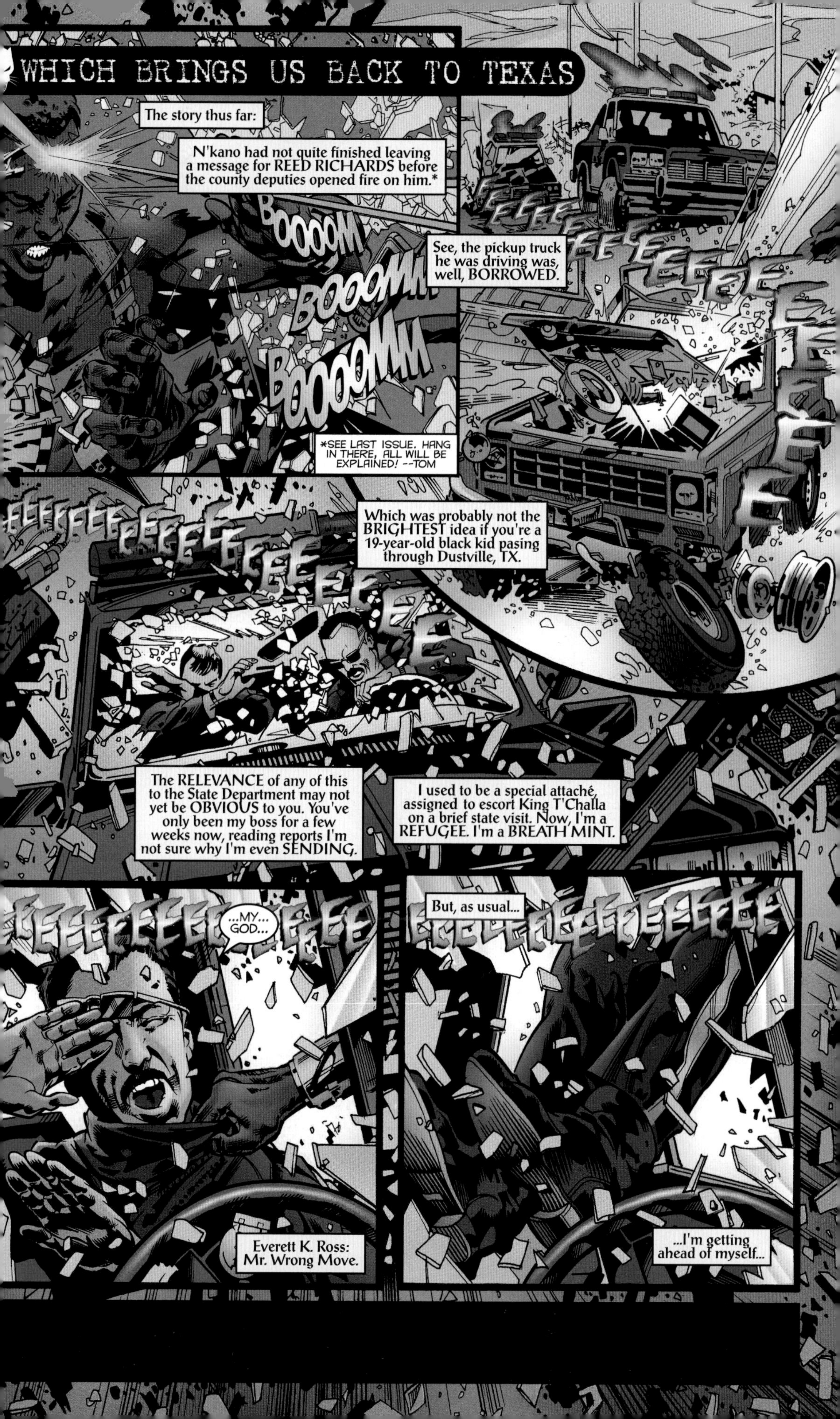

WHICH BRINGS US BACK TO TEXAS
The story thus far:
N'kano had not quite finished leaving a message for REED RICHARDS before the county deputies opened fire on him.*
BOOOOM
BOOOMM
BOOOMM
See, the pickup truck he was driving was, well, BORROWED.
EEEEEEEEEEEEEEEEE
*SEE LAST ISSUE. HANG IN THERE, ALL WILL BE EXPLAINED! --TOM
Which was probably not the BRIGHTEST idea if you're a 19-year-old black kid pasing through Dustville, TX.
EEEEEEEEEEEEEEEEEE
The RELEVANCE of any of this to the State Department may not yet be OBVIOUS to you. You've only been my boss for a few weeks now, reading reports I'm not sure why I'm even SENDING.
I used to be a special attaché, assigned to escort King T'Challa on a brief state visit. Now, I'm a REFUGEE. I'm a BREATH MINT.
EEEEEEEEEEEE
...MY... GOD...
Everett K. Ross: Mr. Wrong Move.
But, as usual...
EEEEEEEEEEEEEEE
...I'm getting ahead of myself...

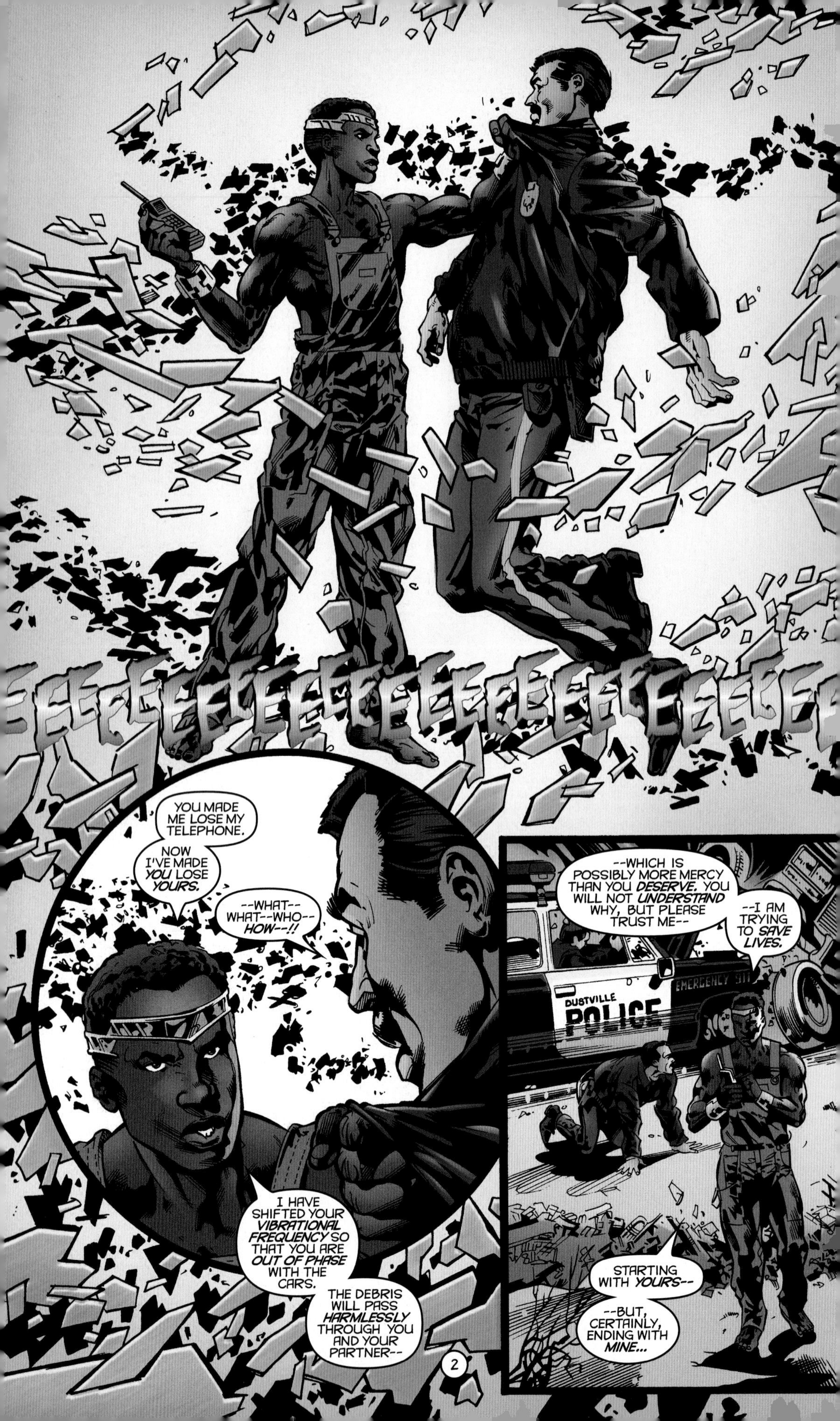
EEEEEEEEEEEEEEEEEEEEEEEE
YOU MADE ME LOSE MY TELEPHONE.
NOW I'VE MADE *YOU* LOSE *YOURS.*
--WHAT-- WHAT--WHO-- *HOW--!!*
I HAVE SHIFTED YOUR *VIBRATIONAL FREQUENCY* SO THAT YOU ARE *OUT OF PHASE* WITH THE CARS.
THE DEBRIS WILL PASS *HARMLESSLY* THROUGH YOU AND YOUR PARTNER--
--WHICH IS POSSIBLY MORE MERCY THAN YOU *DESERVE.* YOU WILL NOT *UNDERSTAND* WHY, BUT PLEASE TRUST ME--
--I AM TRYING TO *SAVE LIVES.*
EMERGENCY 911
DUSTVILLE
POLICE
STARTING WITH *YOURS--*
--BUT, CERTAINLY, ENDING WITH *MINE...*

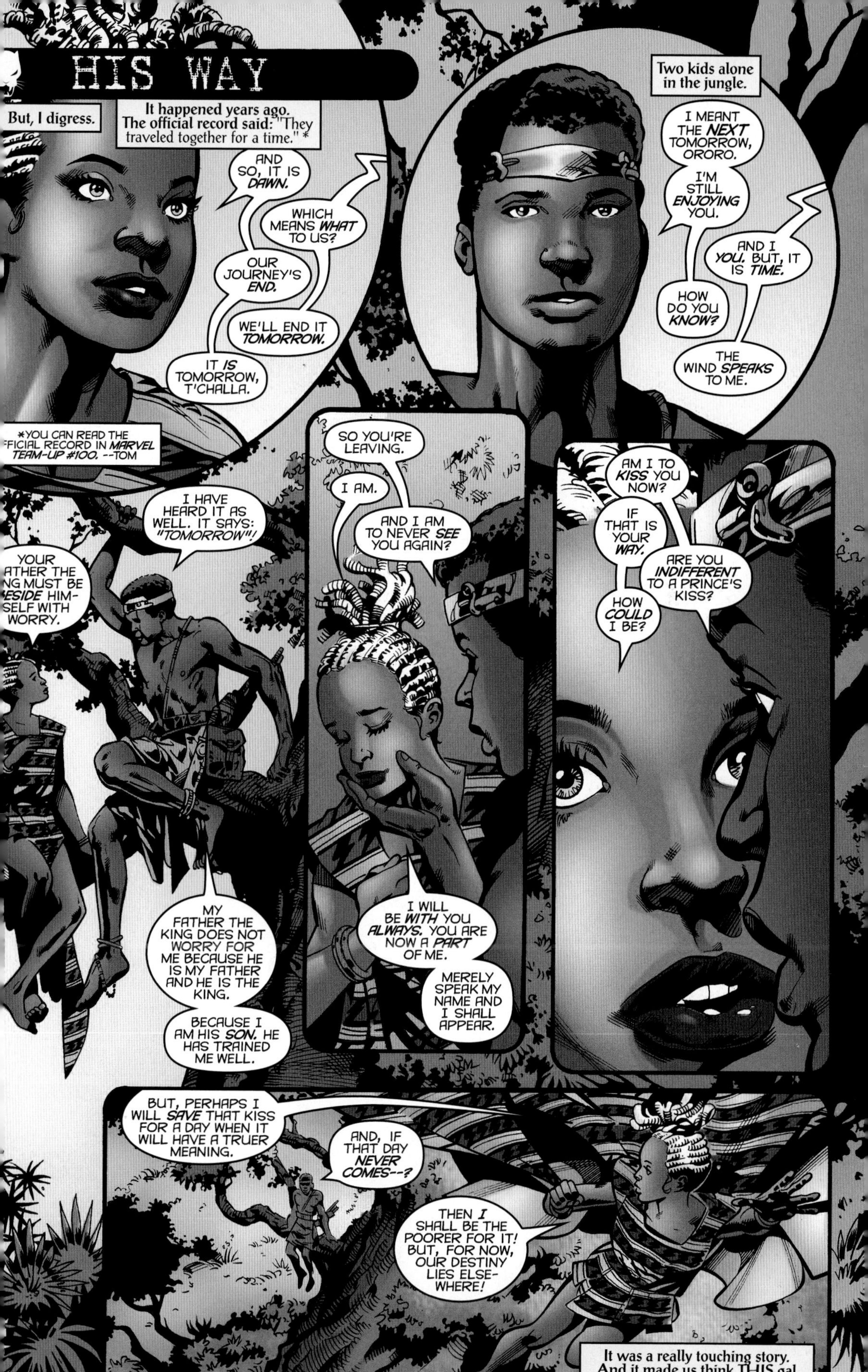
HIS WAY
But, I digress.
It happened years ago. The official record said: "They traveled together for a time." *
AND SO, IT IS DAWN.
WHICH MEANS WHAT TO US?
OUR JOURNEY'S END.
WE'LL END IT TOMORROW.
IT IS TOMORROW, T'CHALLA.
Two kids alone in the jungle.
I MEANT THE NEXT TOMORROW, ORORO.
I'M STILL ENJOYING YOU.
AND I YOU. BUT, IT IS TIME.
HOW DO YOU KNOW?
THE WIND SPEAKS TO ME.
*YOU CAN READ THE FFICIAL RECORD IN MARVEL TEAM-UP #100. --TOM
I HAVE HEARD IT AS WELL. IT SAYS: "TOMORROW"!
YOUR ATHER THE NG MUST BE ESIDE HIMSELF WITH WORRY.
MY FATHER THE KING DOES NOT WORRY FOR ME BECAUSE HE IS MY FATHER AND HE IS THE KING.
BECAUSE I AM HIS SON. HE HAS TRAINED ME WELL.
SO YOU'RE LEAVING.
I AM.
AND I AM TO NEVER SEE YOU AGAIN?
I WILL BE WITH YOU ALWAYS. YOU ARE NOW A PART OF ME.
MERELY SPEAK MY NAME AND I SHALL APPEAR.
AM I TO KISS YOU NOW?
IF THAT IS YOUR WAY.
ARE YOU INDIFFERENT TO A PRINCE'S KISS?
HOW COULD I BE?
BUT, PERHAPS I WILL SAVE THAT KISS FOR A DAY WHEN IT WILL HAVE A TRUER MEANING.
AND, IF THAT DAY NEVER COMES--?
THEN I SHALL BE THE POORER FOR IT! BUT, FOR NOW, OUR DESTINY LIES ELSEWHERE!
It was a really touching story. And it made us think THIS gal was just what the doctor ordered...

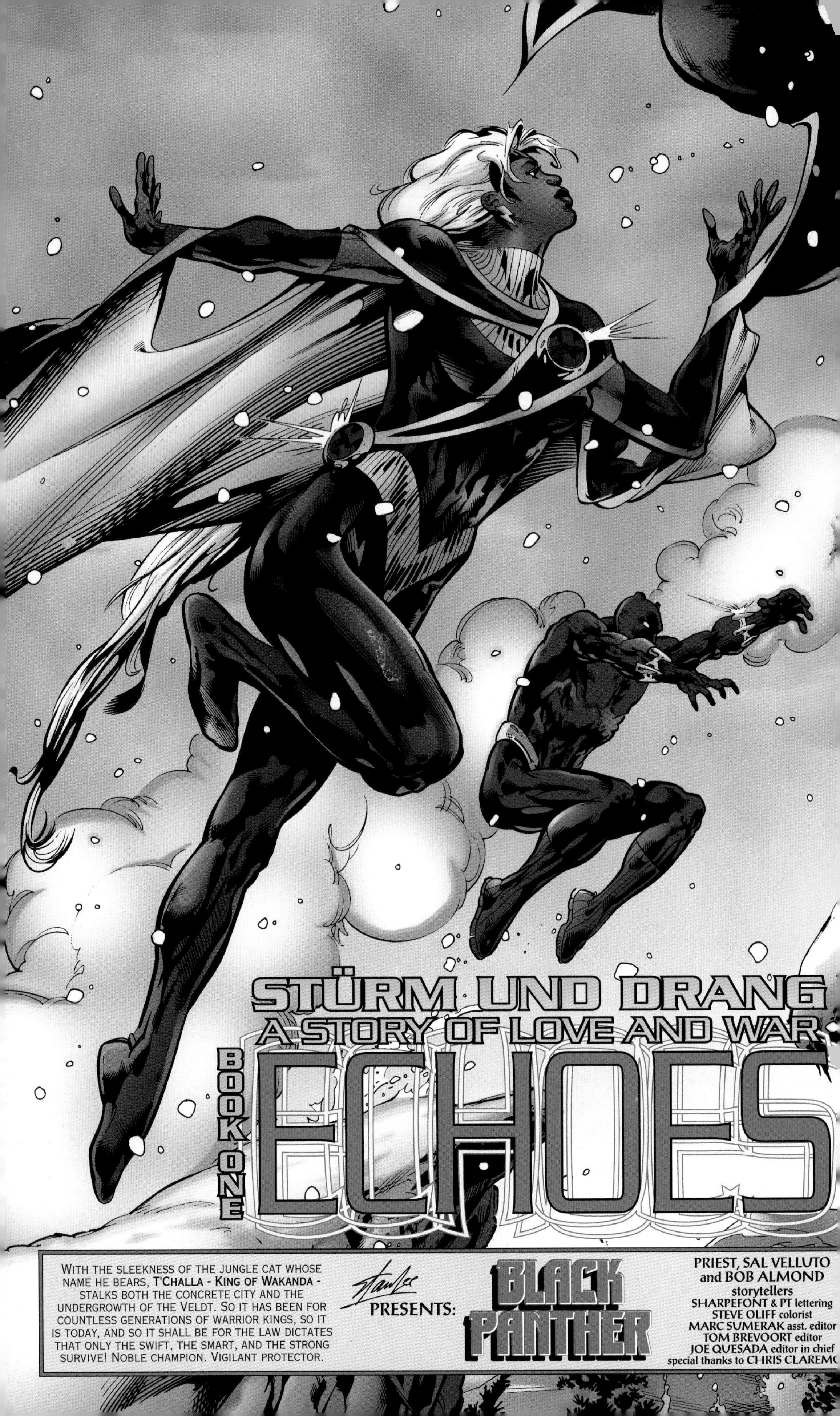

STÜRM UND DRANG
A STORY OF LOVE AND WAR
BOOK ONE
ECHOES
WITH THE SLEEKNESS OF THE JUNGLE CAT WHOSE NAME HE BEARS, T'CHALLA - KING OF WAKANDA - STALKS BOTH THE CONCRETE CITY AND THE UNDERGROWTH OF THE VELDT. SO IT HAS BEEN FOR COUNTLESS GENERATIONS OF WARRIOR KINGS, SO IT IS TODAY, AND SO IT SHALL BE FOR THE LAW DICTATES THAT ONLY THE SWIFT, THE SMART, AND THE STRONG SURVIVE! NOBLE CHAMPION. VIGILANT PROTECTOR.
Stan Lee PRESENTS:
BLACK PANTHER
PRIEST, SAL VELLUTO and BOB ALMOND storytellers
SHARPEFONT & PT lettering
STEVE OLIFF colorist
MARC SUMERAK asst. editor
TOM BREVOORT editor
JOE QUESADA editor in chief
special thanks to CHRIS CLAREM

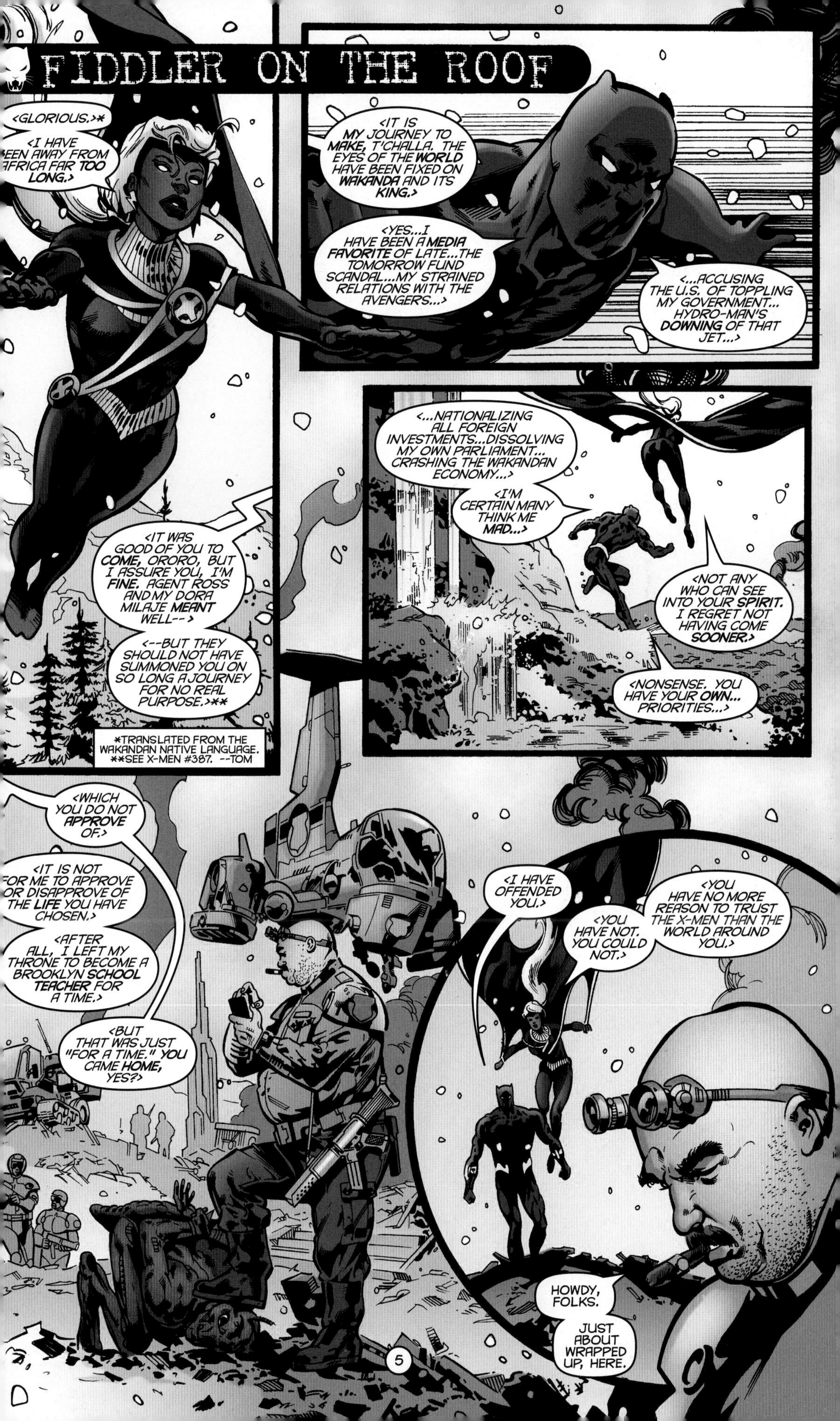
FIDDLER ON THE ROOF
<GLORIOUS.>*
<I HAVE BEEN AWAY FROM AFRICA FAR TOO LONG.>
<IT IS MY JOURNEY TO MAKE, T'CHALLA. THE EYES OF THE WORLD HAVE BEEN FIXED ON WAKANDA AND ITS KING.>
<YES...I HAVE BEEN A MEDIA FAVORITE OF LATE...THE TOMORROW FUND SCANDAL...MY STRAINED RELATIONS WITH THE AVENGERS...>
<...ACCUSING THE U.S. OF TOPPLING MY GOVERNMENT... HYDRO-MAN'S DOWNING OF THAT JET...>
<...NATIONALIZING ALL FOREIGN INVESTMENTS...DISSOLVING MY OWN PARLIAMENT... CRASHING THE WAKANDAN ECONOMY...>
<I'M CERTAIN MANY THINK ME MAD...>
<NOT ANY WHO CAN SEE INTO YOUR SPIRIT. I REGRET NOT HAVING COME SOONER.>
<NONSENSE. YOU HAVE YOUR OWN... PRIORITIES...>
<IT WAS GOOD OF YOU TO COME, ORORO, BUT I ASSURE YOU, I'M FINE. AGENT ROSS AND MY DORA MILAJE MEANT WELL-- >
<--BUT THEY SHOULD NOT HAVE SUMMONED YOU ON SO LONG A JOURNEY FOR NO REAL PURPOSE.>**
*TRANSLATED FROM THE WAKANDAN NATIVE LANGUAGE.
**SEE X-MEN #387. --TOM
<WHICH YOU DO NOT APPROVE OF.>
<IT IS NOT FOR ME TO APPROVE OR DISAPPROVE OF THE LIFE YOU HAVE CHOSEN.>
<AFTER ALL, I LEFT MY THRONE TO BECOME A BROOKLYN SCHOOL TEACHER FOR A TIME.>
<BUT THAT WAS JUST "FOR A TIME." YOU CAME HOME, YES?>
<I HAVE OFFENDED YOU.>
<YOU HAVE NOT. YOU COULD NOT.>
<YOU HAVE NO MORE REASON TO TRUST THE X-MEN THAN THE WORLD AROUND YOU.>
HOWDY, FOLKS.
JUST ABOUT WRAPPED UP, HERE.

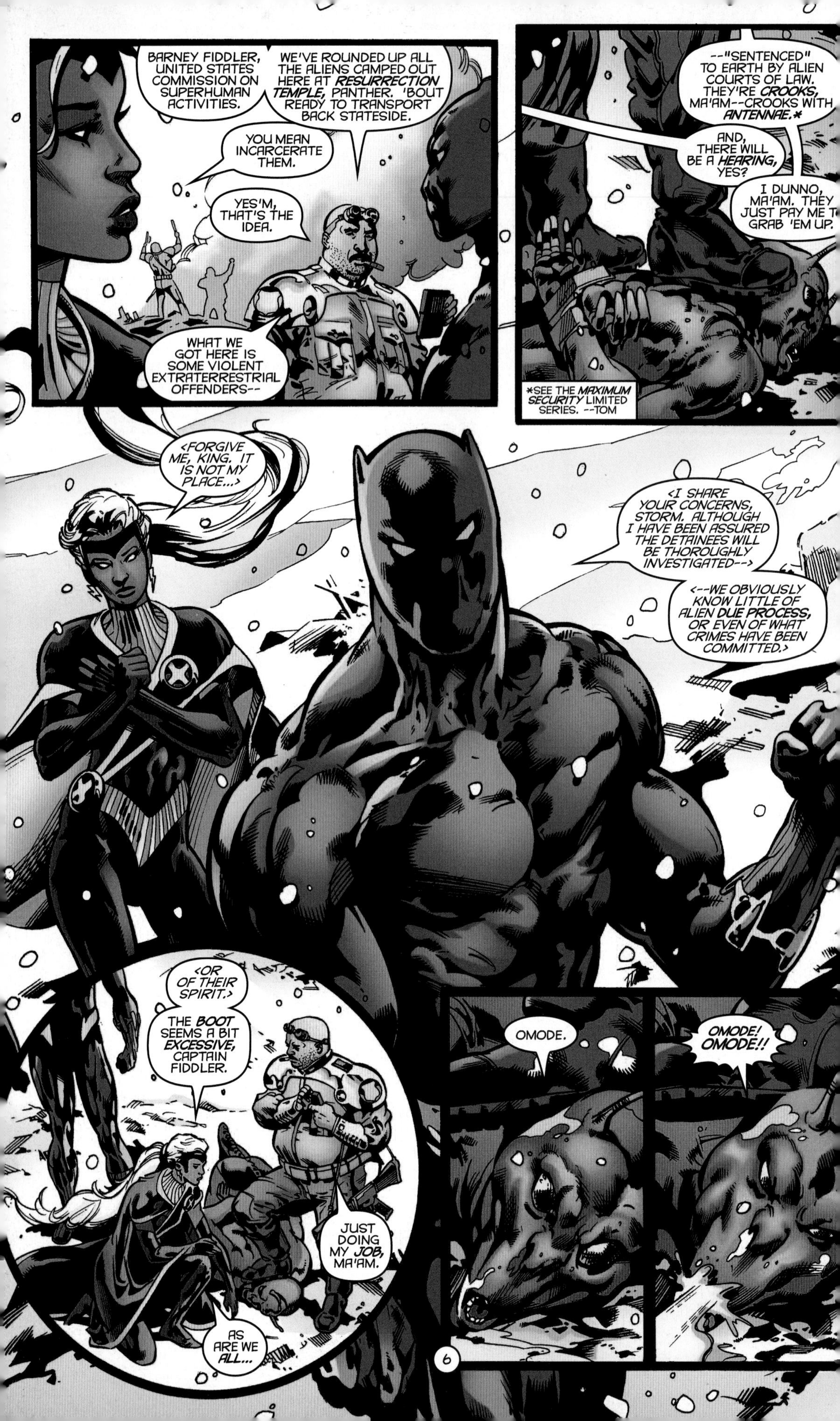
BARNEY FIDDLER, UNITED STATES COMMISSION ON SUPERHUMAN ACTIVITIES.
WE'VE ROUNDED UP ALL THE ALIENS CAMPED OUT HERE AT RESURRECTION TEMPLE, PANTHER. 'BOUT READY TO TRANSPORT BACK STATESIDE.
YOU MEAN INCARCERATE THEM.
YES'M, THAT'S THE IDEA.
WHAT WE GOT HERE IS SOME VIOLENT EXTRATERRESTRIAL OFFENDERS--
--"SENTENCED" TO EARTH BY ALIEN COURTS OF LAW. THEY'RE CROOKS, MA'AM--CROOKS WITH ANTENNAE.*
AND, THERE WILL BE A HEARING, YES?
I DUNNO, MA'AM. THEY JUST PAY ME T GRAB 'EM UP.
*SEE THE MAXIMUM SECURITY LIMITED SERIES. --TOM
<FORGIVE ME, KING. IT IS NOT MY PLACE...>
<I SHARE YOUR CONCERNS, STORM. ALTHOUGH I HAVE BEEN ASSURED THE DETAINEES WILL BE THOROUGHLY INVESTIGATED-->
<--WE OBVIOUSLY KNOW LITTLE OF ALIEN DUE PROCESS, OR EVEN OF WHAT CRIMES HAVE BEEN COMMITTED.>
<OR OF THEIR SPIRIT.>
THE BOOT SEEMS A BIT EXCESSIVE, CAPTAIN FIDDLER.
JUST DOING MY JOB, MA'AM.
AS ARE WE ALL...
OMODE.
OMODE! OMODE!!

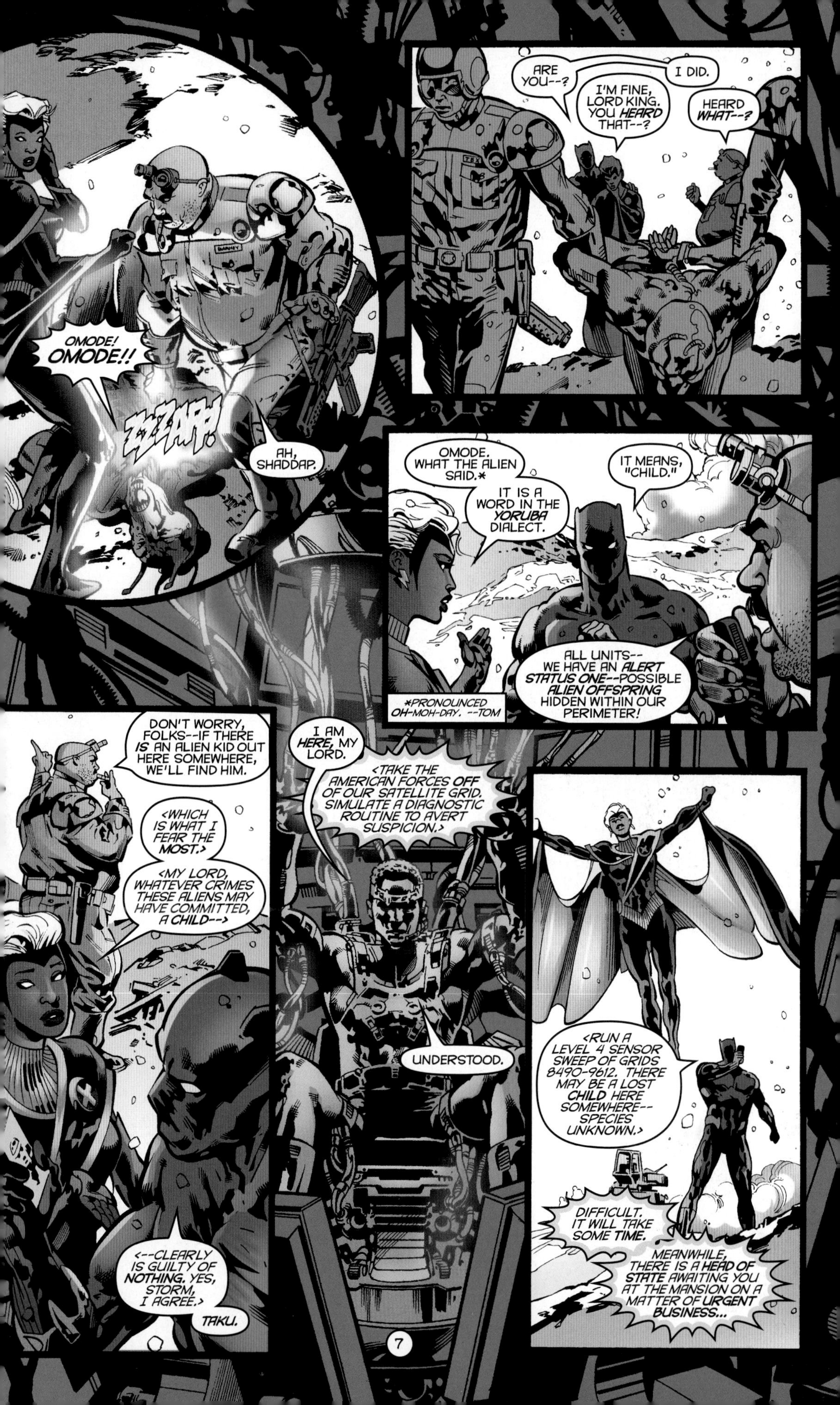
OMODE! OMODE!!
ZZZAPP!
AH, SHADDAP.
ARE YOU--?
I'M FINE, LORD KING. YOU HEARD THAT--?
I DID.
HEARD WHAT--?
OMODE. WHAT THE ALIEN SAID.*
IT IS A WORD IN THE YORUBA DIALECT.
IT MEANS, "CHILD."
ALL UNITS-- WE HAVE AN ALERT STATUS ONE--POSSIBLE ALIEN OFFSPRING HIDDEN WITHIN OUR PERIMETER!
*PRONOUNCED OH-MOH-DAY. --TOM
DON'T WORRY, FOLKS--IF THERE IS AN ALIEN KID OUT HERE SOMEWHERE, WE'LL FIND HIM.
<WHICH IS WHAT I FEAR THE MOST.>
<MY LORD, WHATEVER CRIMES THESE ALIENS MAY HAVE COMMITTED, A CHILD-->
<--CLEARLY IS GUILTY OF NOTHING. YES, STORM, I AGREE.>
TAKU.
I AM HERE, MY LORD.
<TAKE THE AMERICAN FORCES OFF OF OUR SATELLITE GRID. SIMULATE A DIAGNOSTIC ROUTINE TO AVERT SUSPICION.>
UNDERSTOOD.
<RUN A LEVEL 4 SENSOR SWEEP OF GRIDS 8490-9612. THERE MAY BE A LOST CHILD HERE SOMEWHERE-- SPECIES UNKNOWN.>
DIFFICULT. IT WILL TAKE SOME TIME.
MEANWHILE, THERE IS A HEAD OF STATE AWAITING YOU AT THE MANSION ON A MATTER OF URGENT BUSINESS...

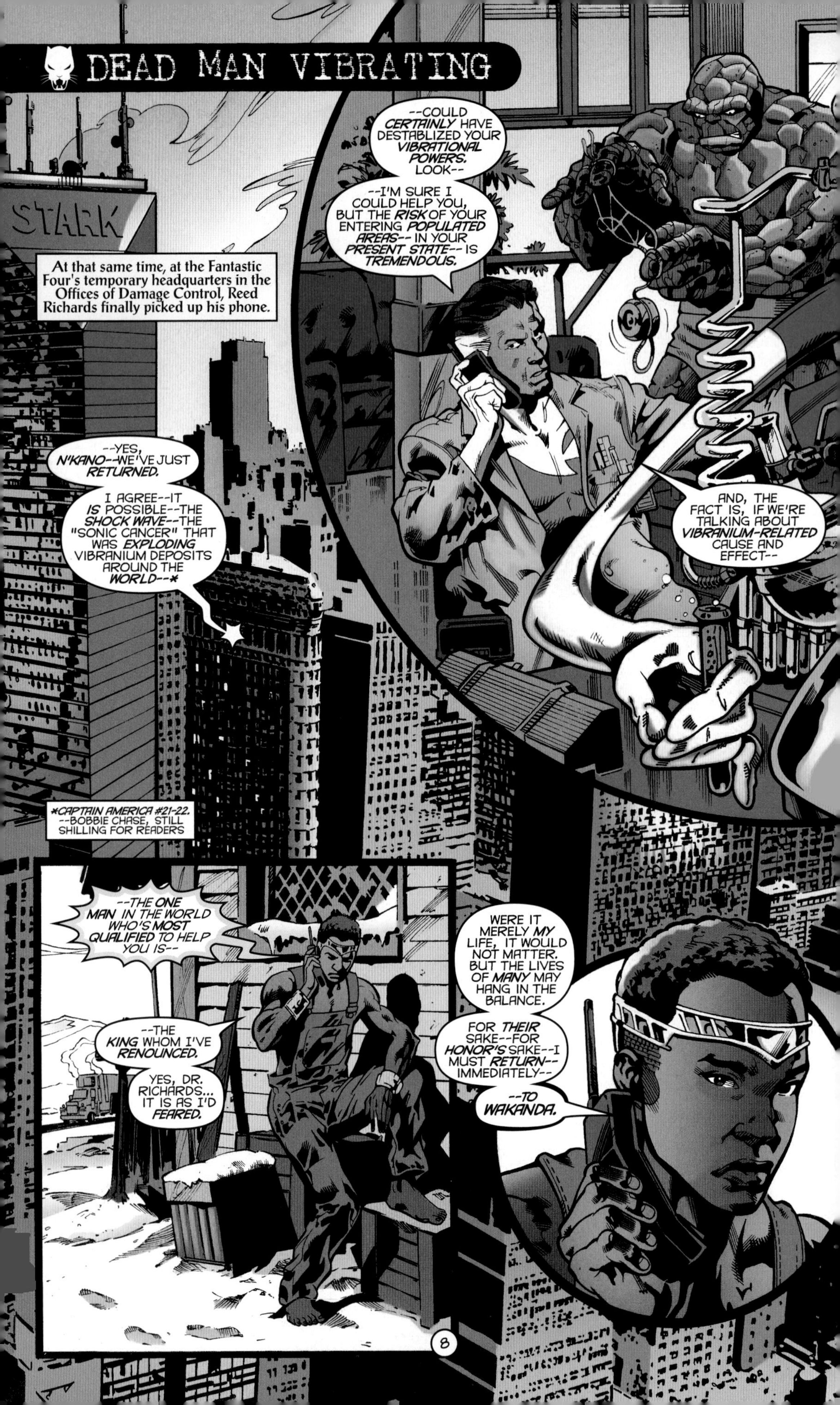

DEAD MAN VIBRATING
STARK
At that same time, at the Fantastic Four's temporary headquarters in the Offices of Damage Control, Reed Richards finally picked up his phone.
--YES, N'KANO--WE'VE JUST RETURNED.
I AGREE--IT IS POSSIBLE--THE SHOCK WAVE--THE "SONIC CANCER" THAT WAS EXPLODING VIBRANIUM DEPOSITS AROUND THE WORLD--*
--COULD CERTAINLY HAVE DESTABLIZED YOUR VIBRATIONAL POWERS. LOOK--
--I'M SURE I COULD HELP YOU, BUT THE RISK OF YOUR ENTERING POPULATED AREAS-- IN YOUR PRESENT STATE-- IS TREMENDOUS.
AND, THE FACT IS, IF WE'RE TALKING ABOUT VIBRANIUM-RELATED CAUSE AND EFFECT--
*CAPTAIN AMERICA #21-22. --BOBBIE CHASE, STILL SHILLING FOR READERS
--THE ONE MAN IN THE WORLD WHO'S MOST QUALIFIED TO HELP YOU IS--
--THE KING WHOM I'VE RENOUNCED.
YES, DR. RICHARDS... IT IS AS I'D FEARED.
WERE IT MERELY MY LIFE, IT WOULD NOT MATTER. BUT THE LIVES OF MANY MAY HANG IN THE BALANCE.
FOR THEIR SAKE--FOR HONOR'S SAKE--I MUST RETURN-- IMMEDIATELY--
--TO WAKANDA.

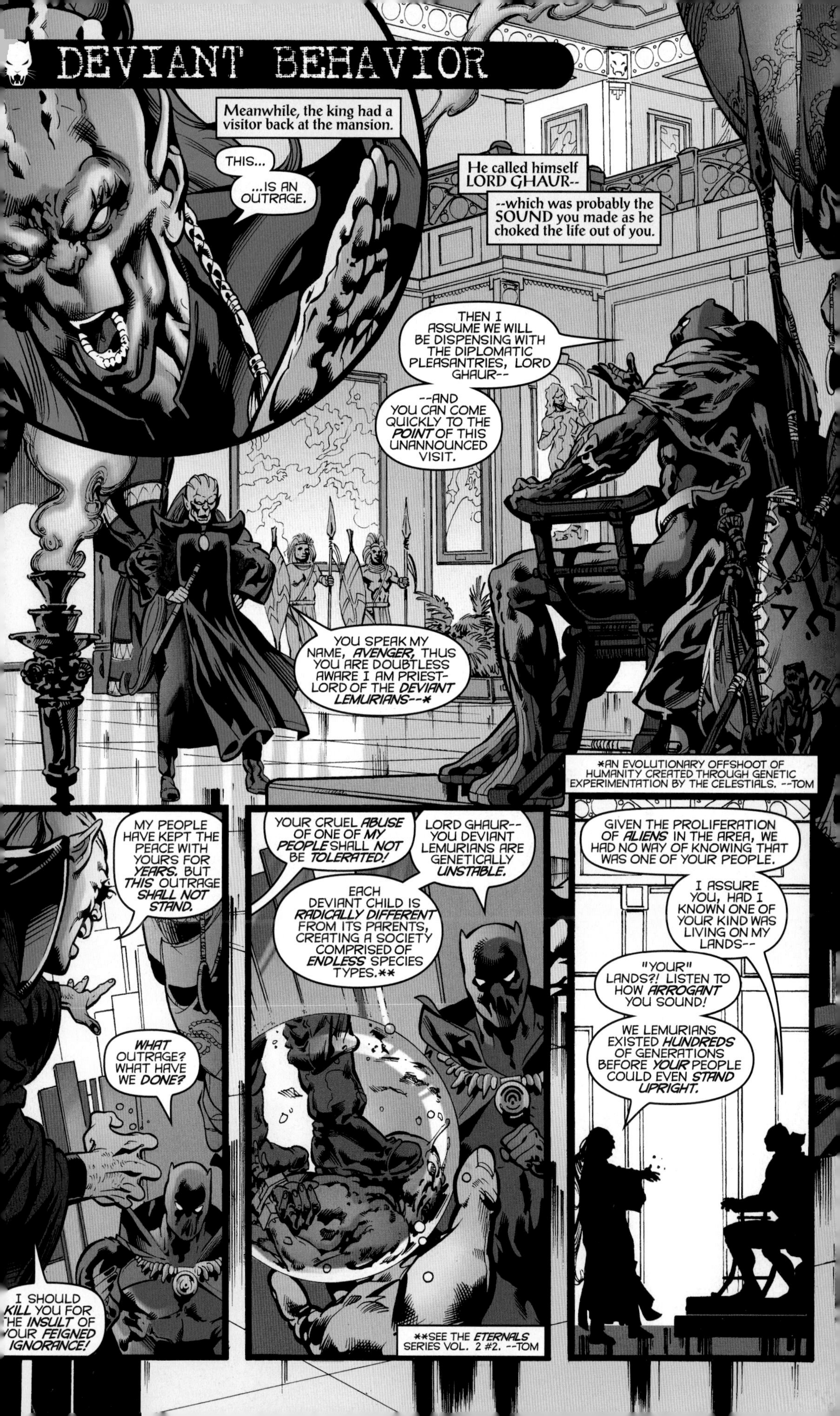
DEVIANT BEHAVIOR
Meanwhile, the king had a visitor back at the mansion.
THIS...
...IS AN OUTRAGE.
He called himself LORD GHAUR--
--which was probably the SOUND you made as he choked the life out of you.
THEN I ASSUME WE WILL BE DISPENSING WITH THE DIPLOMATIC PLEASANTRIES, LORD GHAUR--
--AND YOU CAN COME QUICKLY TO THE POINT OF THIS UNANNOUNCED VISIT.
YOU SPEAK MY NAME, AVENGER, THUS YOU ARE DOUBTLESS AWARE I AM PRIEST-LORD OF THE DEVIANT LEMURIANS--*
*AN EVOLUTIONARY OFFSHOOT OF HUMANITY CREATED THROUGH GENETIC EXPERIMENTATION BY THE CELESTIALS. --TOM
MY PEOPLE HAVE KEPT THE PEACE WITH YOURS FOR YEARS. BUT THIS OUTRAGE SHALL NOT STAND.
WHAT OUTRAGE? WHAT HAVE WE DONE?
I SHOULD KILL YOU FOR THE INSULT OF YOUR FEIGNED IGNORANCE!
YOUR CRUEL ABUSE OF ONE OF MY PEOPLE SHALL NOT BE TOLERATED!
LORD GHAUR-- YOU DEVIANT LEMURIANS ARE GENETICALLY UNSTABLE.
EACH DEVIANT CHILD IS RADICALLY DIFFERENT FROM ITS PARENTS, CREATING A SOCIETY COMPRISED OF ENDLESS SPECIES TYPES.**
**SEE THE ETERNALS SERIES VOL. 2 #2. --TOM
GIVEN THE PROLIFERATION OF ALIENS IN THE AREA, WE HAD NO WAY OF KNOWING THAT WAS ONE OF YOUR PEOPLE.
I ASSURE YOU, HAD I KNOWN ONE OF YOUR KIND WAS LIVING ON MY LANDS--
"YOUR" LANDS?! LISTEN TO HOW ARROGANT YOU SOUND!
WE LEMURIANS EXISTED HUNDREDS OF GENERATIONS BEFORE YOUR PEOPLE COULD EVEN STAND UPRIGHT.

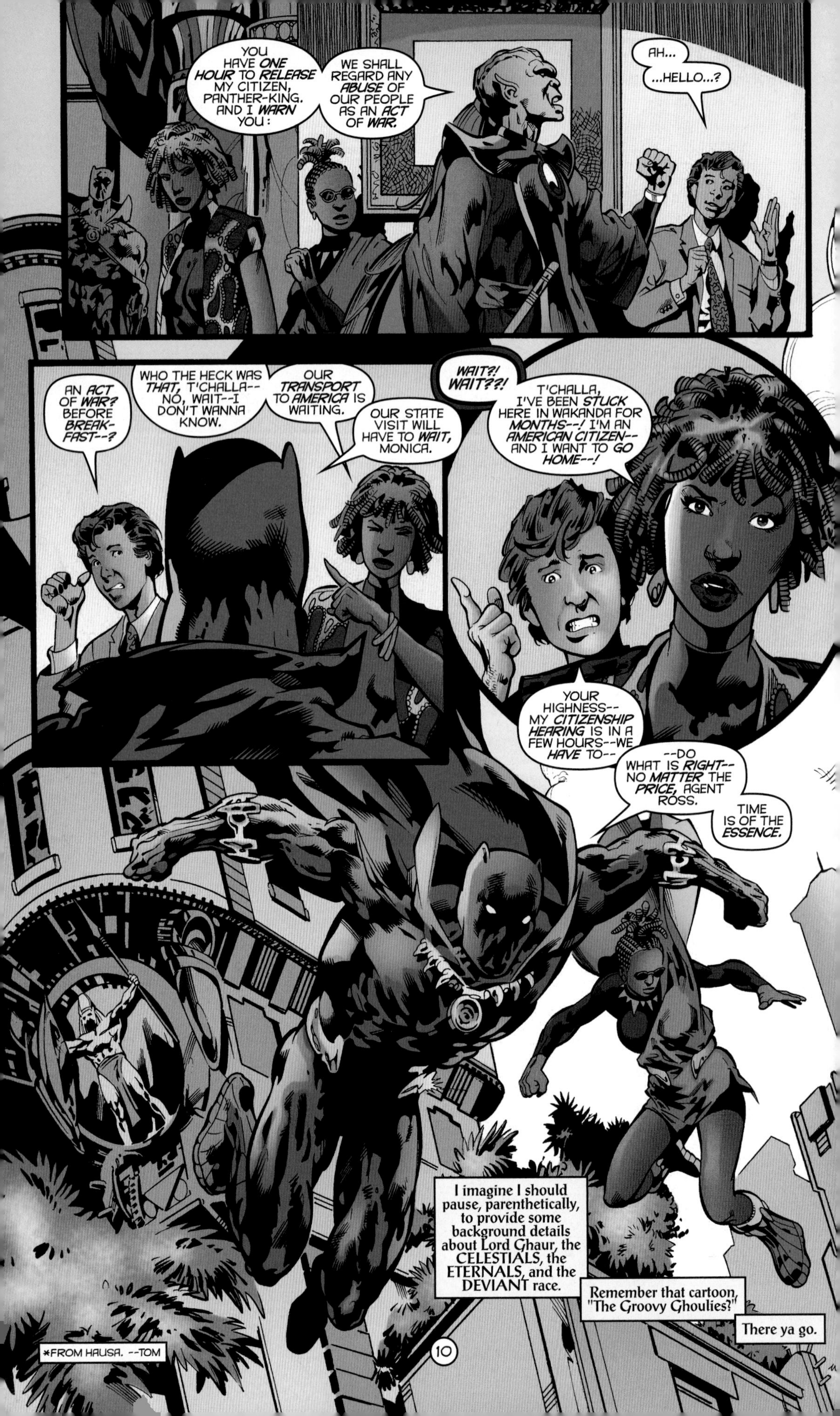
YOU HAVE ONE HOUR TO RELEASE MY CITIZEN, PANTHER-KING. AND I WARN YOU:
WE SHALL REGARD ANY ABUSE OF OUR PEOPLE AS AN ACT OF WAR.
AH...
...HELLO...?
AN ACT OF WAR? BEFORE BREAK-FAST--?
WHO THE HECK WAS THAT, T'CHALLA--NO, WAIT--I DON'T WANNA KNOW.
OUR TRANSPORT TO AMERICA IS WAITING.
OUR STATE VISIT WILL HAVE TO WAIT, MONICA.
WAIT?! WAIT??!
T'CHALLA, I'VE BEEN STUCK HERE IN WAKANDA FOR MONTHS--! I'M AN AMERICAN CITIZEN--AND I WANT TO GO HOME--!
YOUR HIGHNESS--MY CITIZENSHIP HEARING IS IN A FEW HOURS--WE HAVE TO--
--DO WHAT IS RIGHT--NO MATTER THE PRICE, AGENT ROSS.
TIME IS OF THE ESSENCE.
I imagine I should pause, parenthetically, to provide some background details about Lord Ghaur, the CELESTIALS, the ETERNALS, and the DEVIANT race.
Remember that cartoon, "The Groovy Ghoulies?"
There ya go.
*FROM HAUSA. --TOM

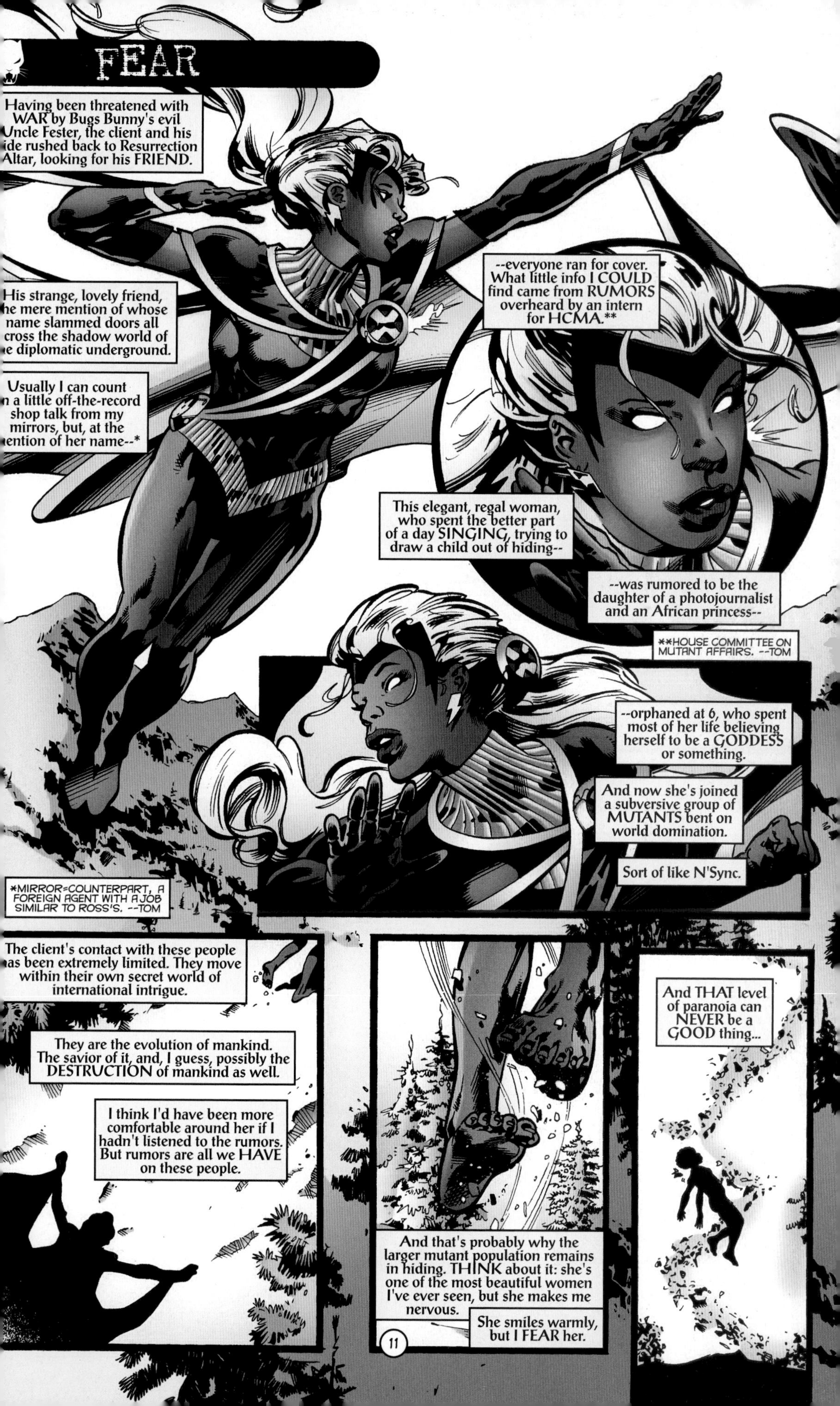

FEAR
Having been threatened with WAR by Bugs Bunny's evil Uncle Fester, the client and his ide rushed back to Resurrection Altar, looking for his FRIEND.
His strange, lovely friend, he mere mention of whose name slammed doors all cross the shadow world of e diplomatic underground.
Usually I can count n a little off-the-record shop talk from my mirrors, but, at the ention of her name--*
--everyone ran for cover. What little info I COULD find came from RUMORS overheard by an intern for HCMA.**
This elegant, regal woman, who spent the better part of a day SINGING, trying to draw a child out of hiding--
--was rumored to be the daughter of a photojournalist and an African princess--
**HOUSE COMMITTEE ON MUTANT AFFAIRS. --TOM
--orphaned at 6, who spent most of her life believing herself to be a GODDESS or something.
And now she's joined a subversive group of MUTANTS bent on world domination.
Sort of like N'Sync.
*MIRROR=COUNTERPART, A FOREIGN AGENT WITH A JOB SIMILAR TO ROSS'S. --TOM
The client's contact with these people has been extremely limited. They move within their own secret world of international intrigue.
They are the evolution of mankind. The savior of it, and, I guess, possibly the DESTRUCTION of mankind as well.
I think I'd have been more comfortable around her if I hadn't listened to the rumors. But rumors are all we HAVE on these people.
And that's probably why the larger mutant population remains in hiding. THINK about it: she's one of the most beautiful women I've ever seen, but she makes me nervous.
She smiles warmly, but I FEAR her.
And THAT level of paranoia can NEVER be a GOOD thing...

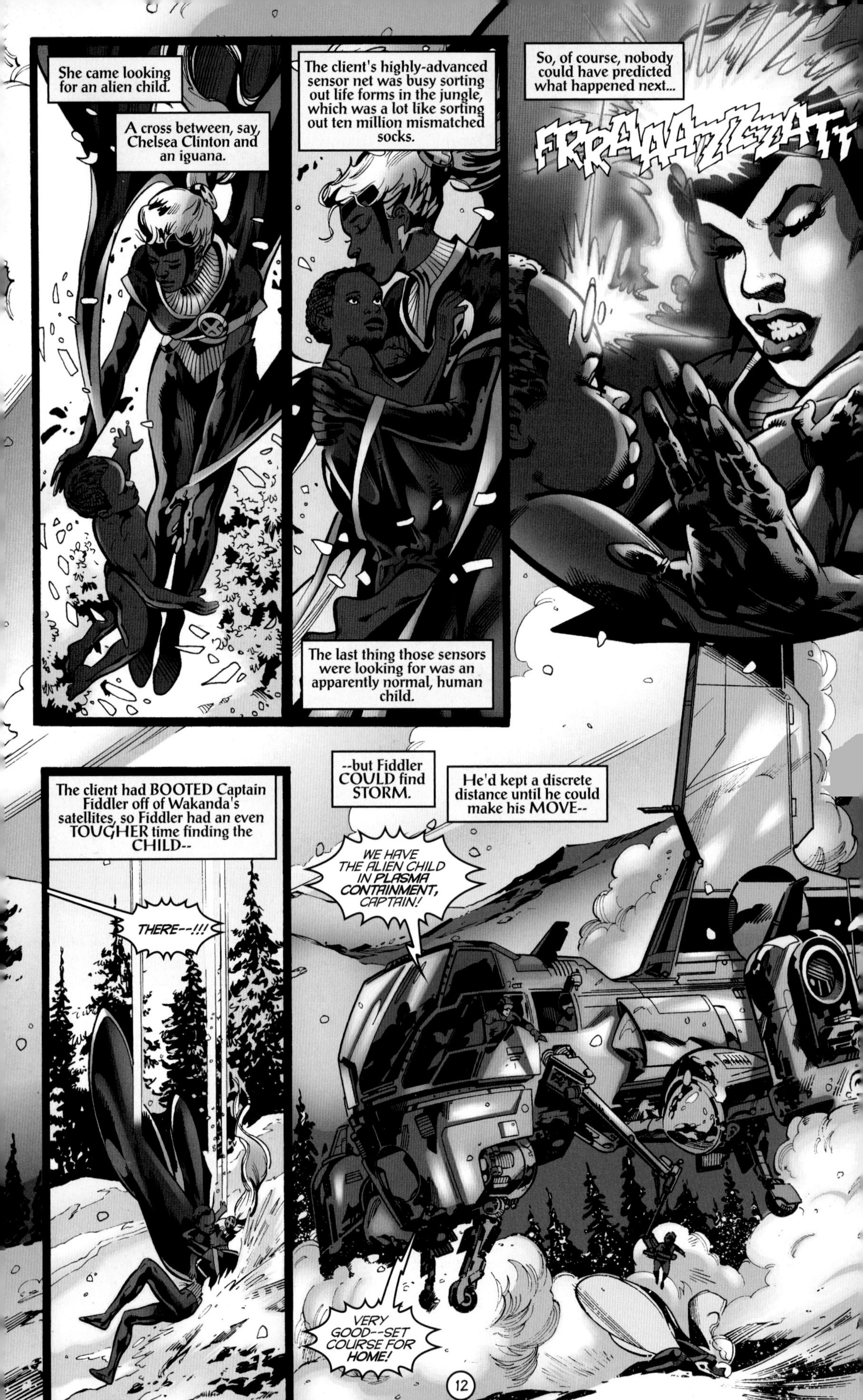
She came looking for an alien child.
A cross between, say, Chelsea Clinton and an iguana.
The client's highly-advanced sensor net was busy sorting out life forms in the jungle, which was a lot like sorting out ten million mismatched socks.
The last thing those sensors were looking for was an apparently normal, human child.
So, of course, nobody could have predicted what happened next...
FRAAAZZZATT
The client had BOOTED Captain Fiddler off of Wakanda's satellites, so Fiddler had an even TOUGHER time finding the CHILD--
--but Fiddler COULD find STORM.
He'd kept a discrete distance until he could make his MOVE--
THERE--!!!
WE HAVE THE ALIEN CHILD IN PLASMA CONTAINMENT, CAPTAIN!
VERY GOOD--SET COURSE FOR HOME!

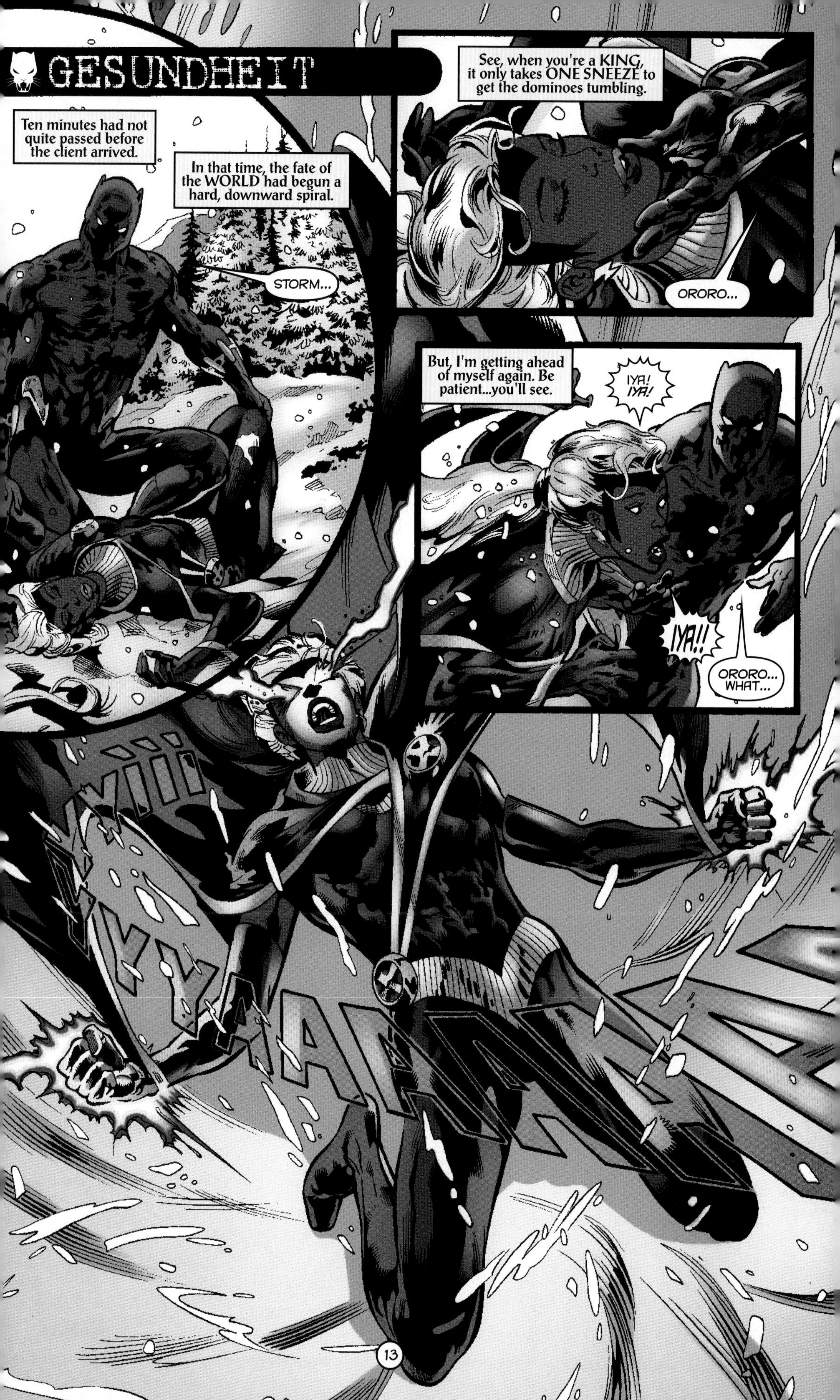
GESUNDHEIT
Ten minutes had not quite passed before the client arrived.
In that time, the fate of the WORLD had begun a hard, downward spiral.
STORM...
See, when you're a KING, it only takes ONE SNEEZE to get the dominoes tumbling.
ORORO...
But, I'm getting ahead of myself again. Be patient...you'll see.
IYA! IYA!
IYA!!
ORORO... WHAT...

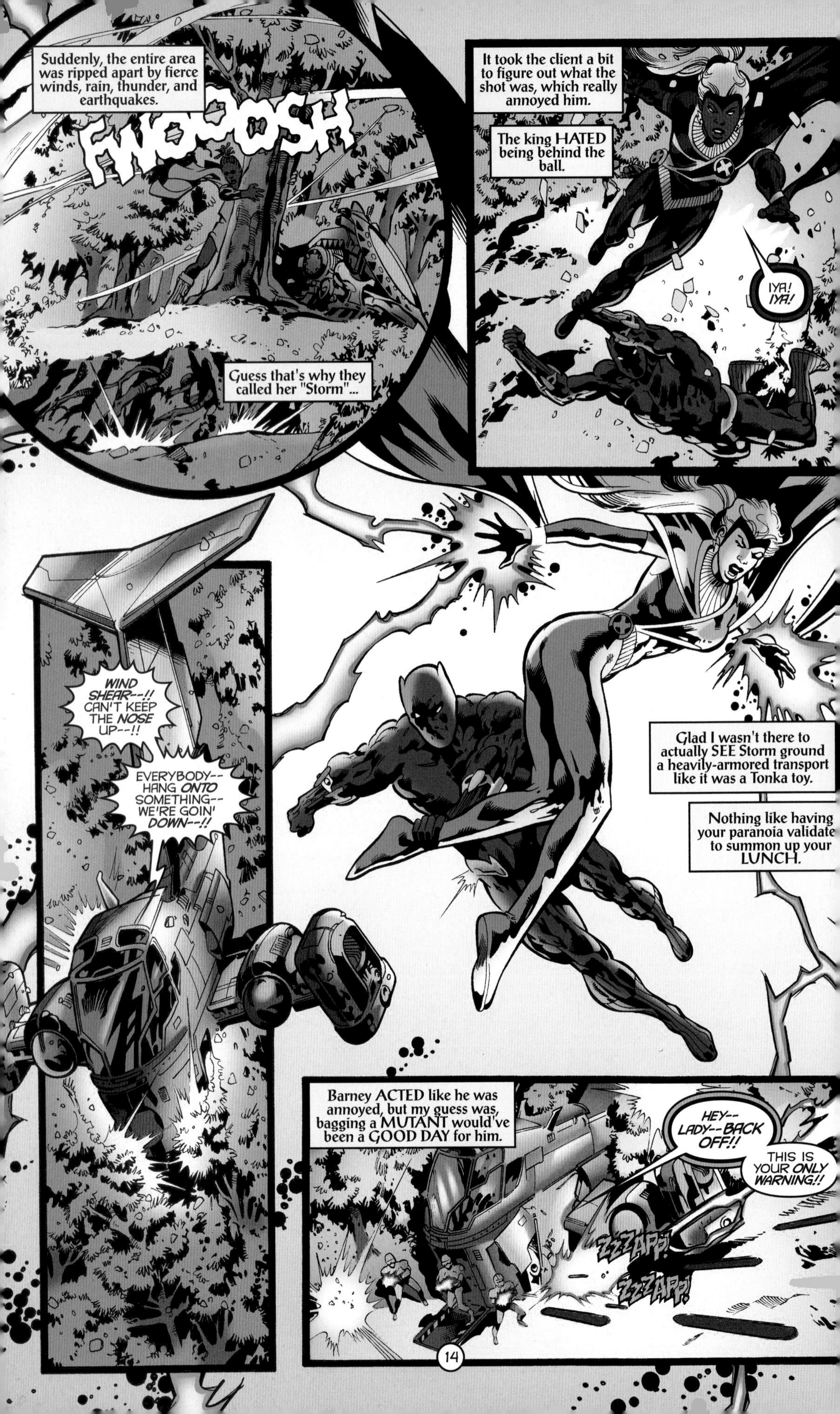
Suddenly, the entire area was ripped apart by fierce winds, rain, thunder, and earthquakes.
FWOOOSH
Guess that's why they called her "Storm"...
It took the client a bit to figure out what the shot was, which really annoyed him.
The king HATED being behind the ball.
IYA! IYA!
WIND SHEAR--!! CAN'T KEEP THE NOSE UP--!!
EVERYBODY-- HANG ONTO SOMETHING-- WE'RE GOIN' DOWN--!!
Glad I wasn't there to actually SEE Storm ground a heavily-armored transport like it was a Tonka toy.
Nothing like having your paranoia validate to summon up your LUNCH.
Barney ACTED like he was annoyed, but my guess was, bagging a MUTANT would've been a GOOD DAY for him.
HEY-- LADY--BACK OFF!!
THIS IS YOUR ONLY WARNING!!
ZZZAPP!
ZZZAPP!

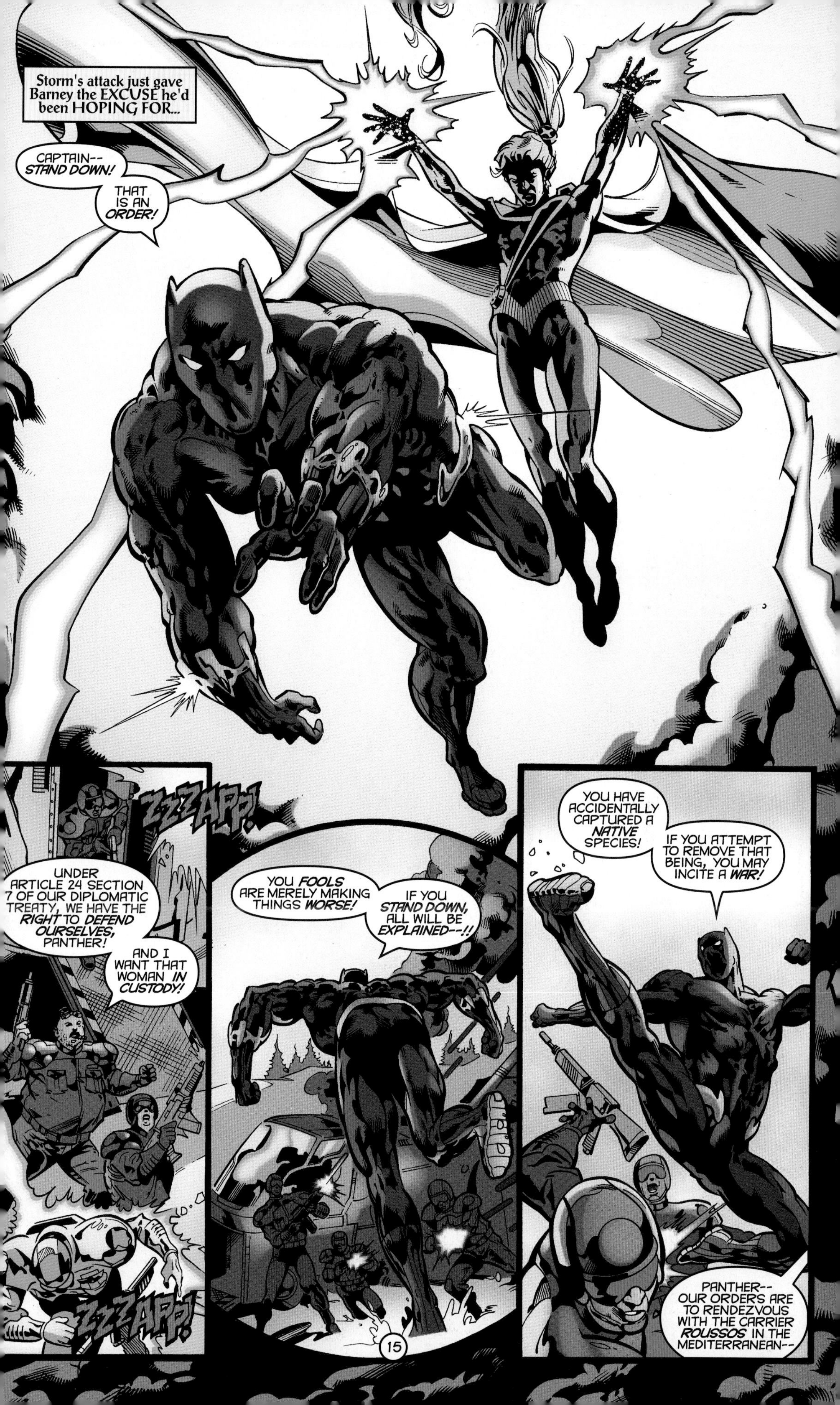

Storm's attack just gave Barney the EXCUSE he'd been HOPING FOR...
CAPTAIN-- STAND DOWN!
THAT IS AN ORDER!
ZZZAPP!
UNDER ARTICLE 24 SECTION 7 OF OUR DIPLOMATIC TREATY, WE HAVE THE RIGHT TO DEFEND OURSELVES, PANTHER!
AND I WANT THAT WOMAN IN CUSTODY!
ZZZAPP!
YOU FOOLS ARE MERELY MAKING THINGS WORSE!
IF YOU STAND DOWN, ALL WILL BE EXPLAINED--!!
YOU HAVE ACCIDENTALLY CAPTURED A NATIVE SPECIES!
IF YOU ATTEMPT TO REMOVE THAT BEING, YOU MAY INCITE A WAR!
PANTHER-- OUR ORDERS ARE TO RENDEZVOUS WITH THE CARRIER ROUSSOS IN THE MEDITERRANEAN--

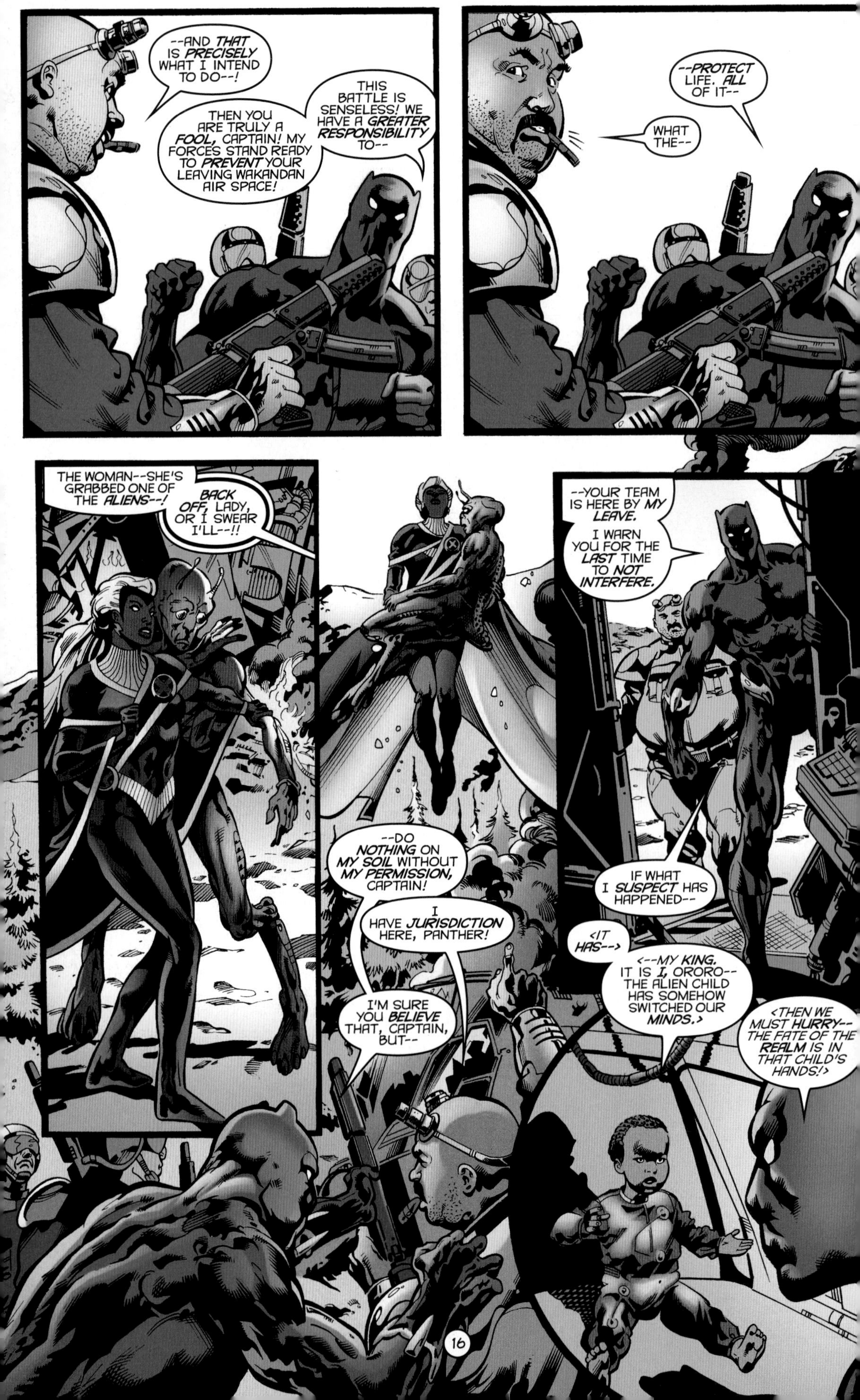
--AND THAT IS PRECISELY WHAT I INTEND TO DO--!
THEN YOU ARE TRULY A FOOL, CAPTAIN! MY FORCES STAND READY TO PREVENT YOUR LEAVING WAKANDAN AIR SPACE!
THIS BATTLE IS SENSELESS! WE HAVE A GREATER RESPONSIBILITY TO--
--PROTECT LIFE. ALL OF IT--
WHAT THE--
THE WOMAN--SHE'S GRABBED ONE OF THE ALIENS--!
BACK OFF, LADY, OR I SWEAR I'LL--!!
--YOUR TEAM IS HERE BY MY LEAVE.
I WARN YOU FOR THE LAST TIME TO NOT INTERFERE.
--DO NOTHING ON MY SOIL WITHOUT MY PERMISSION, CAPTAIN!
I HAVE JURISDICTION HERE, PANTHER!
I'M SURE YOU BELIEVE THAT, CAPTAIN, BUT--
IF WHAT I SUSPECT HAS HAPPENED--
<IT HAS-->
<--MY KING. IT IS I, ORORO-- THE ALIEN CHILD HAS SOMEHOW SWITCHED OUR MINDS.>
<THEN WE MUST HURRY-- THE FATE OF THE REALM IS IN THAT CHILD'S HANDS!>
16

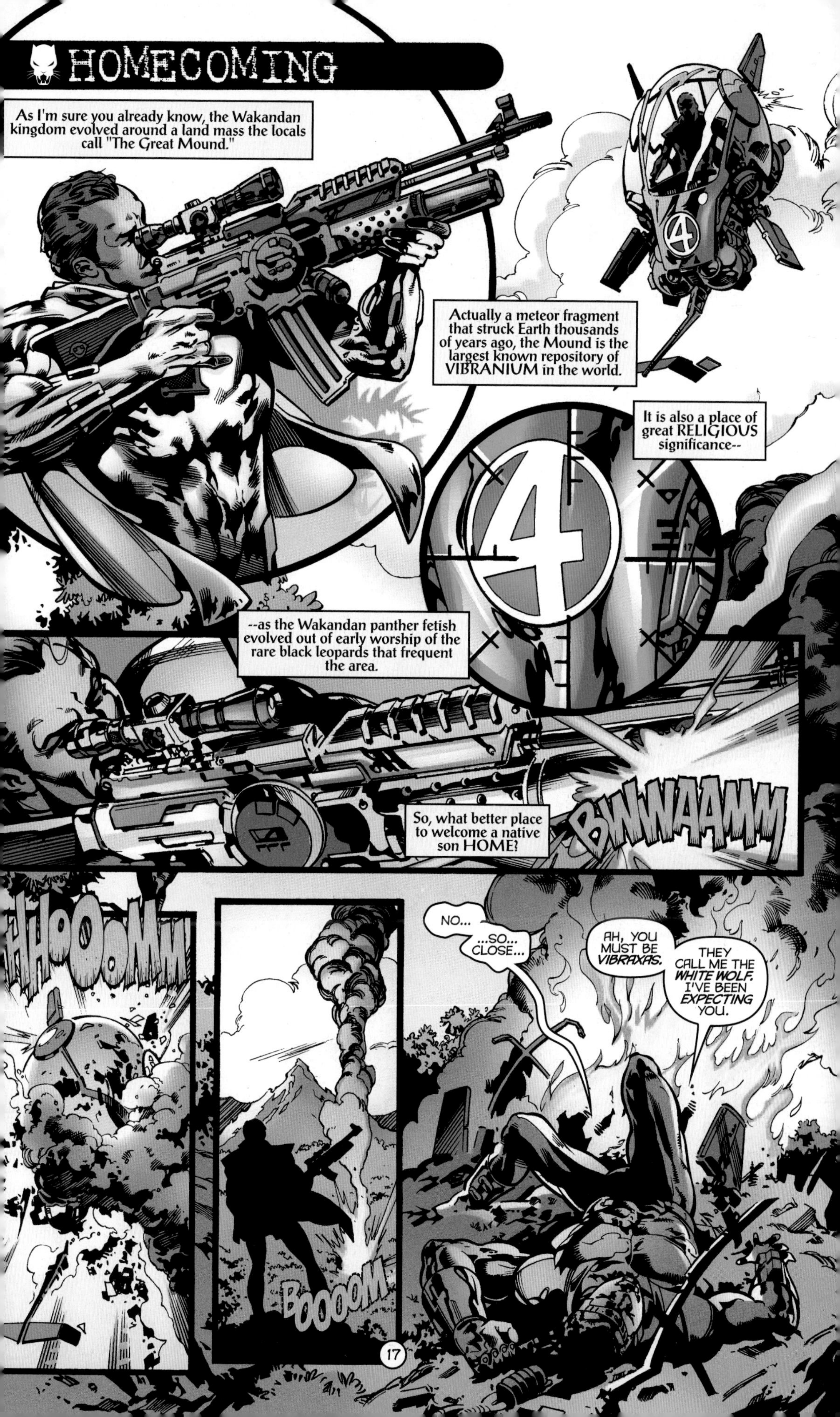

HOMECOMING
As I'm sure you already know, the Wakandan kingdom evolved around a land mass the locals call "The Great Mound."
Actually a meteor fragment that struck Earth thousands of years ago, the Mound is the largest known repository of VIBRANIUM in the world.
It is also a place of great RELIGIOUS significance--
--as the Wakandan panther fetish evolved out of early worship of the rare black leopards that frequent the area.
So, what better place to welcome a native son HOME?
BWWAAMM
HHOOOMM
BOOOOM
NO...
...SO... CLOSE...
AH, YOU MUST BE VIBRAXAS.
THEY CALL ME THE WHITE WOLF. I'VE BEEN EXPECTING YOU.

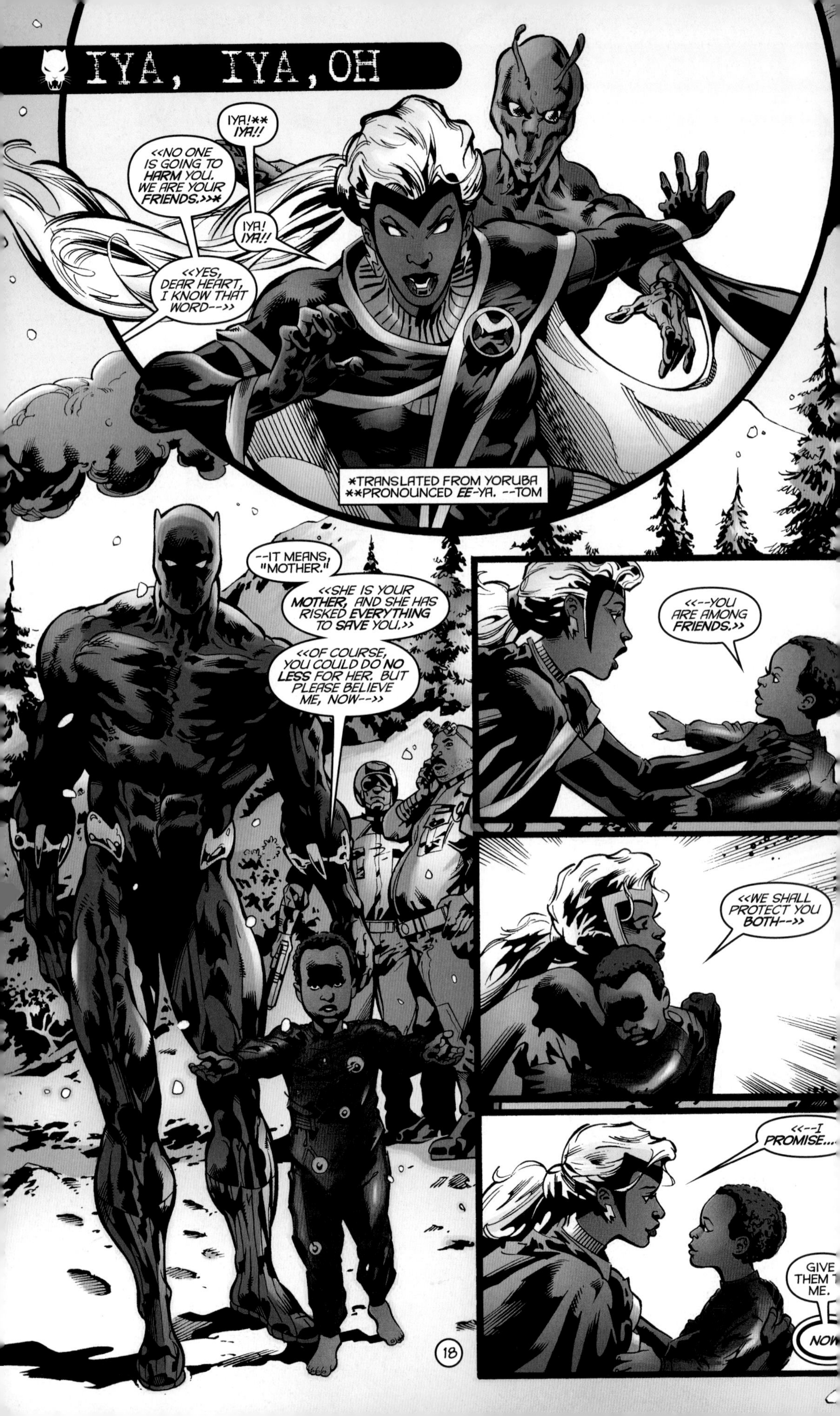

IYA, IYA, OH
<<NO ONE IS GOING TO HARM YOU. WE ARE YOUR FRIENDS.>>*
IYA!** IYA!!
IYA! IYA!!
<<YES, DEAR HEART, I KNOW THAT WORD-->>
*TRANSLATED FROM YORUBA
**PRONOUNCED EE-YA. --TOM
--IT MEANS, "MOTHER."
<<SHE IS YOUR MOTHER, AND SHE HAS RISKED EVERYTHING TO SAVE YOU.>>
<<OF COURSE, YOU COULD DO NO LESS FOR HER. BUT PLEASE BELIEVE ME, NOW-->>
<<--YOU ARE AMONG FRIENDS.>>
<<WE SHALL PROTECT YOU BOTH-->>
<<--I PROMISE...
18

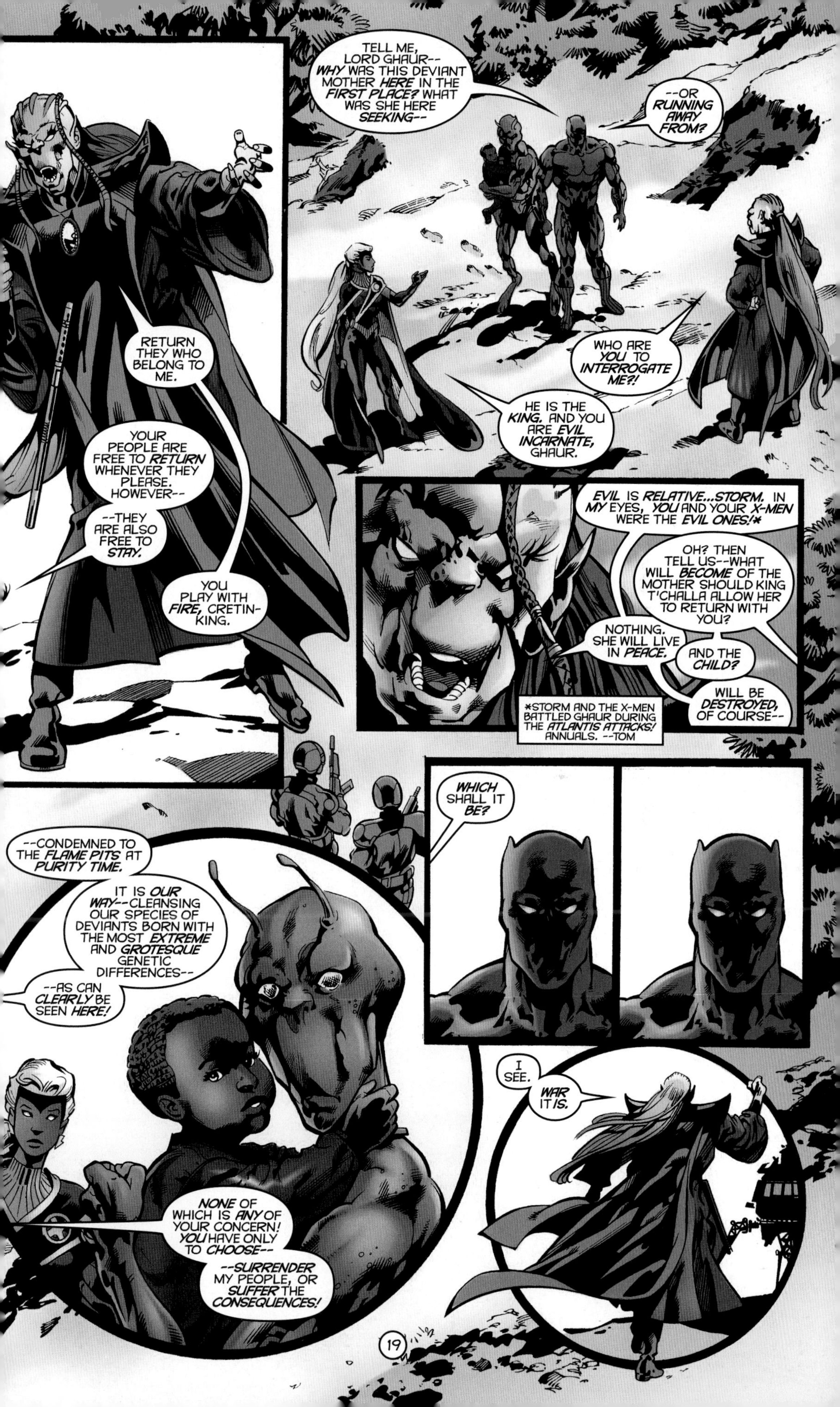
TELL ME, LORD GHAUR-- WHY WAS THIS DEVIANT MOTHER HERE IN THE FIRST PLACE? WHAT WAS SHE HERE SEEKING--
--OR RUNNING AWAY FROM?
WHO ARE YOU TO INTERROGATE ME?!
HE IS THE KING. AND YOU ARE EVIL INCARNATE, GHAUR.
RETURN THEY WHO BELONG TO ME.
YOUR PEOPLE ARE FREE TO RETURN WHENEVER THEY PLEASE. HOWEVER--
--THEY ARE ALSO FREE TO STAY.
YOU PLAY WITH FIRE, CRETIN-KING.
EVIL IS RELATIVE...STORM. IN MY EYES, YOU AND YOUR X-MEN WERE THE EVIL ONES!*
OH? THEN TELL US--WHAT WILL BECOME OF THE MOTHER SHOULD KING T'CHALLA ALLOW HER TO RETURN WITH YOU?
NOTHING. SHE WILL LIVE IN PEACE.
AND THE CHILD?
WILL BE DESTROYED, OF COURSE--
*STORM AND THE X-MEN BATTLED GHAUR DURING THE ATLANTIS ATTACKS! ANNUALS. --TOM
--CONDEMNED TO THE FLAME PITS AT PURITY TIME.
IT IS OUR WAY--CLEANSING OUR SPECIES OF DEVIANTS BORN WITH THE MOST EXTREME AND GROTESQUE GENETIC DIFFERENCES--
--AS CAN CLEARLY BE SEEN HERE!
NONE OF WHICH IS ANY OF YOUR CONCERN! YOU HAVE ONLY TO CHOOSE--
--SURRENDER MY PEOPLE, OR SUFFER THE CONSEQUENCES!
WHICH SHALL IT BE?
I SEE.
WAR IT IS.

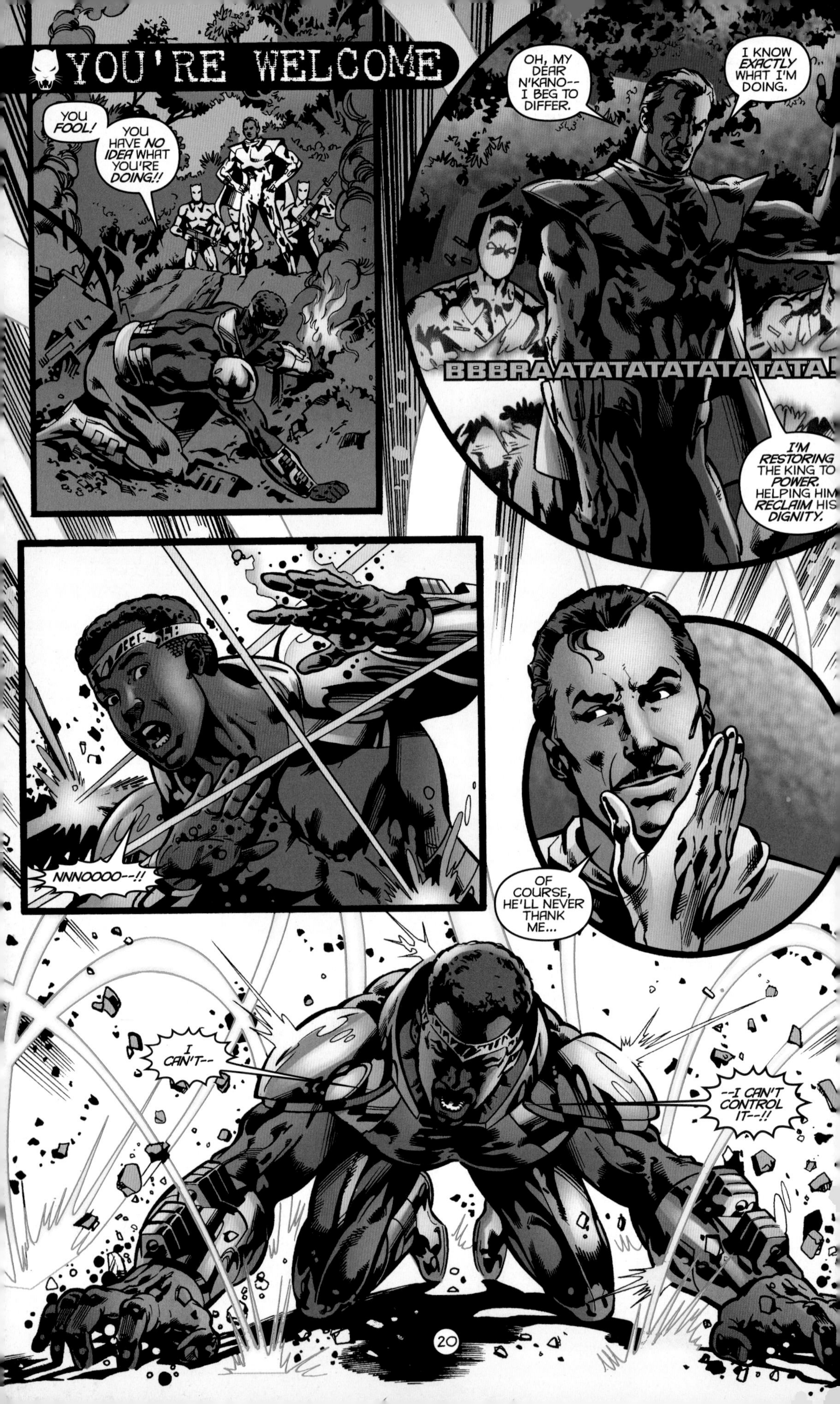
YOU'RE WELCOME
YOU FOOL!
YOU HAVE NO IDEA WHAT YOU'RE DOING!!
OH, MY DEAR N'KANO-- I BEG TO DIFFER.
I KNOW EXACTLY WHAT I'M DOING.
BBBRAATATATATATATATATATA!
I'M RESTORING THE KING TO POWER. HELPING HIM RECLAIM HIS DIGNITY.
NNNOOOO--!!
OF COURSE, HE'LL NEVER THANK ME...
I CAN'T--
--I CAN'T CONTROL IT--!!
20

SSZZAAPZK!

SSZZZZSKFT

SSZZAAACCKKK

WELL,
NOW.

JUST
AS I'D
HOPED.

WELCOME
HOME--

21

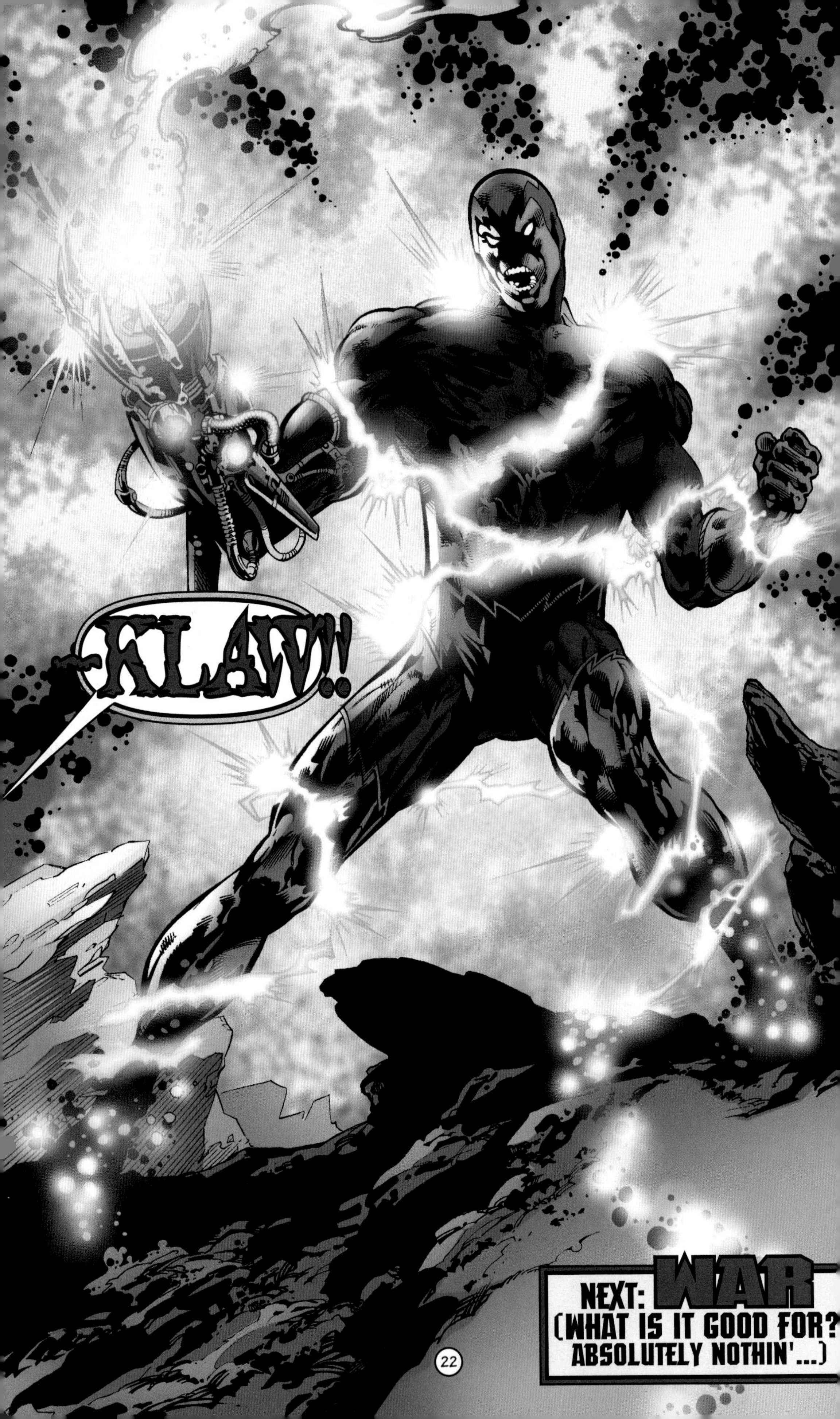
--KLAW!!
NEXT: WAR
(WHAT IS IT GOOD FOR? ABSOLUTELY NOTHIN'...)

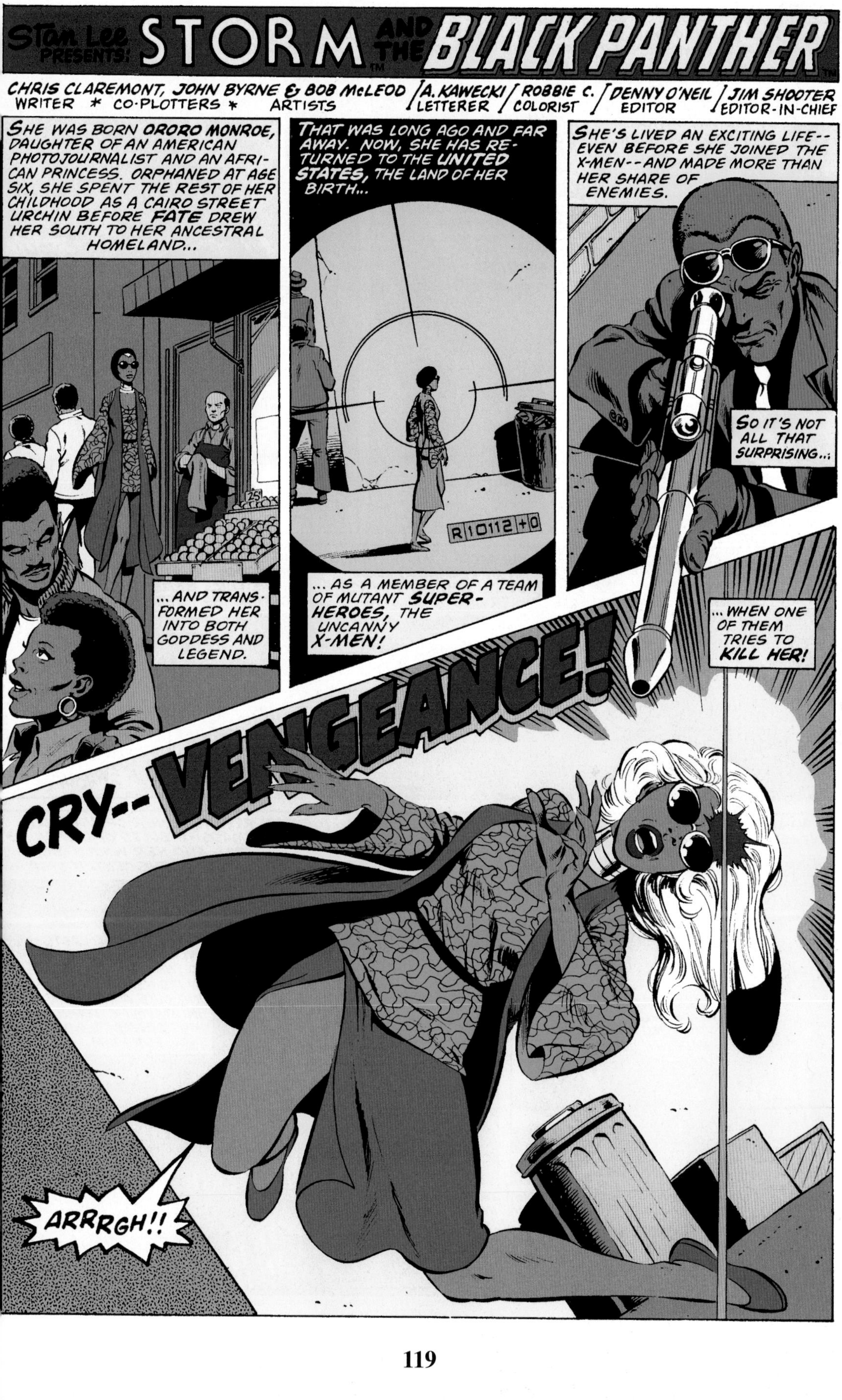

Stan Lee PRESENTS: STORM AND THE BLACK PANTHER
CHRIS CLAREMONT, JOHN BYRNE & BOB McLEOD
WRITER * CO-PLOTTERS * ARTISTS
A. KAWECKI LETTERER
ROBBIE C. COLORIST
DENNY O'NEIL EDITOR
JIM SHOOTER EDITOR-IN-CHIEF
SHE WAS BORN ORORO MONROE, DAUGHTER OF AN AMERICAN PHOTOJOURNALIST AND AN AFRICAN PRINCESS. ORPHANED AT AGE SIX, SHE SPENT THE REST OF HER CHILDHOOD AS A CAIRO STREET URCHIN BEFORE FATE DREW HER SOUTH TO HER ANCESTRAL HOMELAND...
...AND TRANSFORMED HER INTO BOTH GODDESS AND LEGEND.
THAT WAS LONG AGO AND FAR AWAY. NOW, SHE HAS RETURNED TO THE UNITED STATES, THE LAND OF HER BIRTH...
R 10112 +0
...AS A MEMBER OF A TEAM OF MUTANT SUPER-HEROES, THE UNCANNY X-MEN!
SHE'S LIVED AN EXCITING LIFE--EVEN BEFORE SHE JOINED THE X-MEN--AND MADE MORE THAN HER SHARE OF ENEMIES.
SO IT'S NOT ALL THAT SURPRISING...
...WHEN ONE OF THEM TRIES TO KILL HER!
CRY--VENGEANCE!
ARRRGH!!

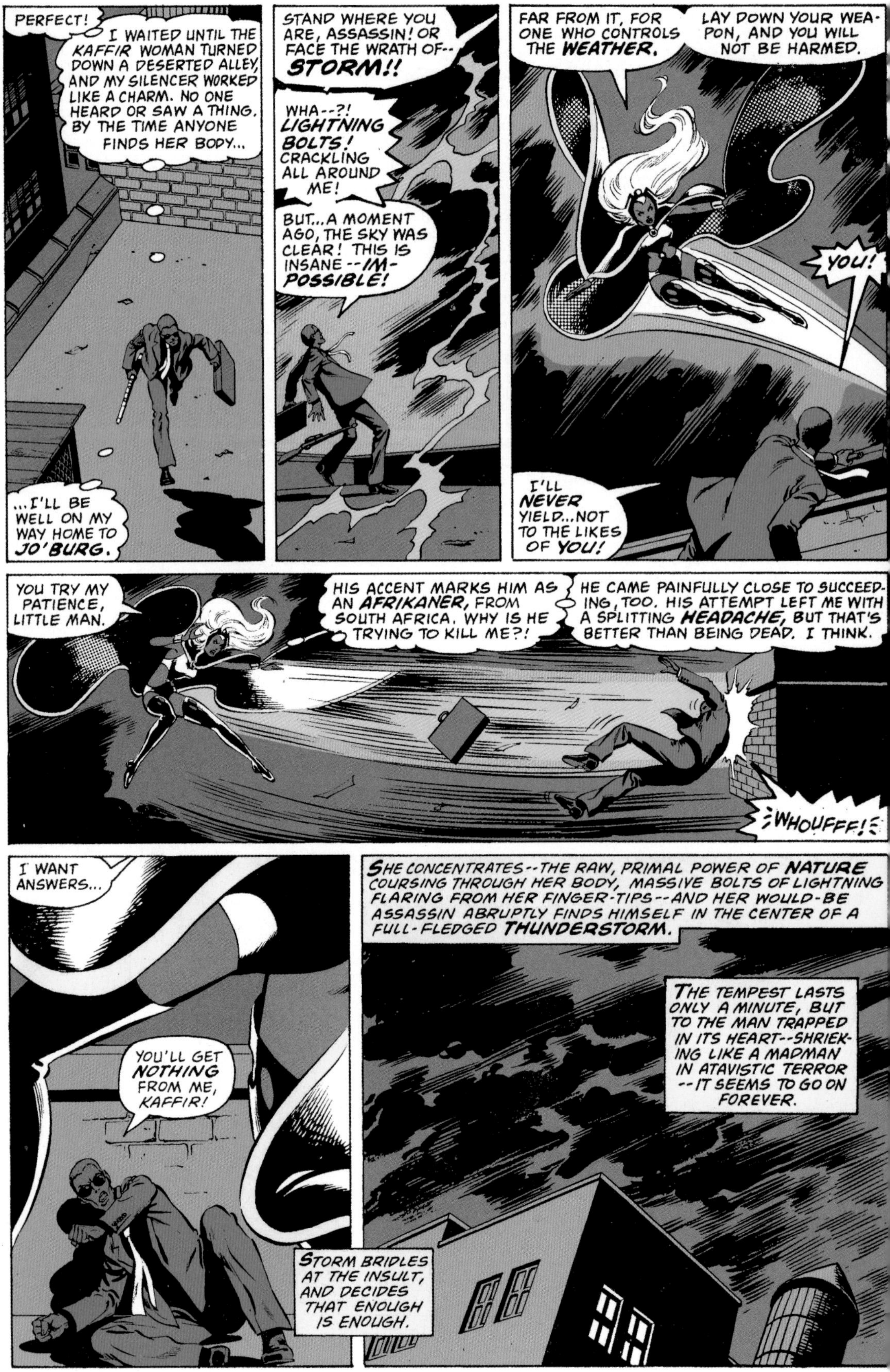
PERFECT!
I WAITED UNTIL THE KAFFIR WOMAN TURNED DOWN A DESERTED ALLEY, AND MY SILENCER WORKED LIKE A CHARM. NO ONE HEARD OR SAW A THING. BY THE TIME ANYONE FINDS HER BODY...
...I'LL BE WELL ON MY WAY HOME TO JO'BURG.
STAND WHERE YOU ARE, ASSASSIN! OR FACE THE WRATH OF-- STORM!!
WHA--?! LIGHTNING BOLTS! CRACKLING ALL AROUND ME!
BUT...A MOMENT AGO, THE SKY WAS CLEAR! THIS IS INSANE --IMPOSSIBLE!
FAR FROM IT, FOR ONE WHO CONTROLS THE WEATHER.
LAY DOWN YOUR WEAPON, AND YOU WILL NOT BE HARMED.
YOU!
I'LL NEVER YIELD...NOT TO THE LIKES OF YOU!
YOU TRY MY PATIENCE, LITTLE MAN.
HIS ACCENT MARKS HIM AS AN AFRIKANER, FROM SOUTH AFRICA. WHY IS HE TRYING TO KILL ME?!
HE CAME PAINFULLY CLOSE TO SUCCEEDING, TOO. HIS ATTEMPT LEFT ME WITH A SPLITTING HEADACHE, BUT THAT'S BETTER THAN BEING DEAD. I THINK.
WHOUFFF!
I WANT ANSWERS...
YOU'LL GET NOTHING FROM ME, KAFFIR!
STORM BRIDLES AT THE INSULT, AND DECIDES THAT ENOUGH IS ENOUGH.
SHE CONCENTRATES--THE RAW, PRIMAL POWER OF NATURE COURSING THROUGH HER BODY, MASSIVE BOLTS OF LIGHTNING FLARING FROM HER FINGER-TIPS--AND HER WOULD-BE ASSASSIN ABRUPTLY FINDS HIMSELF IN THE CENTER OF A FULL-FLEDGED THUNDERSTORM.
THE TEMPEST LASTS ONLY A MINUTE, BUT TO THE MAN TRAPPED IN ITS HEART--SHRIEKING LIKE A MADMAN IN ATAVISTIC TERROR --IT SEEMS TO GO ON FOREVER.

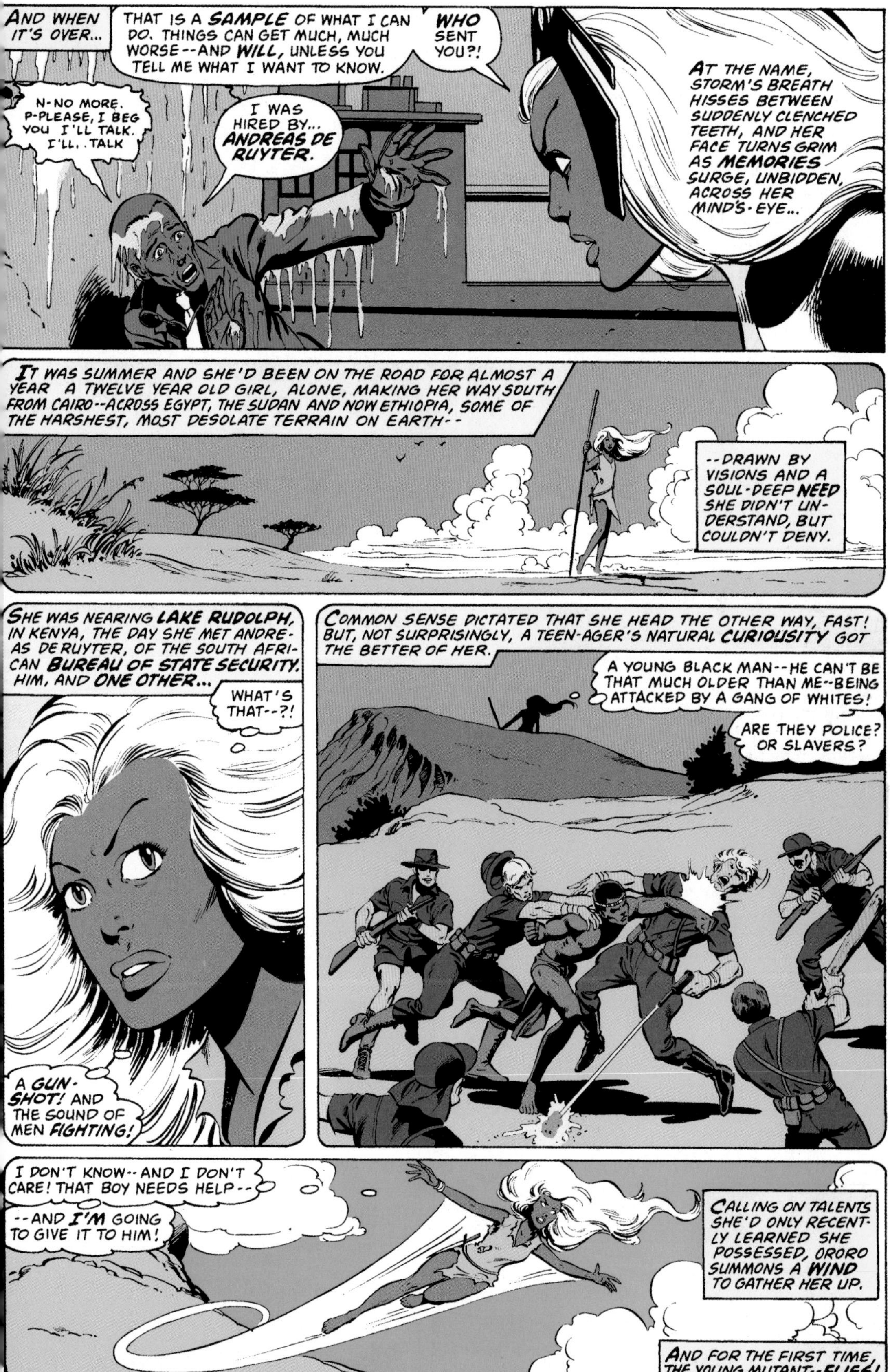
AND WHEN IT'S OVER...
THAT IS A SAMPLE OF WHAT I CAN DO. THINGS CAN GET MUCH, MUCH WORSE--AND WILL, UNLESS YOU TELL ME WHAT I WANT TO KNOW.
N-NO MORE. P-PLEASE, I BEG YOU I'LL TALK. I'LL..TALK
WHO SENT YOU?!
I WAS HIRED BY... ANDREAS DE RUYTER.
AT THE NAME, STORM'S BREATH HISSES BETWEEN SUDDENLY CLENCHED TEETH, AND HER FACE TURNS GRIM AS MEMORIES SURGE, UNBIDDEN, ACROSS HER MIND'S-EYE...
IT WAS SUMMER AND SHE'D BEEN ON THE ROAD FOR ALMOST A YEAR A TWELVE YEAR OLD GIRL, ALONE, MAKING HER WAY SOUTH FROM CAIRO--ACROSS EGYPT, THE SUDAN AND NOW ETHIOPIA, SOME OF THE HARSHEST, MOST DESOLATE TERRAIN ON EARTH--
--DRAWN BY VISIONS AND A SOUL-DEEP NEED SHE DIDN'T UNDERSTAND, BUT COULDN'T DENY.
SHE WAS NEARING LAKE RUDOLPH, IN KENYA, THE DAY SHE MET ANDREAS DE RUYTER, OF THE SOUTH AFRICAN BUREAU OF STATE SECURITY. HIM, AND ONE OTHER...
WHAT'S THAT--?!
A GUN-SHOT! AND THE SOUND OF MEN FIGHTING!
COMMON SENSE DICTATED THAT SHE HEAD THE OTHER WAY, FAST! BUT, NOT SURPRISINGLY, A TEEN-AGER'S NATURAL CURIOUSITY GOT THE BETTER OF HER.
A YOUNG BLACK MAN--HE CAN'T BE THAT MUCH OLDER THAN ME--BEING ATTACKED BY A GANG OF WHITES!
ARE THEY POLICE? OR SLAVERS?
I DON'T KNOW--AND I DON'T CARE! THAT BOY NEEDS HELP--
--AND I'M GOING TO GIVE IT TO HIM!
CALLING ON TALENTS SHE'D ONLY RECENTLY LEARNED SHE POSSESSED, ORORO SUMMONS A WIND TO GATHER HER UP.
AND FOR THE FIRST TIME, THE YOUNG MUTANT--FLIES!

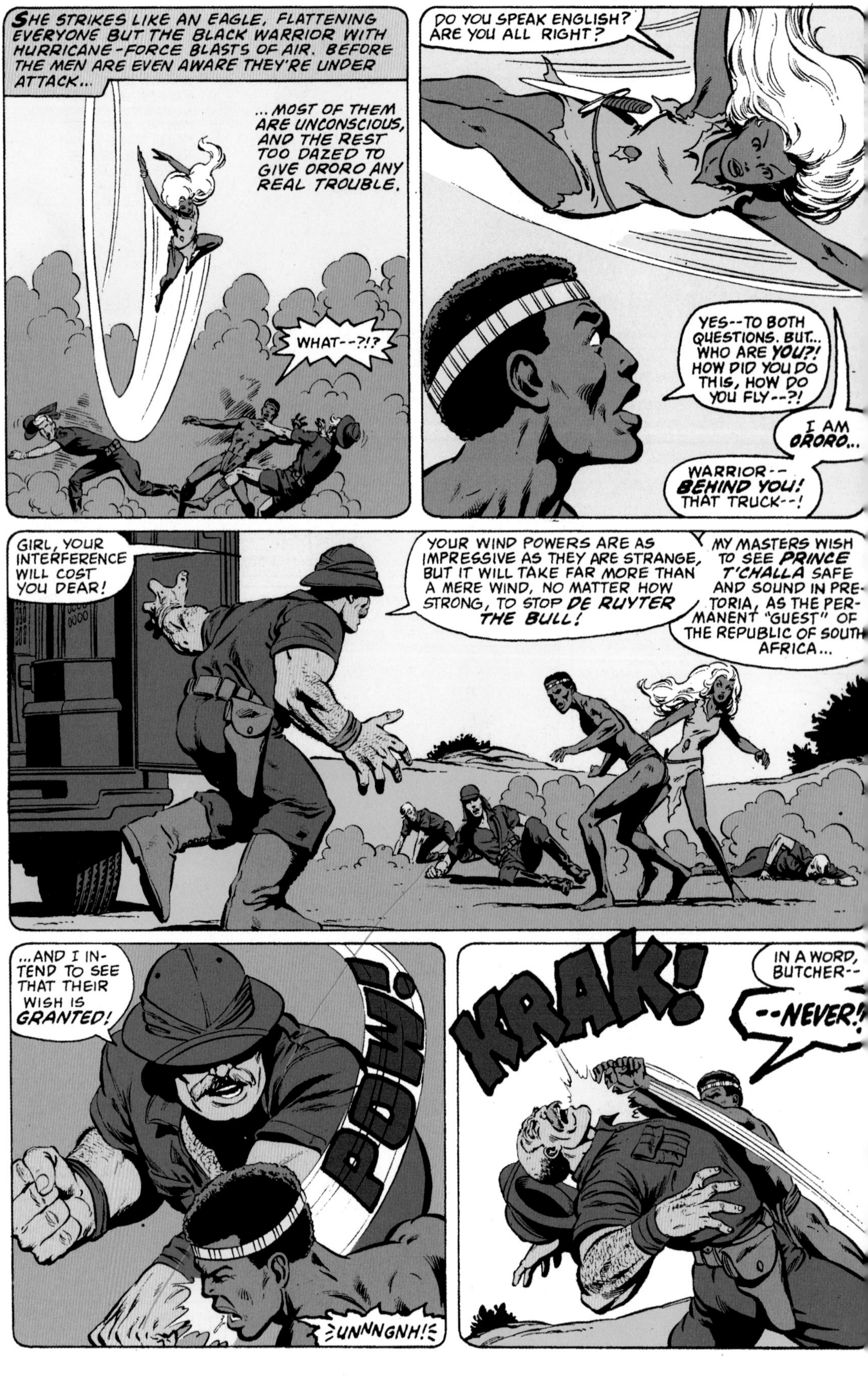
SHE STRIKES LIKE AN EAGLE, FLATTENING EVERYONE BUT THE BLACK WARRIOR WITH HURRICANE-FORCE BLASTS OF AIR. BEFORE THE MEN ARE EVEN AWARE THEY'RE UNDER ATTACK...
...MOST OF THEM ARE UNCONSCIOUS, AND THE REST TOO DAZED TO GIVE ORORO ANY REAL TROUBLE.
WHAT--?!?
DO YOU SPEAK ENGLISH? ARE YOU ALL RIGHT?
YES--TO BOTH QUESTIONS. BUT... WHO ARE YOU?! HOW DID YOU DO THIS, HOW DO YOU FLY--?!
I AM ORORO...
WARRIOR-- BEHIND YOU! THAT TRUCK--!
GIRL, YOUR INTERFERENCE WILL COST YOU DEAR!
YOUR WIND POWERS ARE AS IMPRESSIVE AS THEY ARE STRANGE, BUT IT WILL TAKE FAR MORE THAN A MERE WIND, NO MATTER HOW STRONG, TO STOP DE RUYTER THE BULL!
MY MASTERS WISH TO SEE PRINCE T'CHALLA SAFE AND SOUND IN PRETORIA, AS THE PERMANENT "GUEST" OF THE REPUBLIC OF SOUTH AFRICA...
...AND I INTEND TO SEE THAT THEIR WISH IS GRANTED!
POW!
UNNNGNH!
KRAK!
IN A WORD, BUTCHER--
--NEVER!

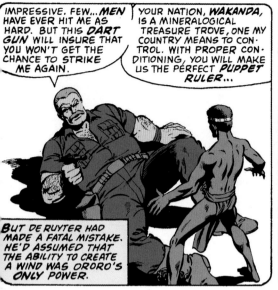

IMPRESSIVE. FEW...*MEN* HAVE EVER HIT ME AS HARD. BUT THIS *DART GUN* WILL INSURE THAT YOU WON'T GET THE CHANCE TO STRIKE ME AGAIN.

YOUR NATION, *WAKANDA*, IS A MINERALOGICAL TREASURE TROVE, ONE MY COUNTRY MEANS TO CONTROL. WITH PROPER CONDITIONING, YOU WILL MAKE US THE PERFECT *PUPPET RULER*...

BUT DE RUYTER HAD MADE A FATAL MISTAKE. HE'D ASSUMED THAT THE ABILITY TO CREATE A WIND WAS ORORO'S *ONLY* POWER.

IT WASN'T.

MY-- *GUN!!*

AAIII--!!

THEY TRAVELLED TOGETHER FOR A TIME--THE *HAPPIEST* TIME OF HER TREK, ORORO REMEMBERS FONDLY--BUT IN THE END, THEY PARTED. T'CHALLA'S DUTY TOOK HIM BACK TO WAKANDA, WHILE ORORO FOLLOWED HER DREAMS TO THE SLOPES OF *MOUNT KILIMANJARO*, WHERE SHE MADE HER HOME.

BEFORE THE *SOUTH AFRICAN* OR HIS FELLOW AGENTS COULD RECOVER, ORORO AND T'CHALLA WERE LONG GONE!

YEARS PASSED. SHE BECAME A GODDESS, HE THE RULER OF HIS NATION. NOW, IRONICALLY, *BOTH* HAD BECOME SUPER-HEROES.

PROFESSOR XAVIER USED HIS *TELEPATHIC* POWERS...

...TO ERASE ANY MEMORY MY ASSAILANT HAD OF MY ACTIONS-- OR EXISTENCE --AS AN X-MAN.

EMBASSY OF THE KINGDOM OF WAKANDA

THEN, WE RELEASED HIM. I WISH WE COULD HAVE TURNED HIM OVER TO THE POLICE, BUT THAT WOULD HAVE CREATED MORE TROUBLE THAN IT WAS WORTH.

YES, MA'AM?

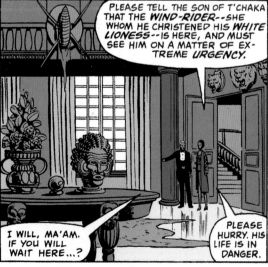

PLEASE TELL THE SON OF T'CHAKA THAT THE *WIND-RIDER*--SHE WHOM HE CHRISTENED HIS *WHITE LIONESS*--IS HERE, AND MUST SEE HIM ON A MATTER OF EXTREME *URGENCY.*

I WILL, MA'AM. IF YOU WILL WAIT HERE...?

PLEASE HURRY. HIS LIFE IS IN DANGER.

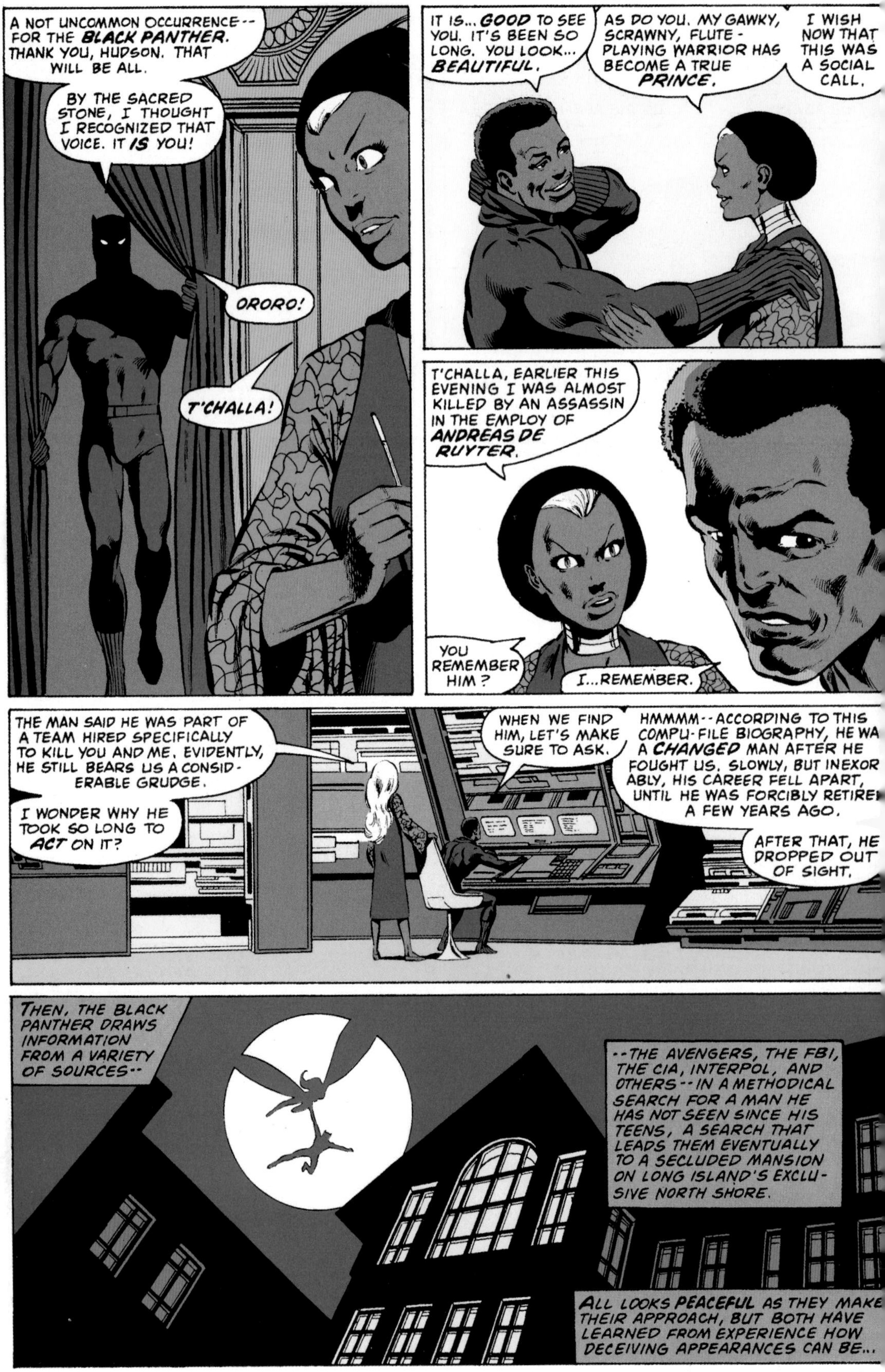
A NOT UNCOMMON OCCURRENCE-- FOR THE BLACK PANTHER. THANK YOU, HUDSON. THAT WILL BE ALL.
BY THE SACRED STONE, I THOUGHT I RECOGNIZED THAT VOICE. IT IS YOU!
ORORO!
T'CHALLA!
IT IS... GOOD TO SEE YOU. IT'S BEEN SO LONG. YOU LOOK... BEAUTIFUL.
AS DO YOU. MY GAWKY, SCRAWNY, FLUTE-PLAYING WARRIOR HAS BECOME A TRUE PRINCE.
I WISH NOW THAT THIS WAS A SOCIAL CALL.
T'CHALLA, EARLIER THIS EVENING I WAS ALMOST KILLED BY AN ASSASSIN IN THE EMPLOY OF ANDREAS DE RUYTER.
YOU REMEMBER HIM?
I...REMEMBER.
THE MAN SAID HE WAS PART OF A TEAM HIRED SPECIFICALLY TO KILL YOU AND ME. EVIDENTLY, HE STILL BEARS US A CONSIDERABLE GRUDGE.
I WONDER WHY HE TOOK SO LONG TO ACT ON IT?
WHEN WE FIND HIM, LET'S MAKE SURE TO ASK.
HMMMM--ACCORDING TO THIS COMPU-FILE BIOGRAPHY, HE WA A CHANGED MAN AFTER HE FOUGHT US. SLOWLY, BUT INEXORABLY, HIS CAREER FELL APART, UNTIL HE WAS FORCIBLY RETIRE A FEW YEARS AGO.
AFTER THAT, HE DROPPED OUT OF SIGHT.
THEN, THE BLACK PANTHER DRAWS INFORMATION FROM A VARIETY OF SOURCES--
--THE AVENGERS, THE FBI, THE CIA, INTERPOL, AND OTHERS--IN A METHODICAL SEARCH FOR A MAN HE HAS NOT SEEN SINCE HIS TEENS, A SEARCH THAT LEADS THEM EVENTUALLY TO A SECLUDED MANSION ON LONG ISLAND'S EXCLUSIVE NORTH SHORE.
ALL LOOKS PEACEFUL AS THEY MAKE THEIR APPROACH, BUT BOTH HAVE LEARNED FROM EXPERIENCE HOW DECEIVING APPEARANCES CAN BE...

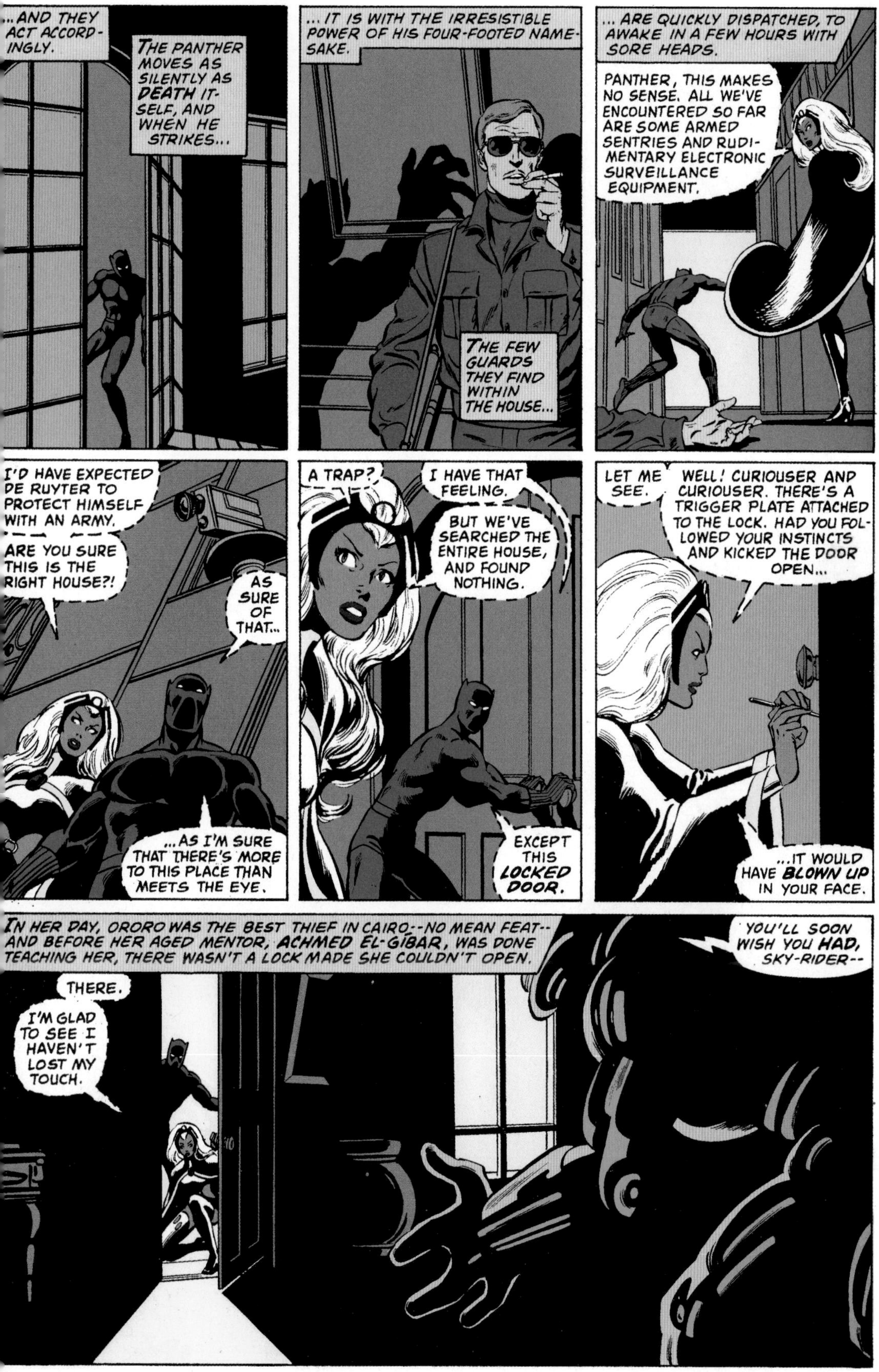
...AND THEY ACT ACCORDINGLY.
THE PANTHER MOVES AS SILENTLY AS DEATH ITSELF, AND WHEN HE STRIKES...
...IT IS WITH THE IRRESISTIBLE POWER OF HIS FOUR-FOOTED NAMESAKE.
THE FEW GUARDS THEY FIND WITHIN THE HOUSE...
...ARE QUICKLY DISPATCHED, TO AWAKE IN A FEW HOURS WITH SORE HEADS.
PANTHER, THIS MAKES NO SENSE. ALL WE'VE ENCOUNTERED SO FAR ARE SOME ARMED SENTRIES AND RUDIMENTARY ELECTRONIC SURVEILLANCE EQUIPMENT.
I'D HAVE EXPECTED DE RUYTER TO PROTECT HIMSELF WITH AN ARMY.
ARE YOU SURE THIS IS THE RIGHT HOUSE?!
AS SURE OF THAT...
...AS I'M SURE THAT THERE'S MORE TO THIS PLACE THAN MEETS THE EYE.
A TRAP?
I HAVE THAT FEELING.
BUT WE'VE SEARCHED THE ENTIRE HOUSE, AND FOUND NOTHING.
EXCEPT THIS LOCKED DOOR.
LET ME SEE.
WELL! CURIOUSER AND CURIOUSER. THERE'S A TRIGGER PLATE ATTACHED TO THE LOCK. HAD YOU FOLLOWED YOUR INSTINCTS AND KICKED THE DOOR OPEN...
...IT WOULD HAVE BLOWN UP IN YOUR FACE.
IN HER DAY, ORORO WAS THE BEST THIEF IN CAIRO--NO MEAN FEAT--AND BEFORE HER AGED MENTOR, ACHMED EL-GIBAR, WAS DONE TEACHING HER, THERE WASN'T A LOCK MADE SHE COULDN'T OPEN.
THERE.
I'M GLAD TO SEE I HAVEN'T LOST MY TOUCH.
YOU'LL SOON WISH YOU HAD, SKY-RIDER--

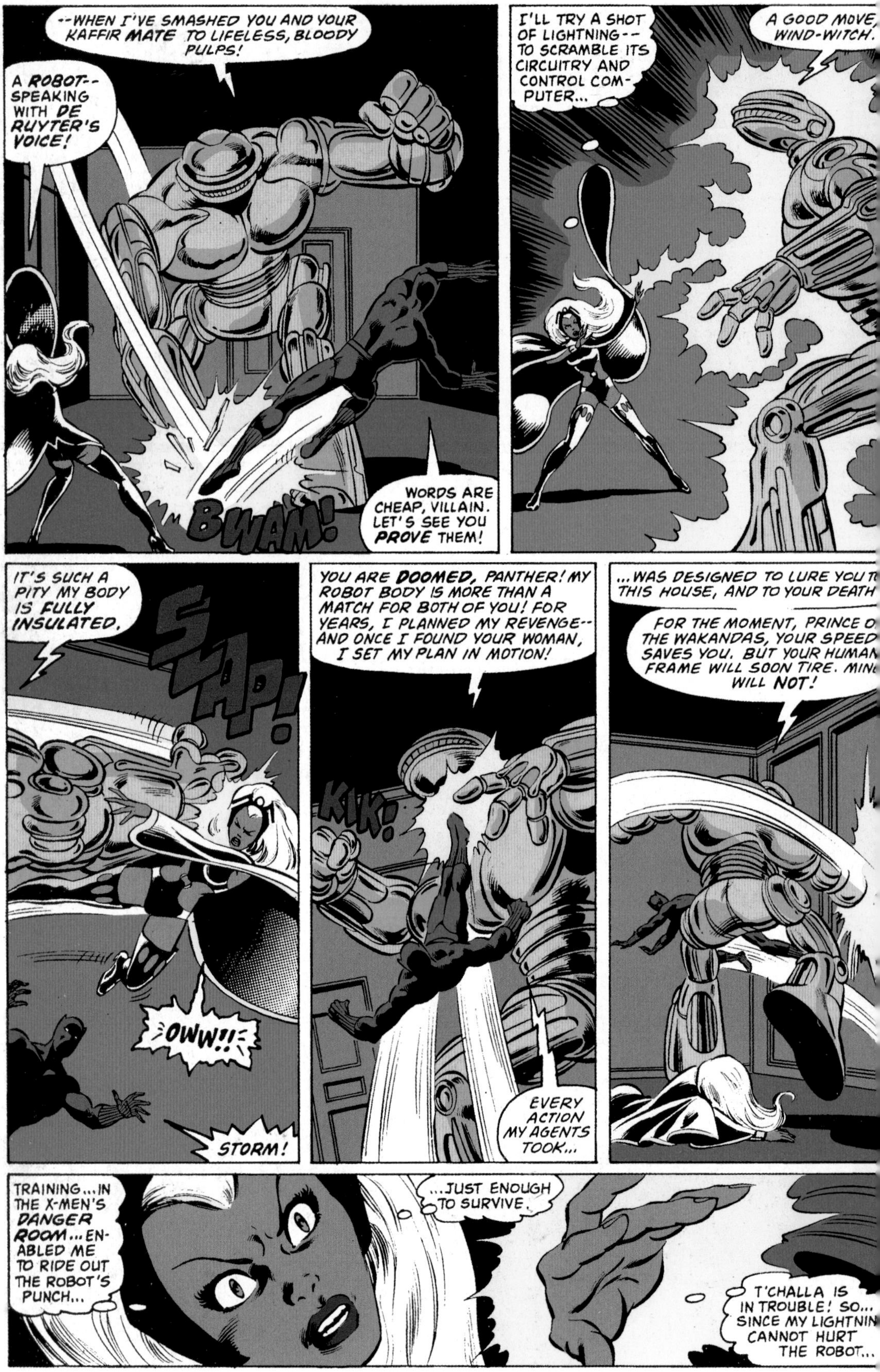
--WHEN I'VE SMASHED YOU AND YOUR KAFFIR MATE TO LIFELESS, BLOODY PULPS!
A ROBOT--SPEAKING WITH DE RUYTER'S VOICE!
BWAM!
WORDS ARE CHEAP, VILLAIN. LET'S SEE YOU PROVE THEM!
I'LL TRY A SHOT OF LIGHTNING--TO SCRAMBLE ITS CIRCUITRY AND CONTROL COMPUTER...
A GOOD MOVE, WIND-WITCH.
IT'S SUCH A PITY MY BODY IS FULLY INSULATED.
SLAP!
OWW!!
STORM!
YOU ARE DOOMED, PANTHER! MY ROBOT BODY IS MORE THAN A MATCH FOR BOTH OF YOU! FOR YEARS, I PLANNED MY REVENGE--AND ONCE I FOUND YOUR WOMAN, I SET MY PLAN IN MOTION!
KIK!
EVERY ACTION MY AGENTS TOOK...
...WAS DESIGNED TO LURE YOU T THIS HOUSE, AND TO YOUR DEATH
FOR THE MOMENT, PRINCE O THE WAKANDAS, YOUR SPEED SAVES YOU. BUT YOUR HUMAN FRAME WILL SOON TIRE. MIN WILL NOT!
TRAINING...IN THE X-MEN'S DANGER ROOM...ENABLED ME TO RIDE OUT THE ROBOT'S PUNCH...
...JUST ENOUGH TO SURVIVE.
T'CHALLA IS IN TROUBLE! SO... SINCE MY LIGHTNIN CANNOT HURT THE ROBOT...

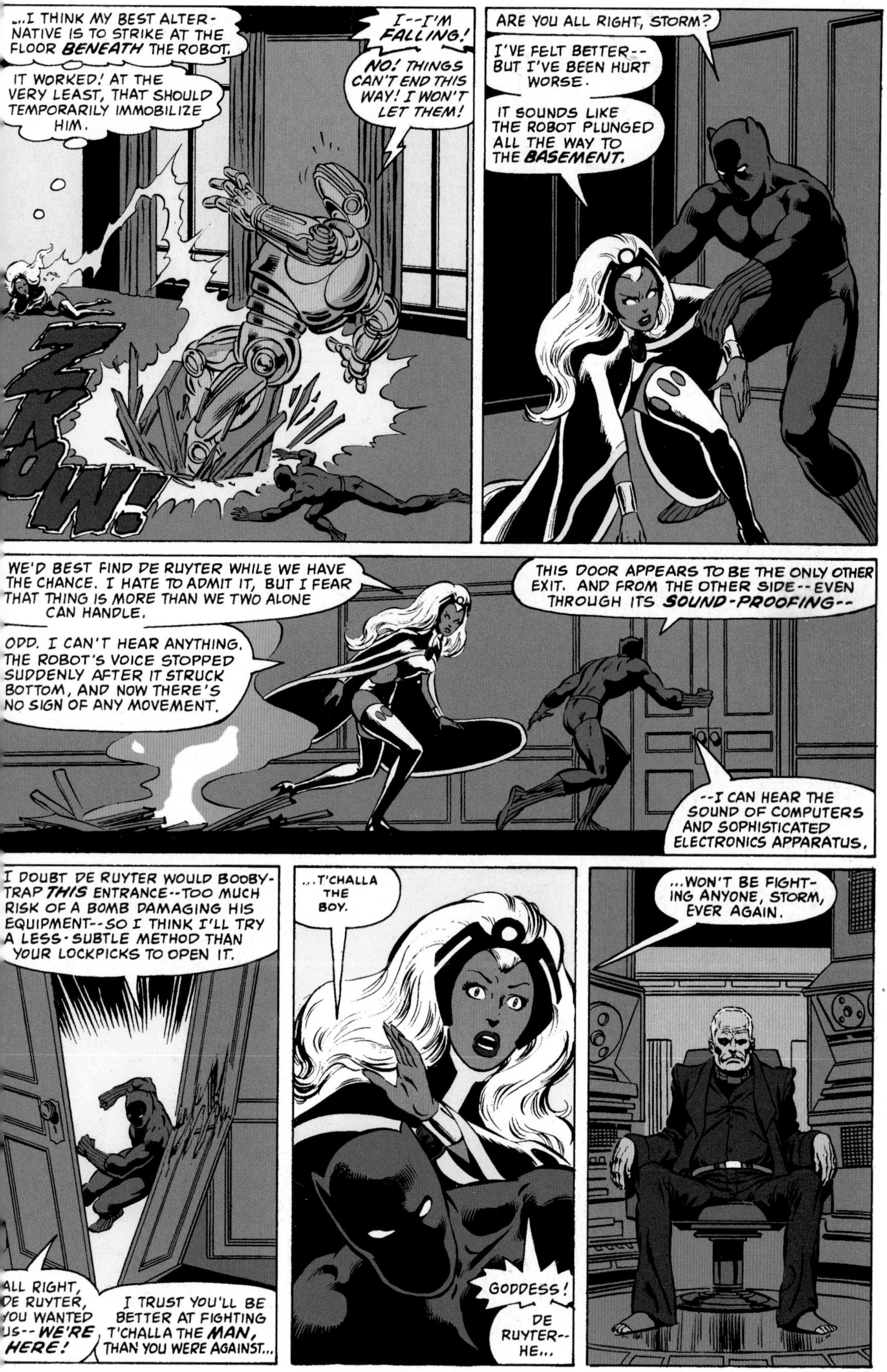

...I THINK MY BEST ALTERNATIVE IS TO STRIKE AT THE FLOOR BENEATH THE ROBOT.
IT WORKED! AT THE VERY LEAST, THAT SHOULD TEMPORARILY IMMOBILIZE HIM.
I--I'M FALLING!
NO! THINGS CAN'T END THIS WAY! I WON'T LET THEM!
ZAKOW!
ARE YOU ALL RIGHT, STORM?
I'VE FELT BETTER--BUT I'VE BEEN HURT WORSE.
IT SOUNDS LIKE THE ROBOT PLUNGED ALL THE WAY TO THE BASEMENT.
WE'D BEST FIND DE RUYTER WHILE WE HAVE THE CHANCE. I HATE TO ADMIT IT, BUT I FEAR THAT THING IS MORE THAN WE TWO ALONE CAN HANDLE.
ODD. I CAN'T HEAR ANYTHING. THE ROBOT'S VOICE STOPPED SUDDENLY AFTER IT STRUCK BOTTOM, AND NOW THERE'S NO SIGN OF ANY MOVEMENT.
THIS DOOR APPEARS TO BE THE ONLY OTHER EXIT. AND FROM THE OTHER SIDE--EVEN THROUGH ITS SOUND-PROOFING--
--I CAN HEAR THE SOUND OF COMPUTERS AND SOPHISTICATED ELECTRONICS APPARATUS.
I DOUBT DE RUYTER WOULD BOOBY-TRAP THIS ENTRANCE--TOO MUCH RISK OF A BOMB DAMAGING HIS EQUIPMENT--SO I THINK I'LL TRY A LESS-SUBTLE METHOD THAN YOUR LOCKPICKS TO OPEN IT.
ALL RIGHT, DE RUYTER, YOU WANTED US--WE'RE HERE!
I TRUST YOU'LL BE BETTER AT FIGHTING T'CHALLA THE MAN, THAN YOU WERE AGAINST...
...T'CHALLA THE BOY.
GODDESS!
DE RUYTER--HE...
...WON'T BE FIGHTING ANYONE, STORM, EVER AGAIN.

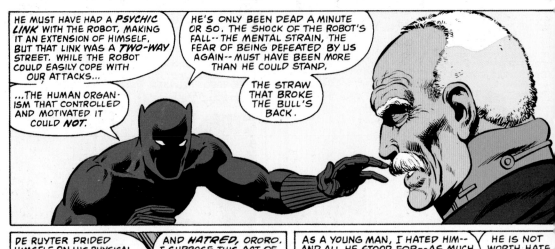

HE MUST HAVE HAD A *PSYCHIC LINK* WITH THE ROBOT, MAKING IT AN EXTENSION OF HIMSELF, BUT THAT LINK WAS A *TWO-WAY* STREET. WHILE THE ROBOT COULD EASILY COPE WITH OUR ATTACKS...

...THE HUMAN ORGANISM THAT CONTROLLED AND MOTIVATED IT COULD *NOT.*

HE'S ONLY BEEN DEAD A MINUTE OR SO. THE SHOCK OF THE ROBOT'S FALL--THE MENTAL STRAIN, THE FEAR OF BEING DEFEATED BY US AGAIN--MUST HAVE BEEN MORE THAN HE COULD STAND.

THE STRAW THAT BROKE THE BULL'S BACK.

DE RUYTER PRIDED HIMSELF ON HIS PHYSICAL STRENGTH, BUT LOOK AT HIM, T'CHALLA--A TWISTED, WASTED, *SHADOW* OF A MAN, CONSUMED BY DISEASE.

AND *HATRED,* ORORO. I SUPPOSE THIS ACT OF VENGEANCE--THE LAST THING HE COULD EVER HOPE TO DO--

--WAS MEANT TO MAKE UP FOR THE LIFE HE BELIEVED WE HAD RUINED.

AS A YOUNG MAN, I HATED HIM-- AND ALL HE STOOD FOR--AS MUCH AS HE DID ME. I LONGED FOR THE DAY WHEN WE WOULD MEET AGAIN, SO I COULD BEAT HIM ONCE AND FOR ALL. NOW I WONDER WHY I BOTHERED.

HE IS NOT WORTH HATE, T'CHALLA. NOT EVEN WORTH *PITY.*

I WOULD RATHER PITY HIS *VICTIMS.*

LATER, AFTER THE PANTHER HAS SUMMONED THE AUTHORITIES...

THERE IS SO MUCH ONE CAN DO WITH A LIFE, YET DE RUYTER CHOSE TO DEVOTE HIS TO THE DESTRUCTION OF TWO PEOPLE HE MET ONLY ONCE.

WHAT A FOOL. WHAT A SHAME. WHAT A...WASTE.

I USED MY *AVENGERS PRIORITY* WITH THE POLICE. YOU WON'T BE INVOLVED IN ANY WAY.

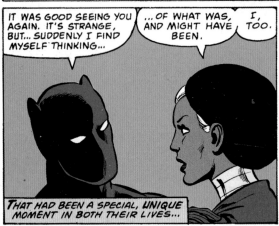

IT WAS GOOD SEEING YOU AGAIN. IT'S STRANGE, BUT... SUDDENLY I FIND MYSELF THINKING...

...OF WHAT WAS, AND MIGHT HAVE BEEN.

I, TOO.

THAT HAD BEEN A SPECIAL, UNIQUE MOMENT IN BOTH THEIR LIVES...

...A MOMENT WHICH--ONCE DENIED--CAN NEVER TRULY BE RECAPTURED. BOTH KNOW THIS. PERHAPS THAT IS WHAT MAKES THEIR PARTING ALL THE MORE *PAINFUL.*

YET... PART THEY DO.

AS FRIENDS. THEY MAY WISH FOR MORE, BUT THAT IS WHAT THEY ARE, WHAT THEY WILL REMAIN. FOREVER.